IN THE LINE OF FIRE

Patton moved into the contact zone, where the ARVN were disorganized and shaken by the loss of their commander. B Troop meanwhile was doing a good job against the enemy, using .50-caliber machine guns and moving rapidly to engage the enemy. Patton, at the same time, was rounding up the ARVN and starting toward a house from which heavy fire was emanating. Patton got a good angle on the structure with an M79 grenade launcher and began to fire against the walls with such intensity that one wall gave way completely. Still, to everyone's amazement, fire continued to come from the mass of rubble, including an RPG round which rocked the American position back and forth like a pendulum. Patton called for a helicopter with a loudspeaker to ask for enemy surrender. The VC refused to give up the fight, and Patton, in a move he later called foolish, advanced with a smoke grenade, found the tunnel opening, and dropped it into the hole.

"Nobody was doing anything and I decided enough was enough."

THE FIGHTING PATTONS

"Recommended for the general reader and the military buff . . . A balanced portrayal of the men and their myths, revealing the father and son to be much alike: dedicated professional men of arms, unswerving in their duty and their devotion to their men."

Library Journal

THE
FIGHTING
PATTONS

Brian M. Sobel

Foreword by
Major General George S. Patton (retired)

A DELL BOOK

Published by
Dell Publishing
a division of
Random House, Inc.
1540 Broadway
New York, New York 10036

Copyright © 1997 by Brian M. Sobel

Dell books may be purchased for business or promotional use or for special sales. For information please write to: Special Markets Department, Random House, Inc., 1540 Broadway, New York, N.Y. 10036.

Dell® is a registered trademark of Random House, Inc., and the colophon is a trademark of Random House, Inc.

ISBN: 0-440-23572-3

Reprinted by arrangement with Praeger Publishers

Printed in the United States of America
Published simultaneously in Canada

July 2000

10 9 8 7 6 5 4 3 2 1
OPM

For Colonel Harold A. Sobel, my father, who passed away in 1987. He was a true American, a proud army officer, a brilliant thinker, and most importantly, my best friend.

CONTENTS

FOREWORD

Several years ago, Brian Sobel first approached me with his idea of a book project in which he would compare eras of two military officer careers—my father's and mine. Our careers certainly were different, but both involved personal and multiple wartime experiences. Between us, we served in five of America's armed conflicts over a period of fifty years. Brian's proposal was intriguing, and so I agreed. Although my current life priorities did not permit my full-time involvement in the book, Brian persisted, patiently obtaining such information and interviews from me as he could persuade me to grant, when my primary attention was on making a go of my second career, farming in Massachusetts. Despite such obstacles, Brian Sobel, as author of *The Fighting Pattons,* has done a fine piece of work, putting into perspective the life experiences of a father and son who shared a love of the Army career, though they served in very different times and circumstances.

When Brian neared the conclusion of the book, he asked me to contribute a few remarks to its Foreword. I am grateful that he thinks I still have something to say and am pleased to respond to his request.

At age seventy-four, as of this writing, I am well into

what my late sister, Ruth Ellen Patton Totten, identified as my "third third." Thus I now approach the end of a very busy life, one with exciting times and moments of adventure, interspersed and intertwined. In his book Brian Sobel has let me travel the old roads, enjoying the recollections of past comrades, many now in retirement or gone to their rewards. He also has reminded me that somewhere long ago I became aware that to unite one's vocation with one's avocation was the secret of happiness in a particular profession or walk of life. I can say without hesitation that this notion applied to my father's life and in my own career, with the possible exception of my two and one-half year tour in the Pentagon as a member of the Army General Staff. In all candor, that was not my most compatible assignment, and I cannot give it very high marks. However, subtracting that period from my thirty-four years of military service, it was a fair trade-off for a lifework that ended up very much on the plus side.

In his efforts to capture or recapture the "fighting Pattons," Brian Sobel faced a difficult undertaking at best. I consider that he has done an excellent job of interpreting my experiences of command, with special attention paid to both the Vietnam conflict and the Korean War. I believe that he has done his utmost to be accurate, candid, and fair without being boring or prejudicial.

As one of the two principal subjects of this book, I do have some regrets as I review the reminiscences I gave Brian. Especially, I regret my personal negligence in not retaining the names of all the great soldiers and noncommissioned officers with whom I shared special incidents or experiences of service. As I could remember them, I credited those I feel deserve to be included. Many were priceless characters, some of whom could scarcely read or write but who blossomed with their knowledge of equipment or their understanding of the young soldiers under them in the structure of tactical command. They were the heart of the Army as I knew it, and as far as I am concerned, the NCOs of today are holding up their end beautifully.

Brian Sobel has taken our history and spun an excellent yarn, gathering into it many of my own experiences in my Army assignments, weaving in some of the characters I had the privilege of meeting or knowing, from John J. Pershing to Haile Selassie and Manfred Rommel. He has included them appropriately and described them with caring skill.

Although this book is Brian's, as its subject I appreciate his letting me acknowledge some of the people who encouraged me to let him write it and to grant him the interviews and assemble the materials he would require. My wife, Joanne, ranks first among this group. Our daughters Mother Margaret Georgina Patton, O.S.B., and Helen Patton Plusczyk, and our sons, George Patton, Jr., Robert Holbrook Patton, and Benjamin Wilson Patton, cheered the effort on and made me feel it was work worth supporting.

Brian Sobel made it so.

George S. Patton
Major General, U.S. Army, Retired
Owner, Green Meadows Farm
February 1997

PREFACE

On the North Shore of Massachusetts a short distance from Boston is the town of Hamilton, named for the early American statesman Alexander Hamilton. With a population of just over six thousand residents, the community retains the look of its colonial past, with expansive estates and meadows that seem to roll on endlessly.

In the center of Hamilton is a park guarded silently by a tank and named after the famous American general George S. Patton, Jr. Patton Memorial Park is but one element of the family presence in town, for a couple of miles away, near the end of a tree-lined country lane, resides retired Major General George Smith Patton, son of the famous World War II hero.

The Patton who lives with his family in Hamilton today, like his father before him, is a tough-talking man and a student of military history and history in general. Although retired from the Army, he remains the consummate West Pointer and general, more in the mold of his father than perhaps even he is willing to admit. This Patton is also a proven combat soldier and leader of men who had to carry the burden of his "old man's" triumphs and failures and not allow it to affect his life or military career. Patton is a physically large man, white-haired now, with a resemblance to his father's pictures. His sister, the late Ruth Ellen Patton Totten, once said, "If he doesn't look exactly like our dad he sure feels like him. He exudes an aura of our father very, very much. Many of his gestures are the same."

George Patton is a thirty-four-year army veteran who admits crying at the loss of his men in battle and yet once saluted an enemy soldier in a way only a professional military man could understand. He fought, was wounded, won medals, and would have gladly perished to preserve the American dream. Today he commercially farms his family estate and spends time speaking with people about his military career, his life and times, and the special place he holds in history because of the Patton name.

Joanne Patton has been married to the general for forty-five years. She is a gentle woman, soft-spoken and well educated. Her attachment to history by marriage to Patton's son has been an exhilarating ride—a life that by her own admission took great adjustment in the beginning. She has often served as a buffer for the General, rounding out what some perceive as his abrupt, no-nonsense manner.

The Pattons had five children. Today George, Jr., works on his father's farm. Margaret is Mother Margaret Georgina, a Benedictine nun. Robert is a writer. Helen and Benjamin, the youngest, are pursuing their own careers in theater and the environment, respectively.

The Patton home one finds in Hamilton was purchased by George S. Patton, Jr., in 1928. *"It was really country at that time, and my mother fixed it up and added a wing in 1939,"* his son recalls. *"When we came the house had no electric lights and the road out front was gravel."* Today, the two-story, white frame house sits comfortably behind a long, high hedge that shields the front of the house and part of the two hundred surrounding acres. Above the front door is a gold-painted, metal eagle and an American flag on a pole, lighted at night, reminding all who enter that this is a house of patriotic values. Joanne points out, "The house has history and personality. Everything has a story."

While the Pattons over the years have donated historically important family artifacts to various museums, the house is still replete with furniture from different historical periods and geographical areas, pictures highlighting the careers of both Pattons, plus a library containing hundreds of books informally shelved by subject. One may discover travel books on various countries and others that detail the great battles that shaped the world. The basic military theme even extends to the outdoors, for just through the back porch screen is a cannon from the days of the Spanish Main, guarding a picturesque meadow and pond. The cannon was brought back from Casablanca by General George S. Patton, Jr., during World War II.

At one time the basement of the home alone held over fifty metal filing cases filled with the late General's personal papers.

"The amount was staggering," says Joanne.

"It was a hell of a thing," comments Patton. *"Ninety-five percent of the items have been sent to the Patton Museum in Fort Knox, Kentucky. Most of my dad's memorabilia is there. His collection of rare books and papers went to West Point and the Library of Congress."*

The Patton military heritage has roots traveling back to the Civil War and even before. Leaders of all ranks can be traced within the family. The first recorded Patton in America, Robert, settled in Fredericksburg, Virginia, in the 1770s. One of Robert's sons, John Mercer Patton, in turn had nine sons of his own, one of whom he named George Smith Patton. Born in 1833, this Patton nineteen years later graduated from the Virginia Military Institute. As a Confederate colonel in the Civil War he received a mortal wound while in command of the 22nd Virginia Infantry. *"He was killed at the third battle of Winchester,"* says his great-grandson, *"in something known as Sheridan's Ride. It was really one of the last campaigns of the war."* In addition to George Patton, several of the other Patton sons also fought for the Confederacy. The role of the Patton family in the Civil War would later be a source of inspiration to the young man born in November 1885, who would rise to become one of the greatest fighting generals in history.

As the child of an increasingly famous military personage, the George Patton who was born in 1923 received great exposure to the military world. Once, for example, he was pulled out of school by his father to see T. E. Lawrence, known as Lawrence of Arabia, who as a soldier in World War I had helped the Arabs defeat the Turks. Another time George was released to see Philippe Pétain, the French marshal and savior of the Verdun front in the First World War. As a child, George also met many prominent people who came to visit, among them the famous General John J. "Black Jack" Pershing and the aviator Eddie Rickenbacker, who, as the top flying ace for the United States, shot down twenty-two planes and four balloons in World War I.

As a boy, George Patton would revel in his father's military historical knowledge, on a few occasions even going to the site of a Civil War battle and analyzing the terrain. *"I would stand where, say, 'Grumble' Jones had his division,"* recalls Patton. *"My sister would be where A. P. Hill's division was located, and we would try to evaluate the distances, which were not very great in those days."*

In keeping with family tradition, Patton attended a military academy when he became eligible. Like his father he attended West Point and, also like his father, soon found himself in academic trouble. *"I got a letter from my dad,"* says Patton. *"He wrote, 'I understand you've been found deficient in Math and for that you're goin to "poop" school* [for remedial instruction], *take the re-entry exam and then repeat the year.' He went on* to say, '*I cannot criticize you for this because the same thing happenend to me.*' " Both Patton and his son attended the U.S. Military Academy at West Point for an extra year before graduating.

George Patton began his army career soon after his father's death and was determined to make his own mark. Eventually he would fight in both Korea and Vietnam. The Vietnam War proved to be a different experience than Korea, however, for both Patton and the nation. "*In Vietnam there were no lines,*" Patton points out. "*It was more a war of the people. And we didn't understand that war nor did we have a clear-cut national strategic objective. It was not clearly defined by the leadership of this country.*" Patton believes the whole experience in Vietnam had a bad beginning that caused early alienation of the media.

The war in Vietnam took its toll on George Patton despite the several medals he was awarded, including two Distinguished Service Crosses. In thirty-three months of fighting he saw many sides of the unpopular war. One battle in particular left him mentally scarred; it occurred in March 1969 in a sector known as the "Michelin plantation." The area had thousands of acres filled with rubber trees and was a North Vietnamese staging area. "*The enemy had a lot of troops in there,*" remembers Patton, "*and I had to go in and tangle with them. We had a hell of a battle that lasted nearly five days.*" Patton lowers his voice to a whisper: "*My outfit did quite well but I lost too many guys in the Michelin. Now every time I see that blue and yellow Michelin sign along the road I look the other way. Those tires may not even come from there, it could be just a trademark, but I still can't buy Michelin tires.*"

Today, information about General George S. Patton, Jr., can be found in countless books and movies. But in earlier years, because the family felt their father was not always represented in a truthful manner, they authorized a military historian, Martin Blumenson, to edit the voluminous material left by the late general.

Blumenson worked it into an accurate record of Patton's thoughts and feelings throughout his adult life. What resulted was a two-volume work called *The Patton Papers,* published in the early 1970s.

The decision to let Blumenson or anyone tackle the papers was a tough one to make. *"We almost had a knockdown family fight on the porch about that book,"* George explains. Ruth Ellen once said, "We felt his story had to be preserved as a whole someplace because the jackals have and will continue to drag out the bones. And each jackal is going to try and prove something by which bone he pulls out. People who have theories will take three things the old man said and take them out of context, and the next will take five and do the same thing. So no matter how they spread the skeleton around, we still wanted to have the context."

Although several books had attempted to tell the General George S. Patton, Jr., story, it was a movie that once again brought the name to public attention in a big way. The movie, simply called *Patton,* starring George C. Scott as the late General, was a box office smash that won three Academy Awards. Released in 1970, the movie is still often shown on home television.

As for the movie, George Patton says, *"The family thought it was really quite good, and we had no association in any manner with the production. In all sincerity part of the reason is due to the stubbornness of George C. Scott. Being a professional, he had done a considerable amount of research on my old man, and when he read the script he went down to the studio and said, 'That's not General Patton. Come up with another script and I'll talk to you.' They did and hence the Patton movie."* Later Scott would once again star as the General, in a sequel entitled *The Last Days of Patton.*

Many years have passed since the end of World War II, yet each year George Patton's name is eulogized in speeches and commemorations of key anniversaries. Pictures, paintings, and statues of Patton can be found in military and nonmilitary museums and settings, the world over. Just a few years ago an intersection of three streets and the Avenue de la Grand-Armée in downtown Paris was named "Place du General Patton." In the dedication ceremony the mayor, now President of France, Jacques Chirac, was quoted as saying, "Patton made a major contribution to the liberation of France and it is the name of this great American that is a symbol of the America we love."

Elsewhere in France, in the Cherbourg Museum, called the Musée de la Guerre et de la Libération, one can find Patton pictured addressing the men of his U.S. Third Army at Christmas, 1944. In the town square of Avranches, France, is a monument to Patton; in the United States, a statue of Patton stands at West Point in the company of George Washington, Douglas MacArthur, and Dwight D. Eisenhower. Its replica overlooks the Charles River Esplanade in Boston. The Patton Museum of Cavalry and Armor, named for the famous general, is located at Fort Knox, Kentucky.

In the small town of Ettelbruck, Luxembourg, townspeople celebrate Patton's liberation of their community from Nazi control in Remembrance Day festivities that occur each summer, and have for over thirty years. Held typically on the last Sunday in June, the ceremonies draw thousands of people to Patton Park, near a nine-foot-statue of the eponymous general. A military parade highlights the day's activities, followed by a trip to the U.S. military cemetery in Hamm, where more than five thousand American soldiers, including Patton, are buried. There are many other Patton memorials in America and Europe, from streets to schools to simple plaques on buildings.

The notoriety that goes with the Patton name has sometimes been a heavy cross to bear. Aside from whatever effect it may have had on his son, it has certainly had a cumulative effect on the family. Accordingly they work very hard to please people. This includes handling a large volume of mail from veterans and other interested followers of the legendary General George S. Patton, Jr. It also involves enduring substantial conjecture and analysis, whether in conversation or in magazines, films or books.

Not long ago appeared yet another volume in which Patton had a large role. The reviewer noted that the author of the book "has particularly sought out and highlighted the sensational, forgetting that although the dead may be gone their families remain." Each member of the Patton family has learned to cope in his or her own way.

The Pattons are noted for their love of country and military service, yet other aspects of the family story are unexpected. For instance, a belief in reincarnation is without a doubt an intriguing aspect of the Patton persona. It was something that was passed from father to both son and daughter. *"I generally believe in reincarnation. I always have,"* says George Patton. *"I feel I fought in the Napoleonic period. I'm not even sure which side I was on. But I can say that I'm intimately familiar with the area in and around Regensburg, Germany. When I got there for the first time I had a complete and total comfort with the area."* Ruth Ellen once said, "It never occurred to me until later in life that everyone didn't believe in it. My father used to say it was the only explanation for inequality and injustice." In addition to reincarnation the Pattons also believe in fate: it was the senior Patton who once wrote, "I can't decide logically if I am a man of destiny or a lucky fool, but I think I am destined."

General George S. Patton, Jr., died in Heidelberg, Germany, on December 21, 1945, from injuries sustained in an automobile accident near Mannheim on December 9th. Patton had been left paralyzed by a collision at less than thirty miles per hour. At the scene most had thought that the accident was minor until, bleeding profusely from a forehead cut, he said, "I think I'm paralyzed." Patton fought tenaciously for his life, but finally a blood clot loosened in his circulatory system and closed a monumental career.

General Patton's son George, meanwhile, as a young army officer, gladly embraced his father's sense of honor and professionalism. These attitudes, as they did for his father, sparked problems with the media on more than one occasion in Vietnam, the most serious occurring on the day he earned his first Distinguished Service Cross. *"It was during a heavy clash with the enemy, following the forced landing of my helicopter,"* says Patton. *"During the fight I shot a couple of VC, including one I hit at some distance with my .357 pistol. After the fight was over, we went forward, and I went into a ditch and brought this VC out of the hole. He was in bad shape, yet I saluted him and said in French, 'You put up one hell of a fight!' And he returned my salute lying there on the stretcher. Later the media said I had honored this VC by saluting him as he was evacuated. I still see nothing wrong in my action. He had shown me his ability as a soldier, and I was saluting him as my honorable enemy whom I had succeeded in conquering."*

George Patton, the professional soldier, could not at times countenance diplomatic protocol. A glaring example occurred one day in 1955 in Belgrade, Yugoslavia, when George and Joanne were being escorted into an elevator. Patton spotted a Chinese Communist delegation already inside and barked for all to hear, "I'll be goddamned. I'm not going to ride in an elevator with the sonovabitch I was trying to kill two years ago."

A soldier in the Patton genre makes for interesting study. *"There were combat commanders,"* says George Patton, *"who were paid to fight and who did it because they were professionals. There are other professional soldiers who were paid to do it and enjoyed it. In my case, I enjoyed it. I'd have done it for nothing, because I truly enjoyed soldiering. The one thing I did not like is losing people. It bothered me greatly, and I lost some good ones."*

Ruth Ellen once said, "I think people totally misunderstand what my father and brother enjoyed about war. They loved the challenge and loved to win. They also loved the mechanics and the interplay of intelligence and historical memory. I don't think anybody can tell me they liked to see limbs fly through the air. Firemen hate fire, doctors hate disease, and soldiers hate to fight, but everyone has to learn a trade, do it properly, and do it fast." George Patton sums it up by saying, *"It takes a special type of person to do the things we have to do, and luckily there are not too many of us, if you know what I mean."*

Most military historians place the late General Patton in an elite group of fighting commanders. In fact, thorough study of his military exploits leaves no doubt that he possessed a greater understanding of the battlefield than most who ever came to fight a war. Of course his vast achievements put pressure on his son, as happens to any relative of a famous person. On October 6, 1943, General Patton wrote to his son, "Naturally with the publicity I've gotten, you are a marked man. It's a good thing to be a marked man if you live up to the reputation."

I first became aware of Major General George S. Patton in 1980. Before that time, like most Americans, I had been aware only of the exploits of General George S. Patton, Jr.; I knew little about his family and nothing of a son following his forebears' military footsteps. Yet in 1980 I saw in a newspaper a photograph of Major General George S. Patton standing at taut attention, retiring at Fort Knox, Kentucky. He was weeping openly. Patton was leaving a profession and a military environment into which he had been born and which had lasted the greater part of his life. Not long after, I arranged to interview Patton for a magazine article. Later we decided to work together to produce a definitive account of the fighting Pattons, father and son.

It has been my intention in this book to let the leading characters in this story, most especially George Patton, share events in their own words, as much as possible. I believe it adds immeasurably to the historical accuracy of this account and gives the reader additional insight into the personalities of the principal figures. For that reason George Patton's reminiscences, his comments and observations to me, and his writings are printed in italics.

John Adams, America's second president, wrote a letter to his wife, Abigail, in May 1780, wherein he remarked, "I must study politics and war, that my sons may have liberty to study mathematics and philosophy, geography, natural history and naval architecture, navigation, commerce, and agriculture, in order to give their children a right to study painting, poetry, music, architecture, statuary, tapestry, and porcelain." So it was true for the Pattons. Today the sons and daughters of Major General George S. Patton (Ret.) enjoy careers not related to military service. The continuous service in war by father and son, from the 1916 punitive expedition in Mexico through the Vietnam War, has completed, if only temporarily, the Patton presence in the Army.

This book, then, is about a remarkable family, a famous father, and his only son, who grew and excelled in a large shadow cast by fate. It is the story of a son who witnessed an ever-changing company of famous names and monumental events, in war and peace.

ACKNOWLEDGMENTS

The process of writing a book, and this one most certainly, is a nearly all-consuming venture. In fact, *The Fighting Pattons* represents years of research, hundreds of interviews, review of countless documents located all over the United States, and cooperation by historians, scholars, research institutions, libraries, military sources, and others connected with the Patton story.

Even with the extensive research, however, *The Fighting Pattons* could not have been produced without the extraordinary assistance of Major General George S. Patton (Ret.), his family, and legions of his friends. Among those who were especially helpful in understanding the contemporary Patton were those who served with him, including Generals John McEnery (Ret.) and Jim Dozier (Ret.), and Colonel Andy O'Meara, Jr. (Ret.)—who once wrote the author, "Keep up your good work. It is an important effort. History should be balanced. I'm afraid the side of the dedicated professional soldier has never been told."

Helpful in telling the story of General George S. Patton, Jr., were the late Hobart "Hap" Gay, Patton's chief of staff; the famed aviator and general Jimmy Doolittle; Patton's wartime driver John Mims; and his driver on the day of the accident, Horace L. "Woody" Woodring. Appreciation is also extended to General Walter "Dutch" Kerwin, who accompanied Beatrice Patton to Europe after the accident and later served as a Field Force commander in Vietnam and as Vice Chief of Staff of the U.S. Army. The late President Richard M. Nixon was also helpful, adding a unique perspective as a great admirer of General George S. Patton, Jr., who also followed the younger Patton's command activities in Vietnam as commander in chief.

On a more personal basis I would like to thank the Patton family, including George's sister Ruth Ellen Patton Totten, who was extremely generous and forthcoming in my interviews with her, especially concerning the family lineage and with observations about her brother. Her death in 1993 closed yet another chapter in Patton history. As the family historian and raconteur extraordinaire, Ruth Ellen offered invaluable input. Her love of Patton family history was passed along to Robert Patton, one of George and Joanne's sons. Robert's genealogical research and subsequent book about the family, stretching back over 250 years, helped augment and round out the extensive family history as told to me by Ruth Ellen. I also wish to highlight the assistance of Joanne Patton. Joanne was extremely supportive; along with George she opened files, diaries, and photo albums, and answered hundreds of questions. The depth of information in this book is in large part owing to the family's assistance and the unprecedented access they gave me to information in their possession.

In addition, my great appreciation is extended to Lois Hunkins and Norma Sosnowski, who work for George and Joanne. Lois assisted me in coordinating my visits and the hundreds of phone calls to and from the General, Joanne, and others. Norma was instrumental in checking numerous manuscript reviews for accuracy, as material was sent back and forth between Petaluma, California, and Hamilton, Massachusetts.

As for members of my own office, I have profound

appreciation for the assistance provided by Kerry O'Brien and Joan O'Brien. Without Joan's extremely competent support this book could not have been completed.

Heartfelt appreciation is also extended to Dan Eades, senior editor for the Greenwood Publishing Group, who embraced this project and helped guide it along the path to publication. His enthusiasm for *The Fighting Pattons* from the very beginning helped immeasurably in producing a balanced portrait of a controversial father and son. Along with Dan, I also wish to thank Maureen Melino, Bridget Austiguy-Preschel, Pelham Boyer, and the many other fine people associated with Greenwood who collectively and individually assisted in bringing this project to fruition. The book, I believe, succeeds because of their unselfish efforts.

I apologize in advance for not noting in this section all the other people who contributed to this book; however, their contribution is appreciated and was instrumental in writing *The Fighting Pattons*.

The time-consuming task of writing a book cannot be accomplished without the support of one's family. In that regard I especially wish to thank my wife Bonnie, daughter Erika, son Ryan, and my mother Josephine. Their patience and support gave me the strength to complete this project. Finally, in everyone's life there is a source of inspiration; in my case, it is my father, Colonel Harold A. Sobel, to whom I dedicate this book. He passed away many years ago, but I think of him each day.

Richard Nixon once wrote to me, "Since I have a passing acquaintance with the ordeal of writing a book, may I wish you well in your project"; since Nixon wrote seven books, "a passing acquaintance" was obviously self-deprecating. Indeed, writing a book is an ordeal, but fulfilling at the same time. As Andy O'Meara, Jr., wished, this is a book which attempts to balance out the Patton story, a story in which two very dedicated soldiers, General George S. Patton, Jr., and

Major General George S. Patton (Ret.), father and son, gave full measure to a nation. To these great Americans and all other veterans of America's armed conflicts we owe an undying debt of gratitude.

Brian Sobel
Petaluma, California
January 1997

BORN OF DISTINCTION

The Patton sons were all either killed, wounded, or otherwise affected by the Civil War.

—Ruth Ellen Patton Totten

It is said that a Patton has fought in nearly every conflict in America's history; yet the first Patton, one Robert Patton, was not a military man but a tobacco exporter from South Carolina, whose name first turns up on a deed in Fredericksburg, Virginia, in 1771. It has been established with considerable certainty that the name was an alias: the young man who called himself Robert Patton, then a popular last name in Scotland, was actually a wanted criminal in the old country. Like so many immigrants of those times, he had set out for America to leave his past behind. From such humble beginnings the family over the next two hundred years would make an indelible mark on the American landscape.

The Patton name has inspired countless literary endeavors, including many books and articles, published especially over the last fifty years. The story of Patton has been chronicled on television and in major motion pictures, including *Patton*, starring the award-winning actor George C. Scott. The name has been brought into the collective consciousness of America and much of the world through the power of Hollywood, with its impact across borders and languages.

An epic major motion picture that wins numerous awards will be seen by hundreds of millions of people around the globe, but it is the story being told that captures the imagination. The Patton saga is just such a story. The leading character is bigger than life, certainly as enhanced by the motion picture screen, which conveys the power and majesty of a persona of inspiring quality, crushing the enemies of freedom and democracy.

While the story of one general and hero is a central part of Patton history, it is not the only one. Importantly and significantly, there is more. The full story involves a son who also became a general, who participated in two of our most controversial wars, Korea and Vietnam. The fact is, the complete Patton military story ends not with General George S. Patton, Jr., but with his son, a general who fought in wars where the enemy was elusive as were the solutions to the problems facing America in the post–World War II era. Telling the story of Major General George S. Patton requires, however, not only recognizing the career of his father, the famous field commander of World War II, but going back to the beginning, to set the scene.

America during the Colonial period was a place where new ideas flourished, where strangers and newcomers banded together to form communities; the young country was flexing its new-found power and allegiance to itself instead of the old country. With just such a backdrop Robert Patton established himself in the Fredericksburg area, ingratiating himself with the local citizens while running a tobacco business. Interestingly, whereas many men of his day fought in the Revolutionary War, Patton did not volunteer, preferring to remain friendly with both the British and Americans alike. During the war, however, Patton killed a British officer in a tavern altercation and was forced to keep a low profile for the remainder of the conflict.

Robert Patton was, if nothing else, a resourceful soul, undaunted by circumstance, who in the late 1770s would marry the daughter of General Hugh Mercer, a close friend of George Washington. The union produced six children; one in particular, John Mercer Patton, went on to a distinguished career, including service in the United States Congress and as the acting governor of Virginia. He and his wife, Peggy French Williams, had twelve children, nine of whom, eight boys and one girl, lived to adulthood.

Seven sons of John and Peggy Mercer Patton would eventually join the Confederacy. The Civil War not only pitted the South against the North in America's greatest tragedy but drew into its wide net members of nearly every family, particularly in the South. The Pattons were no exception, feeling honor-bound to fight, and doing so with a high degree of dedication and bravery. Whether viewed from a Northern or Southern perspective, it was an especially cruel conflict, setting brother against brother and producting horrific and deadly battlefield technology. The famed "minie ball," as an example, designed in 1849 by C. E. Minié, a French Army captain, accounted for 90 percent of the casualties; another 8 percent were caused by increasingly powerful and accurate artillery.

The Civil War, in which the Pattons played a significant role, was especially hard on the family. Ruth Ellen once said, "The Patton sons were all either killed, wounded, or otherwise affected by the Civil War." In addition to splitting families, the war split the military. By 1861, it is reported, 820 graduates of the United States Military Academy at West Point were serving in the armies of both the North and South, though more than 75 percent remained loyal to the Northern cause.

The Pattons, as Virginians and loyal to the South, fought on familiar ground. Virginia evolved as the leading theater of the Civil War; battles, engagements, and campaigns in Virginia exceeded those of any other state, including Tennessee. By war's end just under one-third of all military actions had occurred in Virginia, and extant reports from the field—including specific indications of their movements in battle by generals "Stonewall" Jackson and R. S. Ewell, among others—mention the Pattons in locations throughout the state.

One particular Patton, the fourth child of John and Peggy, was given the name George Smith; he was the first in a line of Pattons with the same first name. Born in Fredericksburg, Virginia, in June 1833, he would eventually attend the Virginia Military Institute, where he graduated in 1852. After VMI, Patton set up a law practice and later formed a volunteer militia company, the Kanawha Rifles, in which he assumed the rank of captain. This company became Company H of the 22nd Virginia Infantry when it was activated in late April 1861. When the entire regiment was sworn into the Confederate service, Patton became a lieutenant colonel and was ordered to report to Brigadier General Henry Wise, a past Virginia governor and now commander of the Army of the Kanawha.

Patton fought courageously. He was wounded in 1862 but returned to the war, to be killed in the third battle of Winchester, often called the battle of Opequon, in September 1864. "At the time Patton was killed in action, his commission as a general in the Confederate Army was in the mail," said Ruth Ellen. It was the second death of a son in the war for the Pattons, who had lost Colonel Waller Tazewell Patton nearly a year before. Today in the Confederate portion of a cemetery in Winchester, Virginia—a town that changed hands seventy-two times during the war—is a statue dedicated on June 6, 1879, "in memory of the 398 Virginia soldiers lying in the cemetery who fell in defense of Constitutional Liberty and sovereignty of their state from 1861–1865 A.D."

Nearby is the simple grave of the Patton brothers, lying among friends and fellow soldiers. The tombstone reads, "In Christ alone perfectly content." Regarding Colonel W. Tazewell Patton, 7th Virginia Regiment, it speaks of a Patton "who fell mortally wounded in the charge of Pickett's division at Gettysburg on the 3rd of July, 1863 in the 29th year of his age"; under Colonel George S. Patton, 22nd Virginia Regiment, it recalls one "who gave his life in Command of his brigade in defense of Winchester on the 19th of September, 1864 in the 32nd year of his age."

The story of Colonel George S. Patton and his life and death was to have great bearing on the future, not only because he and his first cousin George Hugh Smith were born within a week of each other, but also because the two men were devoted friends, both fought for the Confederacy, and both fell in love with a woman named Susan Thornton Glassell. She would marry George Patton, and together they would have four children. In her grief at the death of her husband and concern about the future of the South (for she had no interest in Reconstruction), she left for California with her children to live with her brother, a lawyer, Andrew Glassell.

In California, Susan Glassell Patton diligently went about creating a new life, founding a small private school. Meanwhile, George Hugh Smith, who had been captured and held as a prisoner of war by Northern forces, was released and traveled first to Mexico and then later to California looking for work, but also, and more importantly, for Susan Glassell Patton. Smith found her and, after spending time with her, decided to propose marriage. She accepted, and they were married in 1870. Ruth Ellen reported that Smith was beloved by her children and that her eldest son, George William Patton, even changed his name to George Smith Patton.

As George Smith Patton grew under the tutelage of Susan Glassell Patton Smith and George Hugh Smith, he developed a keen interest in attending VMI, which he finally decided to do. Graduating in 1877, he returned to California within a year and became an attorney and later the Los Angeles District Attorney. Patton also worked in political circles and was considered to be a star of the Democratic Party. Eventually, in 1884, he would meet and marry Ruth Wilson, daughter of Benjamin Davis Wilson, a truly remarkable man of his time, a pioneer, trapper, trader, adventurer and Indian fighter. The union of Ruth, one of Wilson's two daughters, and George produced a son whom they named George S. Patton, Jr. It was this Patton who would go on to fame and glory in World War II.

While the Patton side of the family looked upon themselves as aristocratic Virginians and traced their heritage to George Washington—or "Cousin George," as they called him—the Wilsons reflected the times in California. They drew their eminence from Benjamin Wilson's early presence in southern California, where he helped establish the orange industry, planted the first great vineyards, and was twice elected to the state legislature. Mount Wilson, where the famous observatory now stands, is named after Benjamin Wilson.

The interesting convergence of these two remarkable families produced a military genius and an American folk hero in George S. Patton, Jr. The fighting general would capture the imagination of millions over a span of decades, for he was a man of contrasting qualities. Although tough and quick to anger, he was also thoughtful and sentimental. A man of enormous ambition, he believed that he was fated to be a leader of men in war and worked hard to fulfill that goal. Americans would come to know Patton as a complex and compelling figure.

George Patton's early years were spent in southern California, an area which at the time contained expansive ranches and allowed the young man ample space to ride and pursue his love for horses. At eleven years of age he entered a private school in Pasadena, and at eighteen followed the examples of his grandfather and father and attended VMI. Patton was at VMI for a year before winning an appointment to West Point through a competitive examination held by Senator T. G. Bard of California. He arrived at West Point in June 1904 and immediately established himself as an intensely serious individual. As one historian later wrote, "He had studied military history and West Point customs so thoroughly that he knew them better than most upper classmen. He was hazed unmercifully for it. At the end of his first year he received one of the first setbacks to his military career. He had failed in math and had to repeat his first year again, and as one contemporary would later say, 'with most of the indignities inflicted on lowly plebes.' " Patton's intensity at West Point left some thinking he was cocky; nonetheless, he aggressively sought rank and honors. His habits of discipline and work ethic would continue throughout his life.

Patton's enjoyment of athletics, perhaps born of a love for riding horses and the gallantry of men on horseback in war, extended to fondness for football and acclaim as a swordsman and polo player. He was also an expert shot with a rifle, excelled at track, and in his third year at West Point broke the record he had set the previous year in the 220 low hurdles.

Upon graduation from West Point in 1909, Patton selected the cavalry branch in which to begin his Army career. A few months later he proposed to and married Beatrice Ayer, whose Boston family was immensely wealthy and well known. The wedding on May 26, 1910, was a well-covered event in the Boston newspapers and was attended by family and friends from near and far, including California. Their union, blending Brahmin upbringing and military tradition, produced two daughters and a son. Beatrice, born in 1911, would later marry a career Army officer, John K. Waters. Ruth Ellen, born in 1915, like her sister married a career Army officer, James W. Totten. George S. Patton, born in 1923, would be the youngest of the clan.

Patton began his Army service at Fort Sheridan near

Chicago, arriving for duty in September 1910. Just three years later the young officer, in what would prove to be just one more chapter in his storied career, was selected for the 1912 Olympic team, which competed in Stockholm, Sweden. Patton finished fifth in the Modern Pentathlon, while one of his teammates, the legendary Jim Thorpe, won not only the pentathlon but the decathlon as well.

In 1915 George S. Patton, Jr., was transferred to the 8th Cavalry, located at Fort Bliss, Texas, near the Mexican border. Relations between the United States and Mexico were growing increasingly strained, and bandit chieftains were raiding north of the border. Although American troops were stationed there to assist with the border problem, Fort Bliss also served as a training area for those who would eventually be part of the American Expeditionary Force (AEF) in Europe. In March 1916 the Mexican Pancho Villa and his men raided Columbus, New Mexico, forcing the American government to take action. In response to the attack on Columbus General John J. "Black Jack" Pershing was ordered to organize a punitive expedition into Mexico to capture Villa. Patton quickly persuaded Pershing that he should go along and rode with the cavalry column pursuing the Mexican bandit. Patton performed well in the operation. It was also a great opportunity to study and learn from Pershing's leadership style.

Later, when Pershing assumed command of the American Expeditionary Force and went to France, Patton hooked up again with the legendary general, sailing to Europe with Pershing and a contingent of headquarters troops, leaving on May 28, 1917. Upon arrival in Europe, American troops, with Patton playing a role, moved quickly to establish the groundwork needed to direct the expanding troop deployment. Starting in a staff position was anathema for any aspiring field commander, and Patton longed for a move to the field and a combat assignment. As his orders were being readied for command of an infantry battalion, Patton pursued a new interest in the use of tanks. He attended the French tank school, because he was becoming enamored with the newly emerging fighting vehicle and American tank forces had little armored strength. He also spent many hours as an American observer with the British tank forces.

Patton, excited by the possibilities and advantages of tank warfare, was soon given an assignment with a newly formed U.S. Tank Corps and even became the first officer assigned to it. Patton, portending the future, mastered the skill of running and maintaining tanks and started to develop doctrine on battle employment of armor. He became the AEF's recognized tank expert and, again providing a glimpse of the future as the man who would become synonymous with the tank, also formed an American tank school, where he taught and trained tankers for the AEF. His leadership qualities showed in the excellent performance of his troops.

Patton was always innovating, trying new techniques and inventing. An illustrative aside concerns a visit to the French cavalry school at Saumer, after representing the Army and the United States in the Olympics of 1912. At Saumer, Patton took lessons from the instructor of fencing. When he returned to Fort Myer, Virginia, Patton designed a saber, known as the Patton sword, which was later adopted by the U.S. cavalry.

The end of World War I inevitably brought changes in the Army. The infantry, for example, absorbed the Tank Corps, which was then summarily disbanded. Patton, however, believing that tanks would play a major role in any future war, secured a promise from the Army that he would be able to rejoin his beloved tank outfits if they were ever reassembled.

As a major Patton was transferred to Fort Myer, commanding the 3rd Squadron, 3rd Cavalry. While in Virginia Patton was once again able to spend time riding horses in shows, hunting, and pursuing his love of polo. He trained and rode by the hour, and in 1922 he was manager of the Army polo team that won the American Open Championship.

Patton's assignment to Fort Myer, in close proximity to the nation's capital, was fortuitous also because he met numerous important and influential people, not only in the military but in the world of politics. During this period, for example, he became well known to General Leonard Wood, the Army Chief of Staff, and Henry L. Stimson, the Secretary of War.

During the early years of Patton's career, Ruth Ellen began watching her father closely, finding him very special. She reveled in his dramatic style, observing, "He was an actor, and did so with other people, but not at home." She clearly recalls her father standing in front of a mirror, "practicing that face and reciting to himself." Her father, she learned early, was also emotional. "He was the easiest weeper I ever saw. He'd cry at movies, or when he was reading a book, or when my Mother was reading aloud."

Ruth Ellen would also say years later, "My father had dyslexia. Not many people knew that about him and he was eventually able to overcome it." Through Patton's youth and continuing into adulthood, his family read aloud to him. When he was a child and young man his mother in particular read him books she thought would broaden his education, books such as Xenophon's *March of the Ten Thousand, Napoleon, Alexander the Great, Beowulf, Siegfried*, Hawthorne's *Greek Myths, With Lee in Virginia*, and *Pilgrim's Progress*, among many others. "We used to read to him quite often when we were growing up," remembers Ruth Ellen. "Sometimes he even would be sitting reading his own book, but you could tell he was listening to whomever was reading, because he wouldn't turn a page. He just loved to have someone read aloud."

Life at home was an ever-changing scene of military activity and guests, who would be invited to the house on a regular basis. Ruth Ellen later described her father at home during that time. "He was a most engaging individual, and we learned early that some formality was considered important. In preparation for dinner, as an example, we girls and my mother put on long dresses, and my father always wore a tuxedo. Little George just had to wear something clean. We would have long conversations over the meal, and talk about interesting subjects. He spoke about death and life and destiny. Unlike many families, these subjects were well discussed around our house."

The Patton family through the generations believed in reincarnation, fate, destiny, and life after death. Some may view the acceptance of psychic ability or belief as strange, but for Ruth Ellen, "It never seemed at all strange to me. Just strange that more people didn't believe it." She reported that, for example, her grandmother saw auras around people and believed her father also had that ability. "The Pattons are courageous for talking about it," Ruth Ellen once said. In discussing her father's belief in reincarnation she recounted his saying he could remember being with Hannibal at Carthage and drinking his own urine out of his helmet. "He said you never remembered the good things, you only remembered the scars," she noted. "He also remembered being carried on a shield by four Vikings after being wounded, and hearing one Viking saying, 'He will live, he's not ready to go to Valhalla yet.' " She also recalled her mother telling of a bitterly cold day during a hunting trip in Virginia. "The sky was very blue, and the snow was dirty and the leaves were dead and brown. He was on top of a hill and he turned to my mother and said, 'I never remember it being as cold as this except that time when we were coming back through the snow. I must have had an arm wound because I had my hand stuck in the front of my overcoat and it was so cold my blood was turning brown as it hit the snow.' He thought it was Napoleon's retreat from Moscow."

In another incident Ruth Ellen told the story of her father lying wounded in World War I, looking up and

seeing his ancestors. "He said he never felt so surrounded by love and warmth. Then it came to him, the
line from Bible which says, 'And death shall be the last
enemy to be defeated.' My father later mused that the
line should have been, 'Fear of death shall be the last
enemy.' "

According to Ruth Ellen, the numerous stories about
George S. Patton, Jr., of the time he was a young officer, cut both ways. "He never left anybody feeling
indifferent. You either hated his guts or you liked him.
There was no middle way with the old man. That's how
stories such as his supposedly saying, 'I'll cross the
Rhine if it takes a 2½ [-ton truck] filled with dog tags'
got started. He never said that, but the story was repeated time and again. As anyone knows who served
with him, he was very caring of his men. That's the
kind of thing people like to believe he would have said.
But I think it's also fair to admit that every bit of trouble he got into throughout his life, he got into all by
himself."

Patton is remembered in large part because of his
leadership abilities, honed to a fine edge over many
years. "Practicing that face" and appearing to be every
inch the hardened warrior, which he certainly was, constituted only one of the many ways he sought to moti-
vate his troops. Outlining his leadership qualities, Ruth
Ellen once explained, "To lead others he felt that you
had to be larger than life, and that soldiers would follow somebody who was like them, yet inspiring." Ruth
Ellen also observed that her father was one of the most
erudite men she had ever met. "Having been dyslectic
he memorized everything. You could never catch him
out on a quotation," she said. "He had a spectacular
vocabulary and always had a word for everything. It
was part of his persona, and others recognized it as
such."

Patton made the girls read a chapter of the Bible
every day and give him a report at breakfast of what
they had read. "My father said the Old Testament was

a guiding light and that the Jews had been persecuted for four thousand years by man and God, yet they'd stuck to their laws and that's why they were still in existence," said Ruth Ellen. "He often said if you were ever at a loss to know what to do or didn't have anyone to talk to, that in the Old Testament one would find out just how to behave. He knew the Old Testament practically by heart."

Other early lessons for Ruth Ellen at her father's knee included his belief that "courage was the easiest of human virtues but persistence was the hardest." "He also often quoted the Irish," she reported. "When an Irishman in legend got mad, a so-called 'hero light' shone above his head, and my father believed it was a reference to adrenaline, and when it comes you can do anything. That's how one could get an arm shot off and fire a machine gun with the other hand. He was also fond of reminding us that 'any fool can die for this country because the band is playing and the flag is waving. It takes a real man to live for his country.'"

Patton's sentiments concerning how a country's citizens often forget their soldiers between wars was something the family also knew well, because he would quote the lines, "God and soldier we adore / In time of trouble, not before / When the trouble is over and all things righted / God is forgotten and the soldier slighted."

On a very basic level, Ruth Ellen said of her father, "He was built like a hero, looked like a hero and acted like a hero, and was a hero worshipper. He was a perfect person cast for his own role. He had bright blue eyes, and until he went bald, even had curls. He was angelic looking and often thought that he looked too sissy. He overcame that belief at VMI and West Point."

Later, when all was said and done, Ruth Ellen witnessed what she saw as exploitation of her father. "When my father came home for a visit in 1945 he was being exhibited. He had to go to a ward at Walter Reed Hospital, and there were reporters, doctors, nurses, and

others around. I remember him turning to them and
saying, 'You sons of bitches want to see me slap another
soldier, don't you?' Then he walked in to the huge ward
and looked around. He was moved and took out his
great big handkerchief and burst into tears. He said, 'By
God, if I'd been a better general, most of you wouldn't
be here.' He turned and walked out. I never forgot that,
and that emotion was something I saw from the time I
was a little girl."

Over many years the paths of General George S. Patton,
Jr., and his mentor "Black Jack" Pershing would cross
time and again. Pershing, meanwhile, had lost his wife
and three children, who died of smoke inhalation in a
tragic house fire. "Pershing was absolutely devastated,"
said Ruth Ellen, "so he spent an awful lot of time over
at our house." Later, Anne Wilson Patton, whom the
family called Nita, and General Pershing fell in love and
became engaged. "They were an interesting couple,"
Ruth Ellen recalls. "Nita looked exactly like my father
and was six feet tall with yellow hair and blue eyes, and
of course Pershing was Pershing. When the war came,
Pershing went overseas and the AEF did well and everybody was making a big fuss over him. He got kind of a
big head, and my aunt called off the engagement because Pershing said that, upon reflection, he wasn't sure
he wanted to marry her."

After the war the Pattons were stationed at Fort
Myer again, and Pershing was living at Walter Reed
Hospital in a suite the Army built for him. Pershing was
a frequent visitor at the Patton home. "He and my father would have drinks, and Pershing would start remi-
niscing about Indian fighting and his considerable
military experience," said Ruth Ellen. "My sister and I
were allowed to stay downstairs because he told wonderful stories and loved children. General Pershing
would often start to cry and lament the loss of his own
children. 'Oh, Georgie,' he once said, 'if the accident

didn't happen, I would have children younger than yours with those same true blue eyes.' I remember my sister and I charging up the stairs to look in the mirror to see what true blue eyes looked like.

"My sister Bea said to Ma one day, 'How could Aunt Nita have fallen in love with that horrid old man?' Ma got the saddest look on her face and said, 'You know, the John Pershing that your aunt fell in love with, well, lots of men die but their bodies don't die. The bodies come home and they keep on functioning and the heart keeps ticking, but the man himself is dead, because they've used themselves up completely. That's what happened to General Pershing. He's not General Pershing, he's just a walking image of General Pershing.' "

In addition to knowing Pershing well, the family and most especially George S. Patton, Jr., would get to know Dwight and Mamie Eisenhower, along with their first son. The duty station was Camp (now Fort) George G. Meade, Maryland, a tour that occurred before George was born in 1923. "We got to know the Eisenhowers very well because my father and Ike were serving together there," said Ruth Ellen.

"While the accommodations at Meade were less than satisfactory, Ma said she wasn't ever going to be separated from my father again, so we all went to live with him," explained Ruth Ellen. The officers' quarters during Patton's time at the camp were old, in fact nothing more than wooden shacks with tarpaper roofs. They were such a fire hazard that a regulation was posted prohibiting cooking indoors; families were forced to eat in the mess. "My sister and I thought that was great," laughed Ruth Ellen, "but Ma didn't like it. She didn't like Army mess food, and she told daddy that she had to have a kitchen. So he went off one day and found a deserted shack on the range and hauled it up to our house behind a tank. My father came in and said, 'I realize this is kind of inconvenient, Beatrice,' and Mother replied, 'No, it's just like Mount Vernon,' referring to the summer kitchen at [George] Washington's Mount Vernon which was detached from the main quarters."

While Camp Meade left much to be desired, the Eisenhowers became a source of fascination for Ruth Ellen and young Bea. "My sister and I used to watch Mamie. It could get very hot and humid in Maryland, and we never saw her in anything but a lovely fluffy pink or pale blue negligee. She used to drink what we thought at the time was iced tea and she'd always stir her drink by swishing it. My sister and I came home and started swishing our milk, and that did not go over."

The Eisenhowers, like Pershing, would figure in the Patton family history throughout the years, especially while at Camp Meade. It was around that time that Ruth Ellen first met the Eisenhowers' young son, Doud Dwight Eisenhower, who went by the nickname "Icky." The boy was three years younger than Ruth Ellen, who, even at the age of seven, remembered that Icky would turn up at the Patton house at all hours and that Beatrice Patton used to "worry herself sick about it."

In 1921 tragedy struck the Eisenhowers, when Icky became ill and a short time later succumbed to scarlet fever. Mamie Eisenhower would give birth to another boy, whom they named John. "Interestingly," recounted Ruth Ellen, "I remember Mamie coming to see Mother one time, and Mother telling me later, since I naturally wasn't in on the conversation, that she said, 'With this child, Beatrice, I'm doing just as you do. I'm not taking my eye off him for a minute.' As many people know, John grew up, attended West Point, had a fine military career, served as Ambassador to Belgium, and became a successful writer."

While Ruth Ellen witnessed the transitional years of her father's career, for young George Patton his father's ever-increasing notoriety was a fact of life, a series of momentous events with which he would become very familiar. Knowledge of his father's building fame began in his youth, and the military legacy would be embodied in the young man until he fully realized that he too must take his place in the Patton panoply.

George Patton fondly remembers his early life and has a special place in his heart for Ruth Ellen: *"Without question she knew the stories about the early Pattons, and of course stories about my mother and father which occurred before I was born. Ruth Ellen and I were extremely attached. She was my very close friend and supporter and a partial link to my father. When she passed away on Thanksgiving Day, 1993, it left a great void I feel every day."* Patton's other sister, Beatrice, was not as interested in the history of the family, preferring instead to concentrate on her own family, having married in 1934 Lieutenant John K. Waters, U.S. Army, who later became a four-star general. *"She was a very charming person with an unbelievably sharp sense of humor,"* recalls George. *"She also loved the outdoors and enjoyed riding horses."* Beatrice Waters died in October 1952, at Highland Falls, New York, near West Point, while her husband was serving in Korea. She was just forty-one years old.

2

THE EARLY YEARS

Ever since I was a child I never wanted to be anything else but a soldier.

—George S. Patton

The period after World War I found George S. Patton, Jr., in a variety of assignments, each giving the future general experience in high-level command. In the first half of 1923 he attended the Mounted Service School at Fort Riley, Kansas, and then was selected for the School of the Line, which later became the Command and General Staff College, at Fort Leavenworth, Kansas. The Command and General Staff College was, and remains today, an important step for any Army officer hoping to advance in rank and to greater responsibilities of service.

George S. Patton, Jr., reported to Leavenworth in September 1923, leaving Beatrice in Massachusetts, where she awaited the birth of her third child. As they did whenever separated by war and Army assignments, the two exchanged letters frequently, with Patton explaining his experiences and daily activities in great detail. In a letter to Beatrice, who wanted to come to Kansas, Patton wrote, "If you come here you will be

very lonely for a while. . . . I am not telling you this
to discourage you but simply as a warning." On December 23, 1923, Patton arrived in Massachusetts for
Christmas leave, in time to celebrate the birth of a boy
hours later on December 24th. The baby was named
George Patton IV. The Patton military legacy had been
extended.

Just five years after the Armistice marking the end of
World War I and cessation of fighting on the Western
Front, Patton began the gradual ascent which would
later cast him as one of the most famous generals in
history. However, at the time, high command was well
into the future, and in mid-1924 Patton was completing
Command and General Staff College as an honor graduate, finishing twenty-fifth out of 248 students. After
graduating Patton joined the I Corps Area headquarters
in Boston as the G-1, in charge of personnel.

After eight months in Boston, Patton, who had been
expecting assignment to the War Department in Washington, D.C., was instead ordered to the Hawaiian Islands. Arriving in Hawaii, Major Patton was assigned
to Schofield Barracks and went to work as Acting G-1
and G-2 (operations) of the Hawaiian Division, which
would later became the 24th Infantry Division of World
War II.

Not long after reaching Hawaii and beginning his
new job, Patton summoned his family to join him. *"We
lived at 27th Infantry Loop,"* George Patton recalls,
*"and one of my first memories is of my dad and me
flying a model airplane he had built. I also vaguely remember him telling me a little boy had drowned in the
pool in front of the commanding general's quarters,
and another time when my father and Major John S.
Wood swam out into the ocean to rescue a soldier in
distress. The rumor was that he was taken by a shark.
The soldier's body was never retrieved, but swimming
trunks with his laundry mark were found later in the
belly of a captured shark. I can tell you that incident
stuck with me as a little boy."*

In Hawaii Patton learned how to swim, and when he came home from Hawaii at four years of age he demonstrated it quite effectively at Avalon, the Merrill estate in Pride's Crossing, Massachusetts, where his mother was raised. *"My father dropped me off a pier twenty feet above the surface, and everybody was shocked. I didn't have any problem, I swam right to a ladder."*

In 1928, Patton received orders to return to the United States and was assigned to the office of the Chief of Cavalry, Washington, D.C. The family soon moved into a large home at 3117 Woodland Drive, Northwest. Young George Patton enrolled at Potomac School. Owing to his father's schedule, which involved travel and at times long hours, he saw his dad little, except during the evenings. *"We did have some time together,"* he says, *"and one of the things we used to do was go down in the basement and shoot. He had a movie projector with films of planes flying around. The screen was armor plate, painted white, and he would sit there with a pistol and shoot at the airplanes as they flew by. It was something to see: Here you had various types of aircraft flying toward you and away from you across the screen, and he would shoot and talk about techniques of fire."*

During the time the Pattons lived near Washington, D.C., a magnet not only for politicians but military leaders as well, George recalls a host of interesting people coming to visit. *"Many of the guests that came to that house were well known and I became very much more aware of who they were, what they were, what they had done, and their relationship with my dad. I was invited to sit at supper with my mother and my father and Ruth Ellen, if she was present. The only requirement was to keep my mouth shut and listen. My parents asked me to do that in a very nice way."*

Among the frequent guests was General Charles P. Summerall, who had been Commanding General, 1st Division, in 1918. George remembers one evening in particular when Summerall spent hours talking about World War I. *"At length,"* Patton says, *"he reflected on how he thought he did and how he really did, a sort of a self-criticism session which was absolutely fascinating.*"

The Pattons also hosted Walter Christie, a tank designer and inventor, several times. Christie designed the suspension system that was used on the M4 tank manufactured during World War II. Patton remembers, *"He and my father spent engrossing evenings drawing pictures on pads of paper and discussing tank design, but mainly talking about tank track and how to cushion the bumps.*"

George Patton, like his sister Ruth Ellen, also remembers from his childhood that General Pershing was a frequent house guest. *"My dad and Pershing knew each other well. What a marvelous-looking man he was. Straight as a damned string and with a little bristly moustache. It was hard to believe that he was in the Class of 1886 at West Point. I can remember the first time I met Pershing, my father made me salute him. They were having brandy and cigars and he said, 'Young fellow, it is good to meet you. I've known your dad for years. He is a great man.'*" Patton also recalls sitting on Pershing's lap. *"He was a national figure at the time so I was duly impressed.*"

Along with many others, George Patton, Jr., considered Pershing the father of the American army. As George says, *"At the time America entered World War I with the British and the French, they refused to allocate a sector of the front to Pershing for the American Expeditionary Force. They tried to break up the AEF and put an infantry battalion here, an artillery battalion there, and a machine gun battalion along the line to reinforce the current Allied effort. Pershing just wouldn't do it. Without checking with anyone in Washington he told Marshal Foch, the Supreme Commander, that not one soldier would move until the Americans were provided a sector. He was under tremendous pressure from the French and the English, but he just said, no. Later, the French and British pulled in their horns, and the rest is history."*

Of the many visitors to the Patton home, one guest in particular intrigued young Patton. He was Colonel Wild Bill Sterling, who had been a Texas Ranger in 1916, when George Patton's father was on the border. They became good friends, and Sterling gave him the famous .45-caliber Colt revolver that is now at the Fort Knox Patton Museum. *"He came to dinner when I was going through the cowboy and Indian stage in my life,"* says George Patton. *"At the time I was collecting these little cards of Wild Bill Hickok and Annie Oakley and Billy the Kid and Wyatt Earp that came in chewing gum packs. I was told that if I was a good boy all week I could come down and meet Colonel Sterling after supper. I was bubbling with enthusiasm to meet this guy and he was beautiful, right out of* Gunsmoke *with pipestem trousers, a swallow-tailed coat, string bow tie and an embroidered black vest. I looked at his Stetson out in the hall, which probably cost him $150. I walked in and I said, Colonel Sterling, I've been looking forward to meeting you for so long and I'm just delighted that you're here. He said, 'What questions have you got, boy?' And I said, Sir, I'd like to know how many people you've killed. He said, 'Georgie boy, I've put down more than 35.' That finished me, I'll tell you."*

As a young man Patton remembers being pulled out of school one day to hear T. E. Lawrence, the famed Lawrence of Arabia, make a speech at the National War College. *"He was a slight little man, maybe forty-five years old at the time,"* says Patton. *"It was fascinating. I had read a little bit about him and he was sort of a mystical hero. That day he talked about the Desert Corps and his association with the Arabs. It was certainly worth losing one day in school. When we went into Vietnam many years later, we read Lawrence because it was the only guerilla warfare experience that we could study. My dad felt it was more important for me to see these famous characters than to have one day at school. He felt very strongly about history and the part these individuals played."*

Patton says today that meeting famous individuals had a huge impact at the time. *"My father was very enthusiastic about the link between those people he knew and the current time,"* he says. *"He liked to fill in those gaps by letting me know who these people were and how they had affected his life. I did the same with my children when I could, especially with my two younger sons. When there was a chance I tried to introduce them to famous people as well."*

In 1934 George S. Patton, Jr., was promoted to lieutenant colonel and then learned of his reassignment to Hawaii. The family was delighted to hear the news, particularly Beatrice Patton, who not only spent a great part of her life studying the Hawaiians and Hawaii but would later become a recognized and published expert on the subject. In preparation for his return to Hawaii in mid-1935, Patton bought a second-hand schooner called the *Arcturus*, named after the constellation. The schooner, fifty-two feet overall and forty feet on the waterline, was shipped to San Pedro, California, and made ready for the voyage across the Pacific. Patton says, *"Luckily for our whole family, my father picked up a Swedish fellow, Joe Ekeland, who became the paid skipper of the boat. He had been second mate on the last full-rigged ship to go around Cape Horn and also had been on a boat that was torpedoed in the English Channel in World War I. Joe stayed with us for many years and we were absolutely warm friends all our lives."*

The crew for the adventure to Hawaii included George and Beatrice Patton, Gordon C. Prince (a combat flyer in World War I) and his wife Anna, along with Francis "Doc" Graves (a California Patton cousin) and last but not least, Joe Ekeland.

"I was, in my own way, very concerned," George recalls. *"I really sweated out that cruise, waiting at home to hear if they made it. There was no radio in the*

*boat, no life boat, just a little collapsible dinghy, and
there was a lot of water to be crossed by a fine group of
people who didn't have a whole lot of experience in the
big ocean. They had experience in the Chesapeake Bay,
where they had been practicing for the trip, but there is
a huge difference between that and the Pacific Ocean."*

The trip took fifteen days from California to Hilo
Harbor in Hawaii. The Pattons tell a story about Joe
Ekeland's arrival in Hilo. Not long after dropping anchor, Beatrice Patton suggested that Joe, who had been
at sea a long time, go ashore and have a look around
and enjoy some time off. Joe said he would and left the
boat. Remarkably, four hours later he was back.

Beatrice looked at him rowing up and said, "Joe, I
thought you were going to go downtown and have a
little fun."

Joe replied, "No, no, Mrs. Patton, the thing I wanted
to do I did. I got a bottle of beer and I went to where I
could get a good view of the boat and drank my beer
and then I came home."

At thirteen, young George, now very interested in
helping on the boat, was aboard the *Arcturus* when it
cruised to Palmyra Island and Fanning, about 1,200
miles southwest of Honolulu, Hawaii. Fanning Island,
now called Tabuaeran, is, like Palmyra, part of the
Northern Line Islands. George and Beatrice Patton,
Jimmy Wilder, Lieutenant Maynard Levenick, Joe Ekeland, and young George were the crew for the voyage.
The first leg included about three or four days at Fanning Island exploring the British and Australian coco-
nut plantations while the boat was being resupplied
with water and fresh vegetables.

They then sailed on to Palmyra, located approximately 250 miles from Fanning Island. Uninhabited,
Palmyra Island actually was a series of coral reefs with
palm trees and various tropical shrubs. The channels
between the islands were only about fifty to one hundred feet wide. *"Because of the poor anchorage,"* says
George, *"it was decided that we should not leave the*

boat unattended, so someone would stay on board while the others would go ashore and explore." On the second day George's mother and father and other members of the crew set out for shore. In the mid-afternoon he noted that the small boat they were in had left the island for the return trip. They got to within three hundred yards off the boat when the motor died. There was a very strong current at the time, and George watched as they started drifting away. He remarked to Joe Ekeland that it looked like his parents were having problems getting back. As they made ready to lift anchor and sail out to pick them up, they saw Patton rowing furiously toward the boat and actually making progress, but it was a tough row. "*Finally, after a long time, they came up alongside the boat,*" recollects George, "*and my father yelled 'Shit!' He wasn't happy. But we got them aboard and everything turned out fine.*"

In 1937, becoming ever more experienced on the ocean, George was included as a deck hand for the return of the *Arcturus* to California. "*My dad and I had an outstanding time on the trip. The only time he would get a bit testy with me was when I tried to talk with him when he was navigating, and he had every right since there were no sophisticated navigation aids in those days. We just had the sextant, the compass, the chronometer, an imposing collection of navigation tables, and a good chart requiring great concentration. During the trip I was just one of the crew. I stood watches and was on duty with Joe Ekeland at night. I would do the helm and Joe would do the lines. The trip from Hawaii to the West Coast, despite some bad weather, was generally uneventful. When we arrived at San Pedro I was presented with discharge papers as an able seaman in the merchant marine. My dad arranged that.*"

As the family went to visit relatives upon arrival in California, Joe Ekeland stayed with the boat. It was put up for sale and was almost sold to the actress Greta

Garbo. Patton remembers Ekeland telling his mother, "Oh yes, Mrs. Patton, when she come aboard I looked her over and she vas so pretty. I looked in her mouth and she had teeth just like a healthy dog."

During his second tour in Hawaii, from 1935 to 1937, Lieutenant Colonel George S. Patton, Jr., had a lot of time off, so father and son were able to spend much time together. *"I remember goat hunting in Molokai, and traveling about climbing volcanoes. We also made several visits to the famous Parker Ranch on the big island. Since my father was asked by the Army to procure, at Army expense, what were known as cavalry remounts, we periodically visited the Parker Ranch, and he became great friends with the manager, Mr. Hartwell Carter, who lived there. Later I got a summer job at the ranch paying a dollar a day, but I was on the range with the cowboys, most of whom were either Portuguese or part Hawaiian."*

Patton always loved the Parker Ranch. Even though at that time he was intent on being a soldier, the only ambition he apparently ever had for something other than soldiering was a dream of becoming one of the owners or managers of the Parker Ranch.

A new maturity was also appearing in young George. By the time he was twelve, he began to realize his dad was a *"human being"* and decided that he would lose his fear of him. *"Not my respect, but my fear,"* says George Patton. Finally, one day Patton screwed up enough courage to tell his father things were changing.

His dad laughed and said, "Well, I guess I am sometimes pretty obtrusive."

Young Patton replied, "That's right, sir, you are."

Patton said his father thought about it a moment and said, "I don't always mean to be so tough."

George nodded, "Well, I'm glad to hear that, but from now on we are on different footing. I'm twelve years old and I'm not afraid of you."

After returning from Hawaii in June 1937, Lieutenant Colonel Patton broke his leg in a riding accident; later a serious case of phlebitis set in. He was dangerously ill and would not return to active duty until February 1938. Meanwhile the family and young George were back at Green Meadows in Hamilton, Massachusetts. The estate had been purchased in 1928 when the family was in Hawaii the first time. *"A Mr. Burroughs who owned it had driven his airplane into the ground at about ninety miles an hour,"* says Patton. *"So Green Meadows was offered for sale and my parents received a wire recommending they buy the place. My parents decided to make an offer on the house even though they had not laid eyes on it."*

Patton remembers the first time he saw Green Meadows. *"It was really quite impressive. More importantly, because of my father's military assignments we had never had a home of our own until my parents purchased the house."* Green Meadows had been built around 1786. There was a barn on one side of the road and a large house on the other; there was also a two-car garage, a cottage, and stables with a two-room apartment on the upper level. Additionally, there was a servants' wing and a large sleeping porch, plus a pond and many acres of open land. The house at the time was not yet wired for electricity and had only oil lamps. The road, Asbury Street, which led to Hamilton, was gravel.

The staff at Green Meadows during Patton's youth included a cook, a kitchen maid, a waitress, and an upstairs maid. *"The cook was Rhoda Clements, who had been the cook for President Theodore Roosevelt,"* says Patton. *"We also had two men in the stables and a chauffeur, along with two or three grounds-people. Alice Holmes was also a fixture at Green Meadows. She had been hired to care for me when I was very young and she stayed with us until I was about fifteen. She really was more of a housekeeper as I got older, but was a wonderful seamstress and knitter. She was British, and her father had been a sergeant major in the*

Welsh Guards, so she knew something of the military way of life."

As a young man Patton enjoyed the company of the Green Meadows head groom Gail B. Kent. "*He was an Oklahoman and a soldier from the old Pineapple Army in Hawaii, and my dad hired him to come back with us and take care of the horses. He had a major job, because at one time we had twenty-six horses, most of which were polo ponies. Those ponies were fine animals and I can recall going to many polo games.*" During the intermissions Patton and Kent would go out on the field and cover up the spots where the horses' hooves had dug up the turf. The horses kept Patton very busy, because they had to have exercise every day during the summer. "*We couldn't ride them all so what we'd do is ride one and lead two and go hell bent for leather through the woods,*" he says. "*We ran them for one hour every day of the month unless it was horrible weather. That was the requirement.*"

Young George had learned to ride horses early in life and still fondly remembers Quicksilver, his favorite horse. As a horse-show rider appearing in his first show, Patton rode into the ring on a pony named Jeff. After entering the ring he promptly rode over to his mother to check on protocol.

"Ma," said Patton, "let me make sure I've got this right. If I win I congratulate second, third, and fourth. If I get second, I congratulate the other three. If I don't get anything, I congratulate everybody who gets a ribbon."

"That's what your father always does," said Bea.

Patton's connection to horses and horsemanship impressed others, including young John Eisenhower, whose father would become Supreme Allied Commander in World War II and later president. In his autobiography Eisenhower tells of visiting the Pattons while they were at Fort Myer. "Silver horsemanship trophies covered a complete wall in the living room of their quarters," he wrote.

John Eisenhower also remembers the relationship between the elder and younger Patton as being remarkable. "I was astonished that he not only swore . . . but also encouraged all three of his children to do the same. When young George, a fine boy slightly younger than I, would come out with an appropriate piece of blasphemy, Patton would roar with pleasure. These visits, though rare, were always pleasant."

Patton says the horses and life at Green Meadows provide some of his best memories as a youth. *"My father was moving through a variety of assignments as we spent our summers at Green Meadows. He was gone a lot, mainly in Washington, D.C., but he'd come up on weekends on the train. I can still remember walking down the road and meeting him as he approached."*

During the hot and humid summer months the Patton children were not allowed to do anything in a crowd because of the polio epidemic. Polio was rampant in the area, and so Patton remembers the family staying close to home. *"To pass the time we listened to the radio or read books and played records. We went to the beach once in a while or over to Avalon and went swimming or rode the horses. I can understand our parents' paranoia, because that was before the Salk vaccine was introduced."*

George remembers a great deal more activity when he was in the Washington area, including opportunities to explore the caves in Virginia, fox hunting, and tournaments that his dad arranged. While Patton was considered too young for the hunt operation, he still enjoyed watching. The Pattons also spent time on Civil War battlefields, and, as he says, *"Dad had a great time reliving history."*

Patton as a youth also remembers taking a houseboat trip to Florida and fishing off the side. *"We didn't catch many fish, but the highlight was hunting alligators at night. You could see their two red eyes on the bank and you tried to shoot between them."*

An abiding childhood memory for George occurred

when the family was stationed in Washington and
George S. Patton, Jr., built a boat called the *Menehune*,
which means gnome, or little man, in Hawaiian. He
built it in the garage with the help of a carpenter and
ten-year-old George assisting. *"She was about twenty-
one feet long and the family had her for years. Finally
she started to leak so badly that we towed her out to
sea and sank her. After my dad died we just couldn't
bear to sell the boat."*

The *Menehune* and the *Arcturus*, and later, the
When and If, gave the family a great deal of pleasure.
The Alden-designed schooner *When and If* was built in
1939 by R. E. Pendleton, of Wiscasset, Maine. It was
used for some day sailing, but Patton never got much
use out of it and finally put it up for sale during the
war. Meanwhile, somewhere around 1938 or 1939,
young Patton was having so much fun sailing that he
joined the Pleon Yacht Club near Green Meadows. *"We
raced out of Marblehead on marked courses and members would build up points. Trophies would be
awarded at the end of the season."*

When he was a young man of fifteen, Patton also
recalls, there occurred an incident concerning his father's attention to detail and renowned lack of patience
with historical inaccuracies. One day Patton and
George were at a movie theater watching a film about
the Crusades. *"It was one of the few movies I ever
attended with him,"* explains George. The boy, noting
that his father was shifting around in his chair, asked
him what was wrong. Patton replied, "The armor is
wrong for the time period. It is not even close." Then he
announced he was leaving. *"I protested, since I was
enjoying the movie,"* says George, *"but he replied, 'I
am not staying and if you want to you can walk home.'
Well, it was over five miles to the house, so I got up and
left with him. He just could not bear watching a military film that depicted history inaccurately."*

By the late 1930s the specter of war was looming
ominously. With the war effort mounting in earnest,

George Patton, Jr., was moving from place to place. In 1937, to stabilize George's education, his parents sent the eighth grader to a boarding school, Hill School, in Pottstown, Pennsylvania. *"Their thinking was that my earlier life had been almost totally military in character and that I would benefit from a civilian educational environment,"* says Patton. *"I had wanted to go to a military school called Culver, but my father wouldn't permit it. He said, 'You've had enough military. You've got to experience the other side.'"* Patton would remain in preparatory school for five years, during which time George S. Patton, Jr., came up to see his son several times and even made a speech to the student body about life with the 2nd Armored Division. George recalls, *"I did very poorly at that school. As a matter of fact I had academic help just about every summer. I was a lousy student."*

A lasting impression for Patton from his Hill School days was the attack on Pearl Harbor. After the bombing, which the students heard about in sketchy news bulletins, James I. Wendell, the headmaster, assembled the student body to hear President Franklin D. Roosevelt's address to the nation. *"I remember clearly the famous line, 'Yesterday, December 7th, 1941, a day that will live in infamy . . .'"* recalls Patton. *"After the president's address was over, Mr. Wendell got up and said, 'You heard it, fellows, right now the thing to do is go back and do your work and be normal.' Well, nobody could be 'normal' after something like that. We had one friend whose brother was killed on the USS Arizona. I also recall that several students left school and enlisted in either the Army or the Marine Corps. One of the students even enlisted in the Finnish Army, which later caused him great problems following the surrender of the Axis powers in May of 1945, since the Finns had thrown in with the Germans against the Russians."*

Soon the war would occupy the minds of nearly everyone, although Patton's teen years at Hill School also brought along with it a new interest. *"I guess I was about sixteen and I was starting to run around with girls. There used to be a lot more teenage activities than there are now and we used to go to dances and have fun. But, while I was having fun I also knew things were changing in the world. Listening to the news and watching my father, it was evident circumstances in the world were taking on a serious overtone."*

In reflecting on his years growing up in a military family, Patton generally found satisfaction with a lifestyle dictated by world events or orders from Washington. *"Even though my father was often absent, I was able to maintain a fine relationship with him. He taught me to ride and to shoot and fish and we had the usual father and son relationship."* While George saw his father most during their time in Hawaii when he was going to grade school, later at boarding school the only time he would see his father was on Easter, Christmas, and summer vacations. Patton credits his mother with helping him keep things in perspective. *"She was a fascinating woman who travelled the world. She often visited France and her father, Frederick Ayer, was of course very well known. Among other business interests he was the founder of the American Woolen Company in Lowell, Massachusetts."*

Patton also remembers his mother as one of the most *"beautifully educated"* people he had ever known, although she never went to college. *"As was the custom of the time she had governesses and tutors,"* says Patton. *"Nevertheless, she spoke, read, and wrote French. She authored two books on Hawaii, including one in French, called* Legendes Hawaiiennes, *a collection of legends that she'd picked up from her Hawaiian friends. She also wrote a novel,* Blood of the Shark, *which was published by Paradise of the Pacific Press in 1936–37. It was based on* [George] *Vancouver's* [eighteenth-century] *voyage to Hawaii and a young naval officer who falls in love with a Hawaiian princess."* In

February 1942, young George, surprising no one, settled on becoming a soldier and applied to attend West Point. The form was submitted to the War Department with his father's signature. "I hereby assent to the acceptance of my son of his conditional appointment as Cadet in the military service, and he has my full permission to sign articles binding himself to serve the United States eight years, unless sooner discharged. Signed: G. S. Patton, Jr., Major General." The decision was thus cast in the record; another Patton would join the ranks of the Army.

Patton's decision about his future was never really in doubt. *Ever since I was a child I never wanted to be anything else but a soldier.* Ruth Ellen also couldn't imagine George going down any other path. "Heavens, the first poem he ever learned was, 'Hats off, the flag is passing by.' I remember a little boy with a paper hat on marching around. A soldier was all he ever wanted to be. I don't think he could have done anything else."

3

THE LONG GREY LINE

*While I was never over-romanced by the West Point gradu-
ate, at the same time, I always felt, by God, a West Pointer
ought to be damn good.*

—George S. Patton

In preparation for the United States Military Academy
at West Point, where he had always wanted to go, Patton left the Hill School, in Pottstown, in May 1942,
about three weeks before the graduation ceremonies.
He headed for New York and an odd little place in the
Bronx, next to the East Concourse Hebrew Welfare
Center. *"The place was owned and operated by a truly
brilliant educator, Dr. Jacob R. Silverman,"* says Patton. Silverman ran a remedial educational program
known in those days as a "poop school," with three
distinct missions, all relative to the Military Academy.
The school was designed to:

- *Prepare students for West Point, with a heavy emphasis on the courses presented during the first year.*
- *In the event of academic failure resulting in discharge
  or temporary suspension—known in cadet slang as
  "Foundation," with the individual cadets called*

"foundlings"—to tutor ex-cadets to take and pass the reentrance examination.

- *Finally, to expose certain cadets to other courses in the curriculum, or as Patton says, "generally, to help cadets stay in the Academy and graduate."*

In July 1942, Patton reported to West Point as part of what was then known as the "second echelon" of "plebes" (fourth classmen) brought in for World War II. Congress had only recently approved the expansion of the corps of cadets, and additional appointments were thus made available. Patton was in the second wave. With two echelons, the first group that entered that year was labeled the Class of 1946, but later it became the Class of 1945, because a three-year graduation was instituted in order to get more junior leaders into the war.

Patton will never forget walking with his overnight bag into the central area to begin Beast Barracks, a term referring to a three-month training period for plebes before they officially joined the corps of cadets in September. *"After reporting in, we were lined up and sent through the various supply and issue points drawing uniforms, a mattress, our rifle, a bayonet, and all of the required equipment,"* explains Patton. *"Then, that same afternoon, we were marched to the Thayer Monument and sworn into the U.S. Army."* Cadets then started receiving minimal courses in basic soldiering, which, as Patton remembers, were handled by the first classmen who would graduate, under the accelerated program, in January 1943.

Patton's earliest memories of West Point include standing in formation dressed in a very warm uniform on a hot summer day under the command of an upperclassman known as the "King of Beasts." The "King" when Patton went through West Point, interestingly, was T. Q. Donaldson, a cousin of Patton's future wife, Joanne. Donaldson would call the unit to attention and then march them to meals or to training, as Patton says, *"on the double."* He remembers the first formation very well. *"We were standing at full attention and the upper classes were going up and down, looking us over. The 'King' commanded, 'Left face!' and I will say that in my little platoon, four or five plebes fainted from the heat and stress, only to be carried off by the medics who were standing nearby. I was not one of those who fell but I must say it was 'a near thing,' to quote Wellington after the Battle of Waterloo."*

The training that followed those first days was especially tough on Patton and the others but was designed to put young men brought together from every state in the union through a period of extreme stress. *"Clearly, the regime was designed to eliminate people who were not fully dedicated to a lifelong career in the service. This included a percentage of young men who were interested in little more than avoiding the draft. However, the more important point was that all of those senior to us in rank and time at USMA had been through a similar adventure and had survived, thus being a better man for the experience."*

Patton found early several individuals who stood out among the corps of cadets. He was particularly impressed by Frederick S. Kremer, Class of January 1943. Patton recalls Kremer calling some plebes into his room and telling them to "fall out," or relax. *"He gave each one of us a pint of ice cream, which he had paid for himself,"* says Patton. *"And sitting in the room, after supper, he told us what West Point meant to him as a first classman. He emphasized the fact that he had gone through the identical routine we were experiencing and that he knew that he was a better man for it. The effect was marvelous. I wish I had a tape recorder at the time, because here was this great fellow laying out the meaning of all the things we were doing and all the harassing we were receiving."* Later George would hear that Kremer, his early West Point mentor, had been killed in action as a platoon leader in a Third Army unit.

The intent of West Point, during Patton's day and

throughout its history, has been to mold young cadets in such a way as to develop each into a successful, duty-conscious, and reliable officer. History and tradition also play a major role. Patton remembers Kremer, speaking that day about Colonel Sylvanus Thayer (1785–1872), the father of the Military Academy, and about some of the distinguished personalities who had experienced West Point. *"He mentioned Robert E. Lee, Grant, 'Stonewall' Jackson, Jeb Stuart, MacArthur, and Pershing, and other famous soldiers. He explained to us what they meant not only to the Academy, but to the United States."*

Undoubtedly, even at eighteen years of age, and owing to his family history, Patton had a better understanding of West Point than most of the men in his squad. Nevertheless, he was determined to do well. Academically, however, during his first year (1942–1943) Patton was in constant trouble—from the start of classroom teaching in September to when he was found deficient in analytic geometry, in June. He believes today that his basic problem was failing to learn at an early age the study skills that are vital to all who hope to remain at and graduate from West Point.

Patton became a "D," which is cadet slang for "deficient." In late May 1943 he was notified that he would be "turned out" for receiving a failing grade through the second semester and the written general reviews; the last stage before dismissal would be a "turnout" examination. *"The examination was a final step of sorts to ascertain whether you were going to stay on or not,"* explains Patton. *"If you passed the turnout, you stayed with your class. If you failed the turnout, you were released. The examination permitting an individual to remain was pretty much oriented around the thinking, 'Well, these guys are marginal and we're going to give them a tough examination which most of them will fail, and then good-bye.' At that point you had about ninety days to go and prep yourself to take a reentrance examination. If you were successful you could join the next class, providing you were failing only one subject. If you were turned out in two subjects that would mean automatic dismissal, and one would have to request a re-appointment from Congress. Those were the 1943 rules of the day."*

Patton was asked to report to the Commandant, Brigadier General Philip E. Gallagher, who told him of his being turned out. Gallagher informed Patton that his father had been notified that he had been found deficient in analytic geometry and would have to repeat his plebe year. *"He said my father's response was, 'It's unfortunate, but how can I criticize him, because the same thing happened to me?' My father had also been turned out in 1905 and later repeated his plebe year with the Class of 1909."*

Nevertheless, after being told of his academic status Patton became very depressed. *"I was in bad shape,"* he says. *"I didn't know what in the hell to do. I went down to New York and for probably one of the first times in my life I got roaring drunk. I was in bad shape."* Patton, who had made plans to meet a friend of his parents, *"who was supposed to take me in and soothe my soul,"* didn't show up at the hotel as scheduled and instead woke up in a U.S. Army recruiting station. *"I opened my eyes and saw a huge noncommissioned officer looking down at me,"* remembers Patton. *"I was in my cadet uniform, which was pretty scruffy after a long night, and he said, 'Mister, do you want a cup of coffee?' Then he told me how I had wandered in to the office about seven A.M. just as he was getting ready to open."* The recruiter asked Patton what had happened. He related his story, that he had been kicked out of West Point for failing analytic geometry and wanted to enlist in the infantry and head to Europe and the war. The recruiter replied, "I'll look into your request," and stepped out. The soldier, Patton remembers, was gone for over an hour, and he was beginning to feel better with the coffee.

The soldier returned and, addressing Patton like a

father, smiled gently and said, "Son, where do you really want to go?"

"Sir," Patton replied, "I really want to go to the home of Dr. Jacob Silverman, on Clay Avenue in the Bronx."

He said, "Son, I'll whistle you up a taxi. You don't want to enlist. You are just too damn young and you'd be wasted over there." Patton says today, "I don't remember who he was, but I knew at the time he had already been a member of the 1st Infantry Division in North Africa and Sicily, had been wounded and decorated, and was home recruiting for the Army. I owe much to that NCO, because he refused to enlist me in my condition and then kindly sent me packing back to Silverman's." Later, Patton boarded a train and returned to Green Meadows to discuss the alternatives with his mother, and to "generally sort out my life."

Around the same time, Patton's father, reacting to young George's problems at the Academy, fired off a letter, dated June 20, 1943, to Senator Wadsworth of New York. In it he wrote:

> It seems to me utterly ridiculous to turn cadets back at the Military Academy for failure to pass one subject when at the same time thousands of young men are being commissioned through officers training camps, which while unquestionably splendid institutions, are in no way comparable in education or tradition to West Point.
>
> When a cadet is turned back at West Point all the money which his education cost the government (in my day about $10,000 a year per cadet, now probably much more) is wasted. Moreover, he gains nothing from his second plebe year except the ability to pass in one subject.
>
> It therefore seems to me that, in time of war, cadets who fail in one subject should either be discharged to make room for another cadet, or

conditioned [assigned a special academic requirement upon which graduation is contingent] and carried on at the foot of their class until the condition is passed. If the cadet at the end of a certain time fails to make good his condition, he should then be discharged. In this way neither the cadet nor the government loses. In peace time, if such a happy state ever returns, it may be well to revert to the turnback system, though I personally see no advantage in it; and having been a turnback myself, I speak with considerable knowledge.

I do not know what legal steps, if any, are necessary to accomplish my suggestion, but in view of the urgent need to train officers, I cannot but view with alarm the continuance of a pedantic system, which, in order to maintain a hallowed tradition fathered by a number of ancient professors, few of whom have ever heard a gun go off in anger, should continue to hamper our supply of trained troops.

Soon after, General George C. Marshall, who had received a copy of the letter to Wadsworth, wrote to George's mother:

Dear Mrs. Patton,

Your letter enclosing George's letter to Senator Wadsworth raises a question that is a constantly recurring one, which has been considered from all points of view by those in authority at the Military Academy over a long period of years. It resolves itself briefly into a matter of doing what is considered best not only for the Academy and the Army but also for the cadet himself. The schedules of the Military Academy are so intensive that it is impossible for a candidate to budget his time to be able to carry his regular work and devote sufficient time to study to eliminate a condition. This is particularly true if the subject is mathematics, wherein success in the advanced phase is almost entirely dependent upon thorough grounding in the basic subject. A deficient cadet is required to repeat the groundwork since he otherwise would be placed under tremendous handicap and very likely would lead to deficiencies in other subjects and result in additional expense to the government in further delay in filling a vacancy created in the corps. If young George applies himself this summer, he surely will be successful in his approaching examination. However, and *most confidentially*, I have been told that he is not working hard enough—seems too much occupied in excitement over his father's operations in Sicily to get to hard study. Can't you put on some pressure—but without involving me in this family phase of the matter?

Patton vaguely recalls the exchange of correspondence but says, *"I never operated on it, I mean I was so damned young at that time and so damned naive, I was just trying to survive the academic system."* Specifically, concerning Marshall's comments about the Sicily campaign, Patton says Marshall was wrong. *"I'm sorry to be critical of General Marshall, but I was deep in the books during the Sicily campaign. The Sicily invasion was 10 July, 1943, and I was released from West Point in June."*

At the academy Patton found the powerful early influences of people like Frederick Kremer, but he also reserves great accolades for Jacob Silverman, whom he calls a *"quiet hero of West Point."* Without Silverman, Patton says, the academy would have graduated fewer people. *"We studied hard at Silverman's and I owe him a lot. He knew both cadets and young men in general, very well. We were in the Bronx studying, with no air conditioning, but he knew how to teach. Silverman's basic approach was to have the students take every turnout exam and every reentrance exam administered from 1918 to 1942."* When Patton took the exam to reenter West Point, in August 1943, he opened the test and found ten analytic geometry problems. *"I knew the answers to nine of them before I started,"* says Patton. *"I took out a piece of scratch paper and wrote the answers to the nine problems working backwards from the answer to show the proper calculations, and then took on the tenth problem. As I recall I got a 96 on the reentrance exam, which pleased me, but it also greatly pleased Doc Silverman. The experience put me on the road to recovery academically, and I performed in a satisfactory manner from that point on."*

Silverman remained one of Patton's great mentors and later came to see him at West Point. Patton's lasting memory of Silverman is of a man no taller than five-foot-three, with a bald head and a huge mustache. He taught wearing an old pair of trousers and suspenders, and a striped shirt with elastics around his arms. Patton says, *"We stayed at his house and were fed by him. We'd go to class about eight o'clock and work until eleven thirty, and then we'd have lunch and go back to work until five in the afternoon. I remember, he would sit down with me and say, 'George, George, you son of a bitch, you pay attention, George, and don't write like fly shit!' He was tough. He made us do those problems over and over and over again."* By the time Patton graduated from West Point he had gone to Silverman's three times: first to get into the Academy, then to remain at West Point, and finally in the summer of 1945 to take an advanced course in calculus. For each of these visits Patton recalls being warmly congratulated by his father, who was busy fighting in the campaigns of Europe.

Unlike Patton, who chose to stick it out, some cadets made other choices. Michael J. Daly was such a case. Patton remembers, *"It was one of those hot days and it got to be about a hundred degrees, and old Mike just got fed up and threw his books in the corner, and said, 'See ya later, Doc, I'm going to war.' Next thing we heard, he was in Italy with the 3rd Division, where he later was awarded the Medal of Honor and received a battlefield promotion."*

In September 1943, Patton went back to West Point as a "recognized plebe." In other words, he was a freshman again, but with upperclass privileges. *"For one thing,"* says Patton, *"I could eat at the table like a human being. I could also do things that my former classmates were allowed to do, though I didn't have chevrons on my sleeve."*

Through the war years Patton saw many changes at the Academy. By the winter and early spring of 1945, Patton says, *"A great transformation came over West Point. Many of the staff and faculty who had been there previously were non–combat experienced and had been called up from civilian life. Then in came the new superintendent, General Maxwell D. Taylor, who brought to the Department of Tactics a collection of the finest officers that I have ever known before, or since."* As an example, Patton's tactical officer was Lieutenant Colonel John T. Corley, who had commanded Third Battalion, 26th Infantry Regiment, First Infantry Division, throughout World War II. Corley and many like him, Patton believes, simply threw an entirely different light on cadet service than the cadets had known before. *"We used to go up in one of the clubs and talk about fighting and leadership in battle, and we would sit around with Corley and listen to his war stories. We just really sucked it up. It was an incredible preparation for our later service."*

The life of a West Pointer in Patton's day included academics, discipline, sports, and rigorous military training. Reflecting on his experience, Patton says, *"The lessons of West Point are many, but the Academy has been the source of discipline, courage, and strength for many of its graduates in both peace and war since its founding in 1802."*

Patton's conviction is that West Point and the naval and Air Force academies uniquely prepare officers for war. He cites the case of a West Pointer, Captain Nick

Rowe, who had to live in a cage as a prisoner of the Viet Cong; Patton and others believe that the discipline and religious training he received as a cadet brought him through. *"Admiral Jeremiah Denton, the former Alabama senator, said the same thing about the Naval Academy at Annapolis,"* says Patton. *"He claimed that his faith, learned at the institution. helped save his life. Admiral [James] Stockdale also claims that disciplinary training saved his life while he was a prisoner of war."*

Patton remembers talking to a young widow who would come back every other year to visit West Point. Fearing that the death of her husband in Vietnam had been needless, Patton recalls, she would sit on the chapel steps and try to absorb some of the things that her late husband had also absorbed, so that she could better understand what her husband had died for. *"She told me that she was finally successful in this effort and it had given her a tremendous amount of solace and comfort simply to return and take in the atmosphere,"* says Patton.

In addition to the military aspects of life at West Point, everyone at the academy was required to play sports. Football was king and continues to be today. *"Army had a great football team when I was there,"* says Patton. *"Frankly, because of the draft. At the time the choice was go into the infantry or sign up to play football at West Point. In 1945 and 1946 alone, we had numerous All-Americans, including Doc Blanchard, whom I knew well, and many other truly great players. But I don't think West Point would have ever seen their shadow if the nation had been at peace."* Patton is quick to add that some players, such as Tom Lombardo, an All-American, Class of 1945, made the supreme sacrifice. Lombardo was killed during the Korean War. Don Holleder, Class of 1956, an All-American in 1954, was also killed in action, dying in October 1962 in Vietnam.

When Patton arrived at West Point he weighed 165 pounds and did not particularly want to play sports; he rightly worried more about academics. He had barely made his letter in football at the Hill School; however, since athletic participation in one sport or another at the Academy was a requirement, he participated on various teams. These included varsity hockey in winter and, during the spring and fall, the intercompany competition known as "intramural." Patton remembers that the cadets fondly dubbed it "intra-murder."

Patton found the academic side of the academy very structured. When asked to recite, one did it briefly and accurately. Patton remembers that his first class in algebra was taught by an instructor obviously recalled from civilian life. *"He was an individual who had come into the Army for the duration to teach math,"* says Patton. *"We arrived at his section room and learned that we had to recite problems every day and that our grade would be posted on the bulletin board at the end of the month. We would go into class and he would say, 'Good morning, gentlemen, are there any questions? There seem to be none; take boards.' We would then do our problems on the boards numbered, right to left, one through maybe twelve. 'Odd boards,' he'd say, 'do problem seventeen, even numbers do problem twenty-seven.' Then we'd do them. He would go around and grade our problems and we'd salute and depart. That was class. There's a certain amount of advantage to that; it made you dig and learn how to study, because you knew you would receive no help during the class period. There was no slack. As for the instructors, the regulars were absolutely desperate to serve overseas,"* says Patton. *"The 'recalls' from civilian life were glad to be there and, in a sense, serve their country, but their desire to serve in combat was not strong. Most of the instructors I was exposed to were fine men who were interested in helping cadets who had demonstrated a desire and shown a potential to bite the bullet."*

At the time, Patton sensed pressure on West Point quickly to turn out graduates to win battles, yet the institution held the line. *"I can remember them telling us the maintenance of a standard education, because of West Point's potential for longevity, was more important. So while we did take some precombat training during the summer, quite frankly low-level stuff, and whereas they changed the curriculum maybe 10 to 15 percent because of World War II, they did not change everything and they did not panic. I say that even though in the early years we were getting the hell beat out of us both in Africa and the Pacific."* Patton believes upon reflection that it was a very important decision for the military establishment, and he has always admired West Point for sticking to its curriculum regardless of the international situation.

Under the West Point organization, George Patton remembers, *"the company was the basic structured unit, of which you were a part. For instance, you participated as a company in drill and intramural athletics, and each company was commanded by a first classman with the usual number of sergeants and lieutenants in charge of platoons. Overseeing each company was a tactical officer, who was usually a major or lieutenant colonel. He was responsible for the guidance of that company and the development of cadets. Additionally, there was a regimental commander, a full, active Army colonel with a small staff. The company tactical officers worked for him. The Commandant, a brigadier general, in turn worked for the Superintendent."*

As Patton looks back today, many of the changes subsequently made through the years cause him unease. Changes in curriculum, less emphasis on drill, appearance, and general discipline are special concerns. *"I'm not entirely comfortable with the product that has been turned out of West Point over the last few years. I believe that the Army leadership should tighten the institution."*

Patton is particularly concerned about the honor system at West Point, a topic often discussed by observers of the academy. Patton remembers going through perhaps a half-dozen lectures on the honor system from both the first class and the tactical department. *"The basic rule was clear, cadets do not lie, cheat, or steal, or tolerate anyone who does. Essentially if you fail to report a cadet who breaks these tenets, you also are guilty of an honor violation. This has been, as I'm sure the officials at West Point will testify, an ongoing problem. The guys I served with both at West Point and later, in my view, did not have the same problem with the honor system that later classes had. The first big honor scandal came in 1950–51, at the time my brother-in-law, John Waters, was Commandant of Cadets. It was a mass cheating scandal. The second crisis came in 1977 when Lieutenant General Sidney Berry was Superintendent."* While it would be extremely difficult to pinpoint any societal reasons for the cheating, Patton believes that problems with the honor code rose in proportion with general permissiveness throughout the nation, which he believes started in the high schools and permeated the academies in the 1950s. *"I think this permissiveness caused certain people to keep looking at the honor code of West Point with a jaundiced eye,"* he says. *"Also, there is a problem and continuing discussion about what is an honor violation and what is not."*

West Pointers believe the honor system is the basic foundation of Army service. One does not lie, cheat, or steal because in a combat situation, as Patton says, *"if a fellow on your flank says he has registered the artillery* [specific instructions detailing where artillery fire should be placed] *in front of you, you haven't got time to go check. You must believe him. The honor code is the underpinning of trust, at least for graduates. It is based on the fact that we are honest with one another, that we are honorable people, who have been trained to be honorable throughout our service."*

The cadet honor code would follow Patton his entire career. Many years later, when Patton was commander of the 2nd Armored Division at Fort Hood, a West Point graduate was caught shoplifting a couple of boxes of 35 mm film in the Post Exchange. Patton called him in and confronted him with the charge. The officer immediately handed Patton his resignation. *"It was something,"* recalls Patton. *"He sat there and said, 'I don't know why I did it, I just did it.' I simply said, 'Fella, you're just going to have to pay the ultimate price.'"*

While life at West Point kept Patton busy during the war years, he was also closely watching his father's progress in Europe. Although he didn't see his father very often, one of the rare occasions occurred just shortly after Patton started at West Point. *"My father came to visit and spent about half a day with me during a weekend. At the time, September 1942, he was in a highly classified planning program for the attack on Morocco at Casablanca. He was unable to tell me anything about the operation, except that this would be the last time he would see me before going overseas. He said that I was not to tell anybody that he was going overseas, but that he was leaving soon. Of course, in those days, you didn't have too many privileges as a fourth classman, and besides there were so damned many generals at West Point, and in the Army, that his appearance, as I recall, didn't cause any particular stir. At the time he was a major general and had recently been training in Indio, California."* Patton remembers his father telling him that he knew he was already in academic trouble and that he probably should have had a year of college before going to West Point. He went on to add that all he wanted George to do was try as hard as he could.

Infrequent personal visits from his father may have been the basis of stories suggesting the two might not get along well. *"Those who say that I had a shaky relationship with GSP Jr., my father, are not completely on base,"* observes Patton. *"My relationship with him was a difficult one for both of us to maintain through the mail, although he and I frequently exchanged letters. I'd say I wrote him three times a month and he responded in similar fashion. The problem with his being away was that I was in my formative years and I was learning the hard way. I was not able to visit with Dad, counsel with him, and receive his advice, which I am sure would have been useful. I am the first one to admit that my relationship with him was not nearly as close as his relationship with my grandfather. However, I think in view of the trauma caused by the war it was as good as could be expected."* During his West Point years Patton saw more of his mother, although, as he recalled later, she was very active giving speeches, addressing press conferences, and making public appearances. *"She was living with my sister Ruth Ellen at the time,"* says George. *"We would talk fairly often and she would fill me in on all the family news."*

As for pressure put on young Patton because of his father's successes, he says, *"People were generally interested in his European exploits. The Academy, for example, showed films every Saturday concerning the war and I would go over to the theater with some of my buddies in the company and we'd watch them. After the* [Normandy] *invasion of June 6, 1944, and most particularly after the Third Army started its run across Europe, the faculty and the members of the tactical department were very interested in what my father was doing and they talked to me about it. The upper class was also very interested."*

Patton says that around the time of the D-Day invasion his mother was able to drop a couple of hints concerning events about to transpire in Europe. *"She knew what was going on,"* says Patton, *"although I don't think she knew the precise landing spot or other details. She benefited of course by the fact that general officers censored their own mail and could therefore give a few more details in letters home."*

Patton remembers coming back from an Army football game in New York, earlier in the war, right after he entered at West Point, and going by the New York harbor area. He looked out on the water and saw hundreds of Liberty ships, all anchored and blacked out. His mother had tipped him off that his father was getting set to invade North Africa. "*I remember it gave me quite a feeling, because I was sure that this group of ships was one of his convoys. They took off in mid-October and landed in Morocco in early November.*"

On the downside of having a well recognized name, Patton says, "*As the war progressed and my dad got more famous, things got a little tougher for me because of my father's notoriety.*" He recalls a group of upper classmen making him memorize the battle reports from Africa and Sicily. "*Because of my academic problems in 1942 and '43,*" confides Patton, "*it was taxing on me to sit down at night and memorize the results of the battles when I should have been, for example, studying French. But I got through it all right and as time went on I learned to adjust to pressures from my dad's reputation and his activities in combat, which were making headlines on a frequent basis.*"

Others in Patton's class and at West Point endured some of the same attention. The class of 1946 alone boasted 138 sons whose fathers were in military service. "*Bill Clark (1945), later seriously wounded during the Heartbreak Hill fight in the Korean War, was having many of the same problems,*" says Patton. "*Lucian Truscott, another former classmate of mine, whose dad commanded the Third Division at the time, also endured increased attention, as did Jeff Keyes, also a classmate. His dad was my dad's best friend. Hobie Gay, the son of Brigadier General Hap Gay, and Jimmy Doolittle, whose father was well known, were also in my class, as was the son of Lieutenant General Albert Wedemeyer. But we all got along and tried as best we could to adjust.*"

On Thursday, April 12, 1945, West Point, along with the nation, learned that Franklin D. Roosevelt had passed away. The passing of Roosevelt had enormous ramifications, politically and militarily, but also, in the short term at least, emotionally. For many Americans Roosevelt was the pillar of strength, the steady hand as World War II continued to rage.

Soon after the president's death, plans for a funeral worthy of his stature began in earnest. West Point was selected to send an honor guard to the ceremonies. A meeting was called, and orders were issued concerning the cadets who would be part of the funeral on Sunday morning, April 15th.

Patton remembers the days following Roosevelt's death clearly. "*We had a formation and the company commander got up and told us we were supposed to dress in fatigues and go down to the motor pool and start taking the seats out of buses. Because the uniform for the funeral the next morning was full dress gray over white trousers, they didn't want us sitting down in the buses.*" Patton remembers the ride to Hyde Park from West Point taking at least two hours. Upon arrival he was struck by the scene, thousands of people and cars everywhere. "*It was the goddamnedest crowd of people I've ever seen in my life.*"

As the train bearing Roosevelt's body made its way slowly to Hyde Park, Patton and his classmates were getting ready to provide the honor guard inside the rose garden area where Roosevelt would be laid to rest. "As a proud member of the interior honor guard I had an extraordinary view of the black caisson and the riderless horse, with boots placed backward in the stirrups, which is the tradition in a military funeral. I also saw a distinguished group of leaders right from the pages of a history book. They included Churchill, Chiang Kaishek, Haile Selassie, and Charles de Gaulle, along with President Truman and many others."

In May of 1945, with the war in Europe having come to an end, General Patton was ordered to make a trip to the States for a bond tour and a visit to the president. On the seventh of June, 1945, George Patton, now a first classman, was notified that his father was going to land in Boston and that he was to go and meet him. "*I went home and stayed at Green Meadows,*" says Patton. "*A couple of days later we all went up to Boston and the aircraft landed. I'll never forget it.*

My dad got out of the aircraft and he really looked super; he was fifty-nine years old at the time. With him in the aircraft were a couple of division commanders, including John W. O'Daniel, who had lost his son in the Normandy invasion and who later became my commanding general at the Infantry School at Fort Benning when I went through the basic officers course in 1946. Also aboard was Leon Johnson [USAF], who had been awarded the Medal of Honor for the Ploesti Raid, followed by eight or nine noncoms, not one of whom was wearing less than a Silver Star. All of this was followed by a ticker-tape parade through Boston. That evening my father spoke at the Shell on the Esplanade in Boston. We came home that night quite late and the next morning he came upstairs and woke me up and said we were going for breakfast. I ate breakfast with him and then I got on a train and went back to West Point. It was the last time I ever saw him."

While at West Point, Patton was going to school not only with the sons of well known military commanders but also with a variety of other interesting cadets, including future Nicaraguan dictator Anastasio Somoza, Jr., the son of the then-president of Nicaragua. Somoza, a controversial figure, was overthrown by the Sandinistas in 1979 and then assassinated on September 17, 1980, when a car in which he was riding was torn to shreds by explosives, ending a story of family rule in Nicaragua. *"I roomed with Somoza for a while. It was quite an experience and we got along very well,"* Patton remembers, *"but he had his quirks."* One morning, Patton recalls, he and Somoza were running late for formation and Somoza was shaving. Patton saw that Somoza was cutting himself with his razor and said, "What the hell? Don't you know how to shave?" and Somoza replied that he was always shaved by a servant, so he didn't really know razor techniques.

Patton remembers the one thing that really stuck

with him was the graduation ceremony in 1946, when Somoza went up to receive his diploma. *"His name was announced to the crowd and then a message was read which said Somoza had been promoted to the rank of general and appointed Chief of Staff of the Army of Nicaragua. Everybody clapped and laughed as Somoza sat down, but the irony of course was that the rest of us were still second lieutenants."* Later, as president, when Somoza's grip on power in Nicaragua was coming to an inglorious end, Patton and several West Point classmates recommended to the State Department that they be allowed to talk with Somoza personally to explain how difficult the situation had become from an American point of view. Patton believes that Somoza would have listened to his West Point friends and might have commenced a series of reforms to benefit the people of Nicaragua. *"We wrote the State Department at least two times and received a reply saying they were not interested in any assistance that we might be able to render,"* says Patton. *"Now in my opinion, Jimmy Carter, who was president of the United States at the time, sold Somoza out, just as he sold out the Shah of Iran, also in his term. Somoza, for all his faults, was a United States supporter. So Carter destroyed two dedicated allies to the United States of America and, by God, he has got to live with that."*

As for Patton's impressions of West Point after many years of reflection, he says, *"On the whole it was a tremendous experience. When I graduated with 874 others on June 4, 1946, I was anxious to apply my talents and education as a new second lieutenant. I believe I was a much better person for having attended the Academy. While I was never over-romanced by the West Point graduate, at the same time, I always felt, by God, a West Pointer ought to be damn good. He's got four years of straight, solid military indoctrination and training, and, in most cases, ought to be better than [a graduate of] the Reserve Officers Training Corps [ROTC] out of a civilian university. He should be not only better, but more confident, because he's received a superb education oriented to military service as a lifetime career."*

Even so, West Point has often been accused of fostering what is known as the "WPPA" (West Point Protective Association). *"I'm quite sure over the years certain commanders who attended West Point may well have selected a West Point graduate over officers from other institutions,"* says Patton, *"although I don't think many would admit it. However, much of that has gone away and I know in looking at the general officer selection lists in recent years, I've seen many more ROTC and OCS* [Officer Candidate School] *selections to flag rank. I'm not saying they are exceeding the West Pointers, but they're about even with them as of this writing."*

4

THE WORLD AFIRE

*The Third Army moved further and faster and engaged
more divisions in less time than any other army in the history of the United States, possibly in the history of the
world.*

—General George S. Patton, Jr.

In the winter of 1944 the United States Third Army
raced across France and neighboring lands, heading for
the heartland of tyranny. The mission: to destroy the
powerful forces of Adolf Hitler and liberate millions of
people under the iron fist of the Third Reich.

As the Third Army conquered land and strategic
objectives, sometimes at a forty-mile-a-day pace, their
commanding general was receiving bold headlines in
American newspapers rivaling those given any other
field leader in the history of the United States Army.
Soldiers either loved Patton or hated him, he evoked
such a response in people. To his credit the vast majority respected him as a military leader. The men of the
famous Third Army rode as one with Patton, and to
this day many speak reverently of having served under
his command. Patton placed himself in the chronicle of
military exploits by his fearless actions and sweeping

victories during World War II. In particular he was cele-
brated for his part in the Battle of the Bulge, where he
made history in the forests of the Ardennes, electrifying
his soldiers and the nation when he boasted, "The German has stuck his hand in a meat grinder and I've got
hold of the handle."

Most military researchers place the late General Patton in an elite group of historical commanders. In fact,
thorough study of his military exploits leaves no doubt
that he possessed a greater understanding of the battlefield than most who ever fought a war. His prowess
was not lost on allies or the enemy. Field Marshal Erwin Rommel wrote that although the Americans had
done well in Tunisia, "We had to wait until the Patton
Army in France to see the most astonishing achievements in mobile warfare." Joseph Stalin later concluded
that the Red Army "could not have conceived, never
mind have executed, the Third Army's incredible dash
across France."

Patton brought many elements to the battlefield. He
was an ardent student of history and a superb tactician
as well. His complex personality accepted and reveled
in a belief in reincarnation, extrasensory perception,
destiny, fate, and luck. Two stanzas from unconnected
parts of a long poem called *Through a Glass, Darkly*,
one of many that Patton wrote during World War II,
touch upon reincarnation directly:

> *Through the travail of the ages,*
> *Midst the pomp and toil of war*
> *Have I fought and strove and perished*
> *Countless times upon this star.*

> *So as through a glass, and darkly*
> *The age-long strife I see*
> *Where I fought in many guises,*
> *Many names—but always me.*

Further explaining Patton's long-held belief in fate and luck, Ruth Ellen observes that "he had many reasons to believe in luck and circumstance. He used to say that luck was something you were born with, it was like money in the bank. And a front line soldier spent his luck quicker than a rear area cook. Near the end, my father felt he had spent his luck because the last few shots landed closer to him each time. He used to say, 'Luck is the subconscious realization of the facts of a matter before your brain takes them on.' Even Napoleon, before he promoted anybody, would ask, 'Is he lucky?' "

Patton, as the voracious student of past military leaders and wars, many times seemed to call upon the ages for help in winning a battle. One story epitomizes this: *"This has never been told,"* says George, *"but when my father crossed the Rhine during World War II his main effort was a place called Oppenheim. At the time at West Point I was studying a Napoleon campaign of 1806. I wrote him a letter and said, 'Hey, you crossed where Napoleon crossed.' He sent a note back saying, 'You know, it's very interesting Napoleon crossed there, but I crossed in that spot because Caesar had.' I then did further research and found that Napoleon crossed there because Caesar did—the reason being there was a hidden inlet on the west side of the Rhine. It shows the depth of study my father went through in order to do what he did."*

In every war there are many political considerations and ramifications. In World War II America was tied by alliances mainly to Great Britain, Canada, the Soviet Union, and, to a lesser extent, others. Since the various armies were carrying out the policies of their own governments, certain rivalries and controversies were sure to develop. As an example, over the years since the war many people have come to the conclusion that vital gasoline supplies were withheld from Patton during his race across France and Germany. *"It wasn't to slow him up per se,"* says George Patton, *"but to reinforce the British. There was only so much gasoline to go around.*" Patton goes on to add, "*Issues concerning what resources would be made available to whom were highlighted by the well known fact that there was competition between British Field Marshal Bernard Law Montgomery and my dad.*" Patton, for his part, wanted gasoline to keep the tanks moving. Responding to rumors that his soldiers were employing creative ways of obtaining fuel, he once said, "There was a rumor, which, officially, I hoped was not true, that some of our Ordnance people passed themselves off as members of the First Army and secured quite a bit of gasoline from one of the dumps of that unit. This is not war, but it is magnificent."

His son has given a great deal of thought to British and American cooperation during World War II. "*I believe my dad felt Ike leaned over backwards to support the British, and I have to concur. Ike was selected to do that because of his well known ability to arbitrate. He was selected for that job by Roosevelt and Marshall. While Marshall wasn't well known to Roosevelt, he was known by many others as someone that could find solutions to complex problems and make them work. That's why Marshall was assigned as Chief of Staff, USA [U.S. Army]. My feeling is that Ike did a pretty good job of putting things together.*"

While Patton feels Eisenhower was a compromiser, he also recognizes that his role was one of unity, coalition warfare, bringing the whole allied effort together. "*Therefore,*" he comments, "*I don't think you can criticize Ike too much, but at times he did overstep himself. This may be true, particularly with Montgomery. The attack into Arnhem, the airborne operation called A Bridge Too Far in a book by Cornelius Ryan, was perpetrated by Montgomery and in my opinion extended the war. It was not the right decision on the part of Eisenhower. He should have reinforced success by putting those resources behind the unit gaining ground, which happened to be the Third Army and to a lesser extent the First Army, at the time."*

Patton is also convinced the United States also bent too far for the Russians. *"We could have gone into Berlin ahead of the Russians, and the late General James Gavin confirmed it,"* says Patton. Gavin was commander of the 82nd Airborne division and the senior U.S. Army officer in the occupation of Berlin when it finally occurred. *"But we didn't because of pressure from the Soviets,"* continues Patton. *"It would have been an entirely different story in that area and most soldiers of my generation feel that way. German officers including General Hans Speidel, Rommel's former chief of staff, told me they would have parted like the Red Sea for my father to take Berlin before the Russians. They preferred the Third Army to the Russians."* While Eisenhower would later write, "Berlin was not the most logical or most desirable objective for the forces of the Western Allies," for Patton's part, when asked about going to Berlin, he responded in an uncharacteristically diplomatic fashion that he neither knew nor cared, barking, "I am going to lick the next SOB in front of me."

Patton, as history records, had little patience or respect for the Russians. In addition to feeling they had been accorded too much room in which to operate and occupy, he simply did not trust their intentions and would have preferred not to have anything to do with the Red Army. *"The old man had a big mouth, he said some awful things about the Russians,"* says Patton, *"and as everyone knows we were officially buddy-buddy with them pretty much until the Berlin Airlift and the famous Fulton, Missouri, speech by Churchill wherein he said an Iron Curtain had descended on Europe. But in retrospect, my father had the Russian number from the beginning and he made it quite clear to anyone who would listen that the world would soon see only two superpowers."* True to Patton's prophesy it was the Soviet Union that emerged from the depths of

World War II to become America's chief Cold War adversary.

Allied political considerations aside, on the battlefield, where it counted most, Patton was feared more than any Allied General. General Günther Blumentritt once said, "We regarded Patton extremely highly as the most aggressive Panzer-General of the Allies. A man of incredible initiative and lightning-like action." Captured German records say of Patton, "He is the most dangerous General on all fronts, he is the most modern, and the only master of the offensive." Patton says, *"The Germans were completely aware that he had spent his life studying for this."*

Probably the most famous German general during World War II was Erwin Rommel. Patton thinks he was a brilliant armor commander; however, *"Rommel did have several problems,"* observes Patton. *"He didn't understand logistics and expected everything to be handed to him. Of course, that thought has ruined many people over the years. Hitler also didn't understand logistics. He should have read history in greater detail."*

At times Rommel and Patton have been portrayed as fighting one another, but Patton corrects the record. *"My father never fought him. Rommel was out of Africa at the time of the famous El Guettar battle. So by fate they never were given the opportunity to tangle."*

It was Patton's taking command of the U.S. Third Army in World War II, however, that catapulted him into history. It was the army Patton had waited a lifetime for. It was his great instrument. It proved to be a military machine in the mode Patton had envisioned. Designed to be quick, versatile, dependable, and tough, his army was one that characteristically punched left and right with armored columns. Wherever resistance was particularly tough, he bypassed it. At one point while in France Patton was asked to fight in four directions: VIII Corps fought in a westwardly direction, as XX Corps moved south to clear Brittany of Germans;

XV Corps, meanwhile, was engaged in the east, while XII Corps was pushing north.

According to official documents, the Third Army under Patton's command, in nine months and eight days of fighting, liberated or conquered 81,522 square miles of territory: 47,828 in France, 26,940 in Germany, and the remainder in Belgium, Luxembourg, Austria, and Czechoslovakia. It captured or liberated 12,162 communities, ninety-seven with populations over fifty thousand people. In that time the Third Army killed, wounded, or captured 1,443,888 enemy soldiers. Of the Third Army, 34,840 men were awarded decorations, including nineteen Medals of Honor. The Third Army had maintained a front of seventy-five to a hundred miles, the longest being two hundred miles in the third week of April 1945. It had risen in strength from 92,187 men in August 1944 to 437,860 in May 1945. "History records no greater achievement in such a limited time," said Patton in an Order of the Day wherein he quoted the statistics for the Third Army's campaign.

It was to be a German counteroffensive in December 1944 that gave Patton his ultimate test of fate and his great reward. Many Germans referred to it as the Ardennes Offensive, but to most Americans it was simply the "Battle of the Bulge." The offensive was a carefully conceived surprise attack along an eighty-mile front in southern Belgium. Hitler hoped either to stop the rapidly advancing Allied armies and turn the tide for the failing Axis powers, or force the Allies into a more favorable, negotiated peace. Some military historians have called the operation Hitler's last gamble.

Final gamble or not, none dispute the intensity of the battle, which involved the German Fifth Panzer, Sixth Panzer, and Seventh Armies under the overall command of Field Marshal Gerd von Rundstedt and amounting to well over two hundred thousand soldiers advancing on the weakest sector of the Allied front. The German offensive commenced in the early hours of December 16, 1944, and for all practical purposes was over on

January 3, 1945. The real story, however, lies between those dates, when ferocious fighting produced countless heroes and immortalized a town named Bastogne. It was at this key road junction that a small group of American soldiers under the command of General Anthony McAuliffe were all but surrounded in the wake of the surprise attack. Courageously, the Americans held until Patton's tanks could arrive with then–Lieutenant Colonel Creighton Abrams leading the column.

Not long after the German Army began its devastating Ardennes offensive, Patton was called to an emergency staff conference in Verdun, France. Verdun had been the scene of an enormous battle during World War I that claimed many lives. Adolf Hitler had even been wounded there. It was during the meeting that the ranking Allied generals realized the gravity of the battle then shaping up in the snow-covered Ardennes. It was obvious that defeat would permanently cripple the war effort.

When it was Patton's turn to speak he stunned all present by announcing that his Army could disengage from battle in the Saar, turn ninety degrees, and attack the enemy within seventy-two hours. Amid both skepticism and contemptuous disbelief Patton was given the assignment to lift the siege. In a raging blizzard the Third Army traveled 125 miles to meet the enemy. Patton later said, "During this operation, the Third Army moved further and faster and engaged more divisions in less time than any other army in the history of the United States, possibly in the history of the world." General Omar Bradley would later say, "The speed with which the Third Army turned its forces north astonished even those of us who had gambled in the Ardennes on the mobility of our Army."

"The Bulge was the absolute pinnacle of my father's career," says George Patton, *"when he turned that whole goddamned army and went up in there. And if the Bulge wasn't the pinnacle, then the so-called Verdun conference was the epitome. The beauty of it was he*

had planned a complete action before going to the meeting. That was generalship. It is what they talk about in the history books. All he had to do was get on the radio and say two words, 'Play ball,' and his staff and commanders knew what to do. His order encompassed equipment, fuel, the resupply, the road nets being cleared, and all the things you have to do in order to move that number of people.

"Interestingly," says Patton, "*the Verdun conference is depicted in the movie* Patton, *but for some reason Eisenhower is not shown at the conference, although he was present. I also recall my dad not wanting to immediately relieve the 101st but instead drive toward Koblenz cutting the Bulge off at the base. He was not permitted to do that and instead [was] ordered to relieve the 101st.*"

George Patton in later years was able to talk to many American officers who worked with his father, but was also able to meet several high-level German officers as well. Through those discussions and meetings he has gained a unique understanding of Third Army operations.

Notwithstanding Patton's unequaled ability as a field commander, his aggressive personality seemed always to leave him on the precipice with his superiors. Many times it was deservedly so, for Patton had a way of being in the wrong place at the wrong time or saying something others deemed controversial. For this kind of faux pas Patton paid heavily. Many feel he paid too much, for at different times he was shunned and bypassed for field commands, and he was overlooked for promotion on at least one occasion.

A remarkable story that tends to support the theory that Patton was a victim of jealousy and manipulation was told by Ruth Ellen. "I was living in Washington, D.C., and during a party at my home Walter Bedell Smith's wife [Smith was Eisenhower's chief of staff] said to me, 'You know it's just as well your dad died when he did because Bedell and Ike were planning to

Ward 9 him.' Ward 9 is where they put the mental cases! If my father had ever gone in for a stay in a mental ward nobody would have ever believed another thing he said. It would have been a way of cutting his feet out from under him. I told George but I never told my mother. It would have broken her heart."

A possible explanation of why Patton often suffered at the hands of others, especially in higher military circles, comes from his son. "*Hap Gay* [Patton's chief of staff] *said my father had one major fault. It was that he had a childlike trust in everybody. He just could not believe that people were out to get him.*"

Some accounts of Patton's life have repeated a story about his sending a small task force during the latter days of the war to rescue his son-in-law, who was a prisoner of war. The mission proved to be a debacle, and lives were lost. "*General Gay and all the guys that knew what was going on were aware there was a POW camp at Hammelburg,*" says Patton. "*My father knew there were many officers at that camp and he also knew the Third Reich was in a death throe. Also, that they had been killing Jews and running them up the chimney, so he was fearful that the SS would break loose and just murder those American POWs. And that's the reason he sent the task force. He admitted later that he had made a mistake by not sending more troops.*"

At the close of World War II General Patton was assigned to the Fifteenth Army, which, the *New York Times* reported on October 2, 1945, "consist[ed] of a headquarters and troops engaged in special research work." The newspaper *Stars and Stripes* said the mission was "to prepare an analysis of the strategy of the campaigns in Bavaria and then to formulate recommendations for changes in ground, air and naval tactical doctrine." Patton says his father's transfer was a low point for his father and the family. "*One must understand that he was released from Third Army command*

because as the military governor of Bavaria he contin-
ued using Nazis or people sympathetic with the Nazi
regime to help deliver services to some of these towns
under his control. But the facts were that there wasn't
anybody else to keep the sewerage and the lighting and
essential infrastructure operating. The city of Munich
was 95 percent destroyed, for example. When I visited
some of those cities in 1946 and 1947 you could still
smell bodies rotting in the wreckage that hadn't been
cleaned up."

Patton goes on to add, *"The tone of the time in the*
spring and summer of 1945 in Europe was that they
had seen the death camps and the whole world was
shocked with the carnage and the mass executions. The
whole world, or at least Western Europe, was piteous
of the Jews. My dad's orders were, regardless of the
expertise of the fellow who had a local political job, no
matter what their ability to participate in the rehabilita-
tion of Germany, if they were Nazis, get rid of them.
My dad needed people to keep things running under
terrible circumstances and he was criticized for using
the available help. The criticism grew until Eisenhower
relieved him. MacArthur wrote that he was tempted to
use the Japanese in the same way during the Occupa-
tion there."

The unfairness of asking a field commander to assume and perform well in the task of an administrative
position in a postwar environment was discussed in a
New York Times editorial. "Third Army men, who followed Georgie Patton and the pearl-handled revolvers,
[Patton's revolvers were ivory handled] from Normandy across the borders of Czechoslovakia are in-
clined, most of them, to worship the ground he rolls on.
And most of them will feel no surprise now over his
abrupt return to the doghouse. They admire him ex-
travagantly as a superb tank general and fighting man,
but never thought him cut out to be a politically adept
administrator of a complex occupation problem. . . .
General Patton's spectacular career is another reminder

of the fact that it takes all kinds to make a war—and to make a peace afterward. . . . General Patton is not a diplomat nor a good civil administrator. He remains a top-flight leader of mobile warfare."

Patton remembers meeting a captain who was in Munich the night after his father was relieved and all the people with Nazi ties were removed from their jobs. *"He told me nothing moved,"* remarks Patton. *"The lights went out, the sewerage system, what there was of it, backed up. The utilities went down and the heat went off. He remembered it very clearly since nothing worked in Munich for about several weeks. I'm sure many people, including my mother, felt that Ike had used my father and then threw him aside."*

Over the years, much has been written of Patton's relationship with General Omar Bradley, who commanded II Corps under Patton in Tunisia and later became Patton's superior when he took charge of the U.S. 12th Army Group and Patton was chosen to head the new U.S. Third Army. *"I think basically he and Bradley got along fairly well,"* comments George Patton. *"Bradley was what you would call G.I. He was a colorless kind of guy. My dad was never G.I. There is a book by Bradley, written after the war, in which he had quite a bit to say about my dad. Bradley died before the book was completed and another author finished it; however, Bradley said some complimentary things about my dad, but also criticized him. After all, he had to take the stuff from Ike and the president every time my father goofed. Bradley knew when he had a valuable person."*

On the subject of Bradley and Patton one journalist in particular, the chief of foreign correspondents for *Time* and *Life*, after speaking with Bradley and Eisenhower at length, sent an appraisal of Patton to his home office in New York: "Without Bradley over him Patton would not have been the success he has been in the war. There is in the Third Army almost a conspiracy to glorify Patton. . . . I don't think you want to go into politics in this story but I do think that if Patton were ever persuaded he could be something besides a general he would be a very dangerous man and I hope you bear that in mind. He can be charming and amusing as hell in private and inspiring in public, but his emotionalism is so extreme as to suggest unbalance and I hope he ends his days in the army and not at the head of it."

Despite such an appraisal, Patton, in reviewing his father's life, says, "*I was tremendously impressed with his career. At the time, I knew he was doing a super job, but I didn't realize how super it was until years later when I was able to really study his actions and contrast them with my own experiences and that of others.*"

For instance, George Patton recounts that during the Bulge the most impressive element was his father's shifting of the army to go in a completely different direction. "*This was only possible because he had a marvelous staff that had been with him since the desert,*" he says. "*He knew when his staff had written a plan it contained all the things needed to make a move: logistics, operations, civil affairs, everything. Nobody ever tried taking his staff away from him. One of his favorites was Colonel Walter Muller, the G-4* [supply officer]. *That G-4 operation in the Third Army was a man-killer. They had to supply those armored divisions drinking that gasoline and shooting up huge amounts of ammunition.*"

The strength of Patton's army, but particularly that of Patton as man and leader, was noted early by the German General Frederick von Boetticher, whom George Patton met many years after World War II, when the general was elderly. The German told him the story of first meeting his father before World War II, when he was the military attaché to the United States in Washington. They studied, did a lot of Civil War battlefield touring together, and were good friends. "*Von Boetticher said he had written a dossier on my dad telling the German general staff that they had better watch out for him. He wrote this when my dad was a major.*

Later, because it was well known that senior German generals in the European theater considered my father the most dangerous American general, the Allies devised a deception plan for the Normandy invasion that put my father in a phony command post well east of where they went in. The idea was to make it look like my father's area would be the invasion starting point. In fact the Germans were shocked that he wasn't in the first wave. I agree with the way Ike used him at Normandy, because his forte was the breakout, not the assault."

Over the years Patton, having heard his father compared to MacArthur, has made his own comparisons. *"MacArthur commanded a theater and his responsibilities far transcended those of my dad. MacArthur commanded the Army, Navy, and Marines and had fleets under his command. He was a leader and probably the greatest general this country has ever produced, but he was more on the political-military side than the practical military side. Both he and my dad were prima donnas and enjoyed that form of identification."*

Patton also observes, *"One of the reasons my dad was so successful goes back to his study of history and terrain. He and my mother toured parts of Europe in 1912 and 1913. My father's understanding of history was such that when he crossed the Rhine, in March 1945, he stumbled deliberately and picked up a handful of dirt and said, 'I see in my hand the soil of England.' Of course that's what William the Conqueror once said. He had a hell of a flair for history and it in turn had a tremendous influence on him."*

When hostilities ceased in Europe in May 1945, many adjustments had to be made by officers and enlisted men. General Patton, a military hero, was on ice with the Fifteenth Army, but that did give him a chance to write "Earning My Pay" and "Helpful Hints for Hopeful Heroes," which form an annex to a book entitled *War As I Knew It*, by Patton. *"My dad wrote in his diary at the time, 'No More Horns, No More Honor*

Guards, No More Bugles and Cymbals Clashing,'"
says Patton, "and that probably best sums up his feelings near the end." Ruth Ellen believed that his essay
"Earning My Pay" is as close as anyone who did not
know him personally will ever get to General George S.
Patton, Jr.

George Patton and others believe that his father
would have had a difficult postwar adjustment, mainly
because he would have sorely missed the opportunity to
fight. "My mother wanted him to sit down and continue writing about tactics and strategy," says Patton.
"He also had his schooner, and would have gone sailing, but it would have been a tough transition. When
you're that senior and then BANG, and as the saying
goes, you've got to light your own cigarettes, it is
tough. Also, he wasn't interested in politics like MacArthur and Eisenhower so that would not have been an
avenue either. I recall him saying in a letter that he
wanted to head the [Army] War College when he came
home if he couldn't go to the Pacific, but frankly I don't
think MacArthur wanted him. I think MacArthur felt
that the Pacific was not his kind of war. Of course, the
major operations in the Pacific were pretty much drawing to a close except for the attack cn Japan, which they
were planning." Patton believes the War College would
have been a good option, but to put a four-star general
in charge would have been unusual; at that time it was
a two-star job. "I frankly think they didn't know what
in the hell to do with him," Patton concludes.

The ups and downs of Patton's career stand as lasting memories. "It's ironic," muses Patton, "but my father had so many great moments and triumphs, yet he
had such lows as well, such as after the slapping incident, when Ike made him go around and apologize to
everybody. The furor over the incident was typical of
the lows. Some members of Congress were calling for
his head and my mother got hundreds of crank letters.
She told me an unsigned one said, 'When your husband

goes to Hell, Judas Iscariot will reach out and grip him by the hand.' "

The late General Jimmy Doolittle got to know Patton well during the war years and provided his own view of Patton's highs and lows. At the core, he believed, Patton put his troops first, and that success came because of that attitude. "Patton had in his mind very much the welfare of his men, whether they were under his command or prisoners of war," remarked Doolittle. "In fact one of the things he most dearly wanted to do when he started across Germany was to overtake and overcome the German prisons and release our people. So he had a very, very keen appreciation of doing the very best for his people. He had the reputation for being a chap who was a great leader, a great fighter, and for those of us intimately acquainted with him, we knew he had a deep feeling in his heart for his men. Yet, he would send the men to death if necessary, but he was almost crying when he did so. That was a part of Patton the public rarely got a chance to see."

Doolittle had fond memories of Patton during the war years. "I remember General Eisenhower and General Marshall selected General Patton to be the commander in the field when Torch was to have been a small American operation in North Africa. It later grew up to be a large operation with the British. Patton was selected to be the Army ground leader and I was selected to be the air leader. When we were sent over Eisenhower was a lieutenant general, Patton was a major general and I was a brigadier general. Patton and I went to London to talk to Eisenhower and I made a horrible mistake. He said, 'Now General Patton what would you do under these circumstances,' and General Patton told him what he'd do and Eisenhower was very pleased. He then asked me what I would do under certain circumstances after I moved to Iran. I said General we won't be able to do anything until we have the ground supplies necessary to fuel the airplanes and the bombs and ammunition to arm them. That was a perfectly sound statement except it was stupid. I was saying to him what he knew. What he wanted to know was what I knew. So he telephoned back to General Marshall and said, 'General Patton satisfactory, Doolittle not satisfactory.' "

Doolittle added, "While I think Eisenhower was a fine leader his greatest gift was his ability to get people with diverse ideas and methods of operation to work along in the accomplishment of the common purpose. He got the British, the Americans and the French to work together, a gargantuan job, needless to say. At the same time he knew that Patton was a great leader who required considerable supervision."

As for Patton's view of the postwar world, Doolittle said, "He had a very strong conviction that someday we would have to fight the Russians and we would have to whip them and he felt quite rightly that there would never be an opportunity as good as immediately after World War II when we were still strong and Russia was drained. He was all for carrying the war to Russia at that time. Now while that was sound military strategy, it wasn't acceptable politics. They wanted to live in a war-free society immediately and imagine everything was dandy."

The late President Richard Nixon told this author in an interview that he once asked President Eisenhower about Patton. Nixon said, "He described him to me as one of the most brilliant field commanders in American history. He compared him, incidentally, with Churchill in one respect. He said both were very emotional men and that in arguing their point of view, they would sometimes break into tears. This, in Eisenhower's view, was not a sign of weakness but an indication of the depth of their commitment to a great cause."

General Gay, reflecting on Patton's thoughts and actions in the final years, said, "Patton was misunderstood by some of his superiors at home and abroad and was not always portrayed accurately in books and movies, but I would say his greatest moment militarily was when we broke through the enemy lines and went down into Italy and into Czechoslovakia. Later, I heard Patton ask Eisenhower, beg Eisenhower, to let him go and take Berlin. Eisenhower wouldn't let him do it because he didn't think he could. Patton said, 'Oh, hell, I could take it in two days with a bow and arrow.' "

For Patton's driver, the late Master Sergeant John Mims, of Abbeville, Alabama, the general was a boss, friend, and confidant. One of his fondest memories of Patton was of the general directing traffic near a church in Le Mans, France, while out on maneuvers on a Sunday morning. "Four streets came together at this particular intersection and there was a convoy on each street and traffic was blocked. General Patton got out and started directing traffic and in thirty minutes you couldn't see a vehicle anyplace. When the people were coming out of the church and heard him hollering and cussing, they were taken aback, but when they saw who it was they burst out laughing. It was typical, Patton moving the troops himself."

Mims, remembering Patton during the war, said, "He could get yelling pretty good, but that was all show. You had to really worry about him when he was quiet. He was fixing to tear somebody up. His yelling was an act he was putting on. He knew we were fighting a tough enemy and also knew the effect he had on the troops. When he said take that man's name, rank and serial number and he didn't yell, you better look out. He was fixing to do a court-martial.

"I drove him to a home for dinner one night," Mims remembered, "when we were in England. I got drunk and as we were leaving he said I couldn't drive and told me to get in the back seat with his dog Willy. So he had to drive me home and he laid a cussing on me all the way. When we got back, he put me in jail. His aide came down and got me about six o'clock the next morning. I was so tired I didn't care. At the time I was working seven days and nights a week. I told the aide he and the general could shove the job as far as I was concerned. The aide looked at me and said, 'Aw Sergeant, take it easy and go to bed.' Next morning when I picked up General Patton, not a word was said. I heard later that the hostess talked to General Patton about it and he told her, 'Sergeant Mims gets on one of these sprees every now and then.' "

Mims remembered that Patton did not talk much when they were driving. As a driver Mims was taught to talk to a general only when the general wanted to talk. "You don't start a conversation," said Mims. "Besides, I always felt Patton might be planning for a big battle and didn't want to tear up his thoughts and distract him. Not just anybody could be a general's driver. Knowing how to act is important."

Working as Patton's driver left Mims feeling like others were second-best. When Patton was at the Casablanca Conference an aide asked Mims if he wanted to pick up President Roosevelt. Mims asked Patton if he had to do it; Patton said no, although he thought Mims might like the honor. Looking back, Mims said, "To me it was just more work and I had enough work with Patton."

Driving for Patton was literally a fast-moving experience for Mims. "We were practically wide open all the time. There was a convoy passing a convoy on the autobahn one time and I had to pass both of them. I passed on the right of one and on the left of the other and I was doing seventy miles an hour. I also had diesel engine horns you could hear for five miles. When I was approaching a town, a mile or so before I got there I'd blow the horns and the MPs [Military Police] would clear the traffic so we wouldn't have to lose any time. When we went to a division headquarters the general would immediately send me to the G-3 [Operations] to get the coordinates of the next outfit he wanted to visit. We went from sunup to sundown."

Mims also recalled many close calls. "It's true that

many times we nearly got killed. Once we were up at a company in the front lines and accompanied there by a colonel who was a regimental commander. The Germans started throwing shells all around us. General Patton got to observing and finally told the colonel, 'Let's move.' The colonel said, 'We better not; shells are landing all over.' General Patton said, 'No, they are throwing them out in the field; don't worry about it.' When we started moving they were landing in the roads and everywhere else. There was smoke, sulphur and mud flying around, but Patton didn't seem to care."

Like many other soldiers of this time, Mims had strong opinions about the portrayal of Patton during the war. "Often they pictured him as a bloodthirsty general who didn't care anything about the life of the soldier, that all he was interested in was getting his objective and the glory. That was just the opposite of the man I knew. His main thought was the personal welfare of the soldier. He told a general one day, 'We don't have to worry about machines, we can get plenty of those, but you can't get any more soldiers.' "

Whether Patton would have been able to make a transition to world peace or personal peace, with or without an army, is a question for historians. The end of the war had come, and Patton was starting down the final road of his illustrious life.

5

DEATH OF A HERO

It was sad to see a man of his capacities, a former Olympian, a tremendous horseman, a brilliant general, lying paralyzed in that bed with all those gadgets on him.
—General Walter "Dutch" Kerwin

With the war now a matter of history, Patton concerned himself with inspections of divisions and military bases. He also took time to visit friends, such as General Jean Houdemon, said to have been the last French pilot shot down by the Germans in the First World War. Houdemon was a good example of Patton's long-standing relationships with those in the profession of arms. Patton first met Houdemon, the grandson of a general in Napoleon's Army, at the French Cavalry School in 1913. The future generals spent many hours talking about Napoleon's campaigns and analyzing his successful leadership on the battlefield. Patton throughout his career relished such opportunities to learn more about what made one successful in war.

In addition to visiting friends and making inspection stops, Patton also went to numerous receptions held in cities throughout France that had been liberated by his great Third Army, and he gave speeches to assembled clubs and other groups. While being feted in Europe, Patton also made plans for his arrival in June 1945 for a triumphant visit to the United States. Patton would arrive dressed every inch the conquering hero, the General of Generals. He had, in fact, finally reached the pinnacle. No one would have suspected that less than six months later Patton, as it was once said of Abraham Lincoln, would "belong to the ages." For Ruth Ellen, his passing was the fulfillment of his destiny.

In Europe a story of a different kind would bring a twenty-three-year-old private first class, Horace L. "Woody" Woodring, on a collision course with destiny.

Born in western Kentucky on a dairy farm, Woodring left home to take a job building roads for an atomic bomb plant in Oak Ridge. Tiring of the work he elected to join the Army, attending driver school in Alabama before assignment to Europe. After bouncing from one unit to another, he was sent to the motor pool supporting the Fifteenth Army and lucked into an opportunity to become the chauffeur for the commanding general. Later, when Patton was announced as new commanding general of the Fifteenth, Woodring was asked if he wanted to be the new commander's driver or transfer out. "Patton had been my idol, so I immediately accepted," says Woodring.

Woodring began duty with Patton on a schedule calling for his services seven days a week. "We were always moving somewhere," Woodring recalls. "He always wanted to move fast and that was right up my alley and I loved it. I kind of devoted myself to being able to drive to suit him."

Woodring remembers that Patton was very physically fit. "I tried to keep up with him while he was hunting since I was in good shape myself, but it was tough. He struck me as a very sturdy man and I've always felt his heart was bigger than he was. I also think his mind was extremely sharp. I always admired his remarks; they were always of interest to me. Not being too well educated, I listened to him but I could not always grasp what he was saying because of his brilliance."

On the day of the accident, according to Woodring, he was informed by Patton's aide, Sergeant Joe Spruce, that General Patton and General Gay were going out early to hunt, right around 7:00 A.M., and that they were interested in going to a place between Mannheim and Heidelberg. "Spruce told me he was going to take Patton's dog in a quarter-ton truck and get out ahead of us and would meet us at a checkpoint outside of Mannheim," explains Woodring. "It was a Sunday morning and cold, yet a bright sunny day. As Spruce was getting ready I moved Patton's Cadillac 75 limousine, a vehicle with space for seven passengers and a great deal of interior room, out where I would pick up Patton and Gay to start our trip."

Along the way General Gay said he wanted to see a specific castle, so Woodring maneuvered the vehicle off the road and up a fairly high, snow-covered hill. General Patton and General Gay walked all through the castle and came back to the car, where Patton got in the front with Woodring, because his boots were wet and he wanted to warm his feet next to the heater.

"We drove on," says Woodring, "and after a short time arrived at a checkpoint to leave the autobahn to go on Route 38 through Mannheim. Sergeant Spruce met us there and at Patton's request we took Patton's dog from Spruce and put him in the car with us. General Patton at that point got into the back seat."

As the mini-caravan proceeded, it soon came to a railroad crossing, where a train was approaching. Sergeant Spruce went through the crossing before the train, leaving Patton's vehicle waiting for the train to cross. "While we were at the railroad crossing I observed a quartermaster depot on both sides of the road," says Woodring. "It contained a lot of broken down or blown-up jeeps, trucks and tanks. General Patton and General Gay were busily talking about all this

Army equipment and the waste of the material that was laying all over the place."

Woodring watched the train pass and continue moving down the track. "The only vehicle in sight either way was an Army truck sitting motionless up the road possibly a half mile away. I then noticed the truck pulling out and coming in our direction as we pulled away from the railroad track. As they approached our car, all of a sudden, for no reason whatever, they turned right into the front of our car. If you see a picture of the limousine, you will see the car was hit in the front. To this day I don't know where the truck was going. The only entrance they could have been pointing towards was a large German kaserne [barracks] with a big stone wall around it and an iron gate which was probably fifteen feet from the pavement. The accident happened so quickly I didn't even hit the brake pedal."

"The force of the collision forced Patton forward," relates Woodring, "and he hit the window partition between the front and rear seats. The partition actually caught him just above the eyebrows and ripped the skin from his forehead for three or four inches." When Woodring looked back after the accident he saw Patton lying across General Gay. "The wound hadn't started bleeding yet, but I could tell he had a severe cut. By the time I got out of the car and opened the back door, which took only a few seconds, he was bleeding profusely. General Gay was pinned under him. He was not unconscious, in fact he was saying that 'so and so ran over us.' I very carefully eased him up so General Gay could get out from under him.

"Then Patton said to me, 'Let's get to a hospital,' or 'Drive me on to the hospital.' I replied, 'Sir, the car is just too critical to drive.' Meanwhile Patton had General Gay working his arm and there was no feeling. I heard him say, 'What a hell of a way to die.' Today, as I think about it, I believe in his own mind as soon as he knew he was paralyzed he knew he wasn't going to live."

Woodring remembers an Army ambulance arriving very quickly, along with a medical sergeant who happened by. "He wasn't there by request," says Woodring. "The ambulance driver came running over and I said, 'General Patton's hurt quite badly, can you give us a hand?' He did a masterful job of patching him up.

"I talked to the other driver a very short time after the accident. I asked him, 'Do you realize who you hit? This is General Patton and he is critically injured. What the hell were you doing?' The driver and his passengers were drunk and feeling no pain. It seemed they were having a big time. The driver said, 'Oh, my God, General Patton,' and made kind of clown-like gestures and turned around to his buddies and said, 'General Patton, do you believe it?' It was stupid behavior and I was angry. This was just minutes after the accident. Perhaps later when they sobered up the seriousness of the accident hit home. I don't know."

Meanwhile, one of the first MPs that came on the scene after the accident was giving Woodring trouble and said he was going to arrest him for being involved in the accident. General Gay, who had quickly assessed the situation, "very sharply straightened him out," according to Woodring.

Soon other people began to arrive at the accident scene, including a colonel who was a doctor. He quickly began attending to General Patton. A few moments later the General was put in the Army ambulance and taken to Heidelberg and the hospital. Woodring, shaken and disbelieving, gathered Patton's dog, Sergeant Spruce, and the truck, and headed home.

Legend has it that a large crowd gathered at the accident scene, but Woodring disputes that assertion. "It wasn't a huge crowd at all; actually, traffic was kind of quiet. After all, it was Sunday morning and we weren't in a residential area. There were no houses on either side of the road and the only building around was the one we were in front of, which was locked. The people who came along were those who were going down the road. By the time General Patton was placed in the ambulance, there were quite a few people on the scene, but it wasn't a record crowd by any means."

Woodring, in the hours and days following the accident, barely left his quarters. "I was totally dismayed, like a kid who had lost his father I guess, because that's how I felt about him. I had every admiration in the world for the man. I just thought he was the greatest. He never failed to excite me. Everywhere we went, he was always an attraction. Anytime there was more than five officers, or even less, they all had questions for him and the amazing part was he always had answers to any question they posed. The man was just phenomenal."

The following afternoon the Army allowed the press to talk to Woodring, and the young soldier gave details of the story as he knew it. "Unfortunately no one printed that story," claims Woodring. "They chose to tell their own story, each looking for their own sensational angle about the accident."

As fate would have it, Woodring would not see Patton again, but he later got a telephone call from General Gay, who asked if he would take a staff car and go to the airport and pick up Beatrice Patton in Frankfurt and bring her to the hospital.

"The accident left me thinking a great deal about General Patton and some impressions have never left me," says Woodring. "He used to talk to me like a father talking to his son. One day he asked me to hand him a bottle of whiskey and I did. He asked me if I'd like a drink. We were going pretty fast and I didn't answer quickly enough and he said, 'Goddamn it, you either do or you don't.' And I said, 'Yes, Sir.' Well, he handed me the bottle and here I am going seventy or eighty miles an hour and I took a drink and handed it back to him. Then he started lecturing me on how to drink, how to govern yourself. 'Don't ever get drunk,' he said, 'because when you get drunk you are no longer your own boss.' You know, to this day, every time I start drinking, I remember what the old man said, stay sober."

A lasting memory for Woodring is a conversation that occurred four days before the famous accident which would eventually result in Patton's death. "We were chatting this day about different things when he said he would be leaving the Army in the near future and asked me if I would like to be his civilian chauffeur. I was scheduled for discharge around the same time and told him it would be an honor, but it wasn't to be."

Woodring views the accident as the saddest day of his life, next to the death of his mother and father. "There was nothing I could have done differently that I know of; if there had been I'd certainly have done it."

At home, in Washington, D.C., the late Ruth Ellen Patton Totten remembered the day of the accident vividly. "Ma was staying with me. She used to come down and visit my sister and me. We lived very close to each other. Her husband was at Walter Reed and my husband was in the Pentagon. The phone rang while I was sitting in this little room mending the corner cabinet where some of the veneer had fallen off. I can remember that perfectly. I picked it up and knew it was a long distance call for my mother. Ma said, 'Something's happened to your father.' She came and sat at a little desk in the hall, and they told her that he'd been hurt in an automobile accident."

George Patton recalls being at West Point when he heard about the accident. *"I was right in the middle of examinations when they called me up into the Tactical Department Office,"* says Patton. *"Colonel Russell 'Red' Reeder told me what had occurred. He went on to explain that my father had suffered a broken neck and was paralyzed. He also said they were in communication and would keep me informed. I went back to my room and wrote a cable which I sent on December 10, 1945. It said: All of us here are praying for your speedy recovery and return home. I know you can do it. Your affectionate son. George."*

Lieutenant Colonel (later General) Walter "Dutch" Kerwin was at home on that Sunday morning when he received a call from the Pentagon to report to the Chief of Staff, General Dwight Eisenhower. Eisenhower had just assumed the job on December 3, 1945, taking over from the venerable George C. Marshall. (Marshall had opted to retire from the Army and was honored in a White House ceremony on November 26, 1945, only to be asked by President Truman to return to government service one day later as a special emissary to China, with the rank of ambassador.) Just six days after becoming Army Chief of Staff, Eisenhower would have to deal with the accident to and subsequent death of General George S. Patton, Jr.

Kerwin at the time was the executive officer of the European/African/Middle East branch of the Operations Division of the War Department Chief of Staff, and in that capacity he was the briefer for General Eisenhower for those areas. "I quickly went to the Pentagon and was told that General Patton had been in an automobile accident. We didn't know a great many details about the accident at that time," says Kerwin, "but I was ordered to contact Mrs. Patton and a Dr. Glen Spurling, a doctor who had been the chief neurosurgeon for U.S. Army Europe." (Later Kerwin was to learn that Spurling, a fifty-one-year-old Kentuckian, was a renowned expert in his field.) Additionally, Kerwin was ordered to arrange for an airplane and accompany Spurling and Mrs. Patton to Europe. He was to see General Patton and report directly to the Chief of Staff concerning the accident and the General's medical condition.

Beatrice Patton was not difficult to locate, but Spurling was another matter. Kerwin was informed by Walter Reed Army Hospital that Spurling had been there recently and was en route by train to Kentucky, going home for discharge from the service. The question was, exactly where was Spurling and on what train?

As he was considering his dilemma, Kerwin continued making plans for the trip to Europe including arranging for the airplane, a C-54 four-engine aircraft, to
take off from Washington National Airport that night
with Mrs. Patton and the doctor, assuming he could
find him. It so happened Kerwin knew the chief of the
Maryland State Police; he called him and asked for his
assistance in finding the train. The chief, in turn, made
several calls to people he knew to find out what train
Spurling was on. Actually, Spurling was not where Kerwin was at first led to believe; instead of heading to
Kentucky, Spurling was on a train from his home in
Kentucky to Washington, D.C., for discharge at a later
date.

Spurling received a message from the Army Adjutant
General to leave the train at Cincinnati, where he
would be met and taken to the airport for a flight to
Washington. Spurling was also briefly informed that
Patton had been in a serious accident. Later, when Kerwin received a report from the State Police that Spurling
was debarking at Cincinnati, everything seemed to be
on time despite the confusion.

In the meantime, Beatrice Patton and Kerwin were at
Washington National Airport, in one of the back
tarmac areas, waiting to see if Spurling would arrive.
"Mrs. Patton was of course anxious to leave, so we
were all relieved when Spurling finally arrived," says
Kerwin. "He still didn't quite know what was going on,
but we got him on the plane, with just the crew, Mrs.
Patton, and myself," explains Kerwin. "We then told
Spurling what we knew about Patton and off we went."

The trip to reach the stricken general was long and
required several stops. "In those days you just didn't fly
across the ocean," says Kerwin. "We made several stops
and changed crews and then tried to get into Paris, but
were turned away by the weather. So we then flew on to
Marseilles.

"When we got there we were met by General John
'Courthouse' Lee who was the commanding general of

the Communication Zone at that time. We loaded up in another plane and flew to Frankfurt where we were met and transported to Heidelberg where General Patton was hospitalized."

Kerwin stayed in Germany six or seven days, and each day would call back to the Pentagon. At times he spoke with General Eisenhower himself, otherwise to one of the officers on the general's staff. "I reported on how he was doing and what the situation was," Kerwin explains. "Basically, he was paralyzed completely from the neck down and it was quite obvious to most people that he was going to have a very difficult time. The end product was that after I completed my assignment I was told to come back home. I returned to the airport and loaded up and started that long trip back to Washington, D.C."

Kerwin has many memories of his sudden trip to Europe, but the most lasting impression was the pleasure of getting to know Beatrice Patton. "I had met her before, but I didn't know her. She was a perky little gal. She wore a hat with a feather in it and she sat up in that swing seat between the pilot and copilot in front of the navigator for most of the flight. She chattered away. Nobody knew much about the General's condition and under circumstances like that you try avoiding the subject. The doctor didn't know much either, just what we had told him. Near the end of the trip, at Marseilles, he received a report, but essentially he didn't really know what to expect, although the initial reports were not good."

In the hospital Kerwin visited General Patton several times, but, he confides, "Because of his condition, we talked to him, but only barely. The real problem was making sure he and Mrs. Patton could spend as much time together as possible. Meanwhile, I got the readout from the doctors concerning his prognosis and how he was feeling. Today, I don't recall whether the doctors said they thought he would live or not, but I do recall he was in very poor shape. It was sad to see a man of

his capacities, a former Olympian, a tremendous horseman, a brilliant general, lying paralyzed in that bed
with all those gadgets on him. He was unable to do
anything but talk. The hospital staff showed great concern because, after all, he was an individual with a tremendous reputation. I left for Washington before he
passed away and then heard about his death after I got
home."

Patton's last hours have been written about before,
usually describing a theatrical-like scene where Patton
utters, "Too little, too late," or words to that effect,
before passing away. The truth according to Ruth Ellen
was less dramatic. "The fact is, my mother told me that
she had been reading aloud to him and he said, 'I'm
getting sleepy. Why don't you go eat your dinner and
we'll finish the chapter when you get back.' The nurse
in the room told Ma that she was sitting there and she
suddenly realized how quiet the room had become. He
had stopped breathing and slipped over to the other
side."

George Patton read about his father's passing in a
newspaper. *"I was en route home for leave on December 21st. They had been trying to contact me at West
Point but I had already left on a train to New York.
After I arrived I went to board the ferry to cross over to
Grand Central Station where I was to head for Washington, my residence at the time. I was walking along
when I glanced over to see a newspaper, an extra edi-
tion, in the ticket office. The headline announced my
dad's death. I continued home and a few days later met
my mother who arrived on the 24th of December. She
had just returned from the funeral, escorted by then-
Colonel Paul Harkins. We had a solemn Christmas dinner with the family on the 25th. It wasn't a pleasant
time and everyone was very, very sad.*

*"My sister and I often talked about the accident and
knew he would not have been happy as a paraplegic.
He would have probably asked us to pull the plug or
something. In a way, I'm glad he did go on because,*

had he been saved, he would have been either in a wheelchair or flat on his back for the rest of his life."

It is said that General Patton foresaw his own death, a statement supported by Ruth Ellen. "In fact my dad knew since he was a child that he'd die in a foreign country," she said. "My sister, George, and I were brought up on that. The last time I saw him in June of 1945, on the occasion of his last visit home, he said good-bye to my sister and me. Ma had gone upstairs and the old man said, 'This is really good-bye. I won't be seeing you girls again; I'll see your mother but I won't be seeing you. Keep an eye on your kid brother.' I replied, 'Daddy, the war is over.' He shook his head, 'It's not over for me. Luck is something you're born with, and you spend it.' Then he said, 'A front line soldier spends his life a lot faster than a rear-echelon cook and I've been out in the front line for a long time. I can feel my life running out because every round toward the end of the shooting war got closer. Don't you girls let them bring me back. Remember what Napoleon said, "The boundaries of an empire are the graves of her soldiers." ' I really deeply believe, and I had a talk with General Gay on it the last time I ever saw him, that my father's death was fate."

Strangely, yet prophetically, Ruth Ellen tells a story about how she knew her father had passed away. "I was sleeping," she says, "and woke up and looked at a window seat beyond the foot of our bed. There in front of me was my father in full uniform. I looked at him, and he smiled at me and nodded his head, and then he wasn't there. I thought, well, he's gone. Since I was alone and this was very moving, I almost called my sister, but I thought since it was late, why wake her up, she'll be startled. So the next morning I called her and she said, 'I was just about to call you. The strangest thing happened last night. The phone rang and I picked it up and it was long distance, I could tell. I heard Daddy say, 'Are you OK, Little Bee?' and that's all. And then I was cut off. I called the operator and said, 'I just had an overseas call,' and the operator said, 'You haven't had any calls, Mrs. Waters.' My sister and I just knew he was saying a final good-bye."

For years after the accident there was talk of an assassination plot in regard to Patton's death, but those rumors have been discounted over and again. Even an Army investigation, which also debunked the stories, failed to prevent the plethora of articles, books, and a motion picture, called *Brass Target*, purporting to show how and why an assassination attempt was constructed. General Patton's driver for most of the war, Mims, discounted any assassination talk, although he acknowledged that some suggested through the years that had he been driving the accident would not have occurred. "I believe that it was just something that was meant to happen. Of course, Woodring was a young guy and he wasn't as experienced as I was. I know that in my case we could have gotten killed several times if I hadn't been noticing what was happening. I always looked out for the other person. A lot of times we left the road or went into a ditch to miss a tank or a truck. We had many instances like that. But, I believe in what will be, will be. I can't help but believe anything else because General Patton and I went through thirty-two months of combat and had good chance of getting killed every day and we didn't even get a scratch."

Mims related that after he left Germany he wrote a letter to General Patton saying he was thinking about reenlisting and was going to try to get back to him. Patton died before the letter reached him; however, General Gay took the time to write Mims a response telling him about the accident. "There is no way it could have been an assassination," said Mims.

Replacing Mims with Woodring has been described in some conspiracy theories as a key part of an intricate assassination plot. George Patton scoffs at the notion, remembering how Mims was sent home before the accident. *"He came to my dad right after the war in September of 1945 and said, 'I've been with you a long*

*time but I've got a family and I want to go home.' The
old man said, 'Go, just get me another driver. You've
got the points [for demobilization], you've done a great
job for me and I appreciate your service.'*"

Woodring recalls that he appeared on a Boston
"Good Morning" TV show with Ruth Ellen concerning
the movie *Brass Target*. "I was delighted and quite
amused by her because she was very much like her dad.
She told me the only reason she came was to meet me
and let me know the family had no ill feelings concerning my involvement as the driver of the car on that
day."

As for assassination plots, Woodring says, "The
plans for the hunting trip were made the night before
we left. We always knew ahead of time what was happening but there was no way others could have planned
an assassination. For instance, when I dropped him off
on Saturday afternoon, and he wanted to go hunting
Sunday morning, he would tell me. He always told me
what he was doing the next day. However, this particular trip was not mentioned to me until the morning of
the drive. Now how anyone could have set up a trap for
him that quick I don't know. I don't think it is possible.
If I had to bet my life on it I would say it was an accident."

General Hap Gay, before he passed away, confirmed
Woodring's memory, telling this author, "Patton was
going to leave the next day to go home and he was
nervous and pacing the floor and we decided the best
way to calm him down was to go hunting. There
wouldn't have been any way for anyone to know that
we were going hunting. No one could have known because we decided to do it at the last minute and we
didn't even really know where we were going to go, we
were just going to go out and hunt." George Patton
muses that the only odd thing about the accident was
that his father was so badly hurt, while Woodring and
Gay were untouched. *"It's an incredible irony."* Ruth
Ellen summed it up simply: "It was just destined to be."

After Patton's passing, tributes flooded in from around the world, from military colleagues to heads of state and common people, including a message from General MacArthur that read, "General Patton was a gallant, romantic soldier of unquestioned greatness. All army forces in the Pacific will mourn him." President Truman, a Patton favorite, wrote Bea Patton saying, "Mrs. Truman and I extend our deepest sympathy to you in the passing of your distinguished husband. The entire nation, to whom his brilliant career has been a constant inspiration, has suffered a great loss." Dwight Eisenhower wrote, "His presence gave me a certainty that the boldest plan could be even more daringly executed. It is no exaggeration to say that Patton's name struck terror at the heart of the enemy."

A day after his death, General Order Number 121 was released by the War Department in Washington, D.C. In part it read: "General Patton as Commanding General, Third Army, inscribed his name in the annals of military history by bold and brilliant leadership of troops in Africa, and Sicily, and from the Normandy Peninsula across France, Germany, and Austria, inspiring them to many brilliant victories. His sound tactical knowledge, skillful, farsighted judgement, and masterful generalship contributed in the highest degree to the success of the Allied arms."

On December 23, 1945, a memorial service was held in Christ Church in Heidelberg. In attendance were representatives of nearly every major command and division in the European Theater. The moving twenty-two-minute service concluded in song from the thirty-six-voice choir of the 1st Armored Division, which had served under Patton in North Africa. The casket was then placed on a halftrack for transport in a funeral procession to the train station for its final trip to Luxembourg. It was reported that nearly seven thousand soldiers and civilians lined the half-mile route to the train.

General George S. Patton, Jr., was buried at the U.S.

military cemetery at Hamm on Christmas Eve morning, young George's twenty-second birthday. The funeral at the cemetery included guards of honor from the British, French, and Belgian armies, and most importantly, soldiers from the U.S. Third Army. Twelve high-ranking officers acted as honorary pallbearers, and as the crowd looked silently on a twelve-man honor guard fired a farewell salute to the departed general. His grave marker, like those of his fallen soldiers, is a simple white cross containing his name, rank, and serial number.

As for George Patton, he was unable to attend his father's funeral owing to a decision made by the Department of the Army. *"Naturally I wish I had gone; however, the Army recommended that I not go. I don't know why they made that decision even today, but I just didn't go."* Beatrice Patton, meanwhile, according to Ruth Ellen, never got over his death. "Ma didn't carry on. She said it was like learning to live without a leg or arm or eye."

For Woodring, who attended the funeral, and for many others, Patton remains a lasting memory. "I think about General Patton and the accident nearly every day. In so many ways he was misunderstood." Indeed, a one-dimensional Patton, garnered from a movie screen or a description in a magazine, has emerged over the years. Such a characterization is in part attributable to the circumstances of his tragic death. It meant that Patton would be unable to refute errors or, indeed, review his own accomplishments with the passing of years. It is something most of his contemporaries certainly had a chance to do.

But, while some over the years have continued to stress the eccentric aspects of Patton's personality, General Dwight Eisenhower may have captured his true essence when he remarked at the end of the war, "No one but Patton could exert such an extraordinary and ruthless driving power at critical moments or demonstrate the ability of getting the utmost out of soldiers in an offensive operation."

For young George Patton, the death of his father simply meant having to forge ahead, pursuing an Army career in the long shadow cast by one of the most successful generals in history. Such shoes would be tough to fill, but George Patton not only accepted but looked forward to the challenge that awaited him.

6

A SOLDIER CARRIES ON

George need not worry about missing a war. The next is on the way.

—General George S. Patton, Jr.

In 1946, using most of his West Point graduation leave, Patton and his mother Beatrice left the United States for an extended visit to Europe. *"My dad had originally planned to make this trip to show the whole Third Army campaign to my mother and me,"* says Patton. *"Following his death she still wanted to grant his wish. The trip was unique since our escorts were veterans of the Third Army, including Lieutenant Colonel James Hayes, a former battalion commander with the 80th Division and a Third Army advisor for the entire campaign, and General Gay, my dad's chief of staff."*

The trip to Europe caught the attention of the *Stars and Stripes*, which reported the trip in an article dated June 11, 1946, under the headline, "Patton's Wife and Son Continue Battlefield Tour." The article's lead paragraph, written from Cherbourg, said, "Continuing the pilgrimage of the battlefields where her husband led the 3rd Army to victory, Mrs. George S. Patton arrived here today with her son George."

Patton and his mother started their retracing of history from Nehou, where elements of the Third Army were held in reserve until it was activated in Normandy, and followed the course of battle up to Kassel and Fulda. *"We went to all the various command posts and toured the entire battle sequence, looking at the area and the surrounding terrain,"* Patton recalls. *"We also visited Bastogne and the very road that the Fourth Armored Division traveled with Creighton Abrams's task force leading the way. At the time there was still all kinds of abandoned material lying around, and many of the buildings had sustained considerable damage. People talked continuously about my father, and particularly in France, local VIPs would also escort us through the villages. My mother was a national figure at that time and we were treated exceptionally well. I was terribly proud of how well she did considering her husband had been dead only seven months."*

During the trip the Pattons also had an opportunity to attend several hours of the Nuremburg war crimes trials, listening to lengthy testimony on headsets. Patton recalls the particular phase of the trial concerning the Katyn Forest massacre, where an entire Polish officer corps was taken out to the woods and gunned down. *"The Germans were claiming the Russians did it and the Russians said it was the Germans,"* says Patton. *"Much later it developed that it was the Russians."*

While in Europe the group also took time to call on the Grand Duchess and Prince Felix at Luxembourg. *"My father had been buried in the military cemetery in Luxembourg, and at the time of our visit, there was no lawn, just dirt surrounded by a barbed-wire fence. There were no monuments yet created, and the American Battle Monuments Commission had designated his burial spot among the troops. My mother wanted him moved to the head of the cemetery, and I remember her telling the Grand Duchess about the situation and the Grand Duchess saying, 'Bea, if there is any problem the government of Luxembourg will exhume the remains*

and put them in the national cathedral.' They were
very, very aware of what had been done and they
looked upon General Patton as the national liberator of
Luxembourg." As Patton toured he was struck time
and again by the general sense of war; it continued to
hang in the air. As he viewed the battlefields he also
could not help but wonder what his own military future
would be. Perhaps young Patton would have gleaned
the answer from a letter his father had written his
mother in September 1945, wherein he commented,
"George need not worry about missing a war. The next
is on the way."

The younger Patton's Army career began when he
returned from his European trip. For further branch
training he was assigned to the Infantry School at Fort
Benning, Georgia, in April 1947. His ability and dedication were recognized there by Colonel Charles E.
Johnson, a school official, who wrote: "This officer
showed promise as an instructor and troop leader as
demonstrated by his energy and ability in commanding
small units and tactical problems. He is very serious
about his work and has considerable potential value to
the service. From other than an academic viewpoint,
this officer is rated excellent."

While at Fort Benning, Patton considered himself
fortunate to meet the famous Field Marshal Bernard
Law Montgomery, Eisenhower's senior British commander in Europe. *"He was at a commandant's reception,"* Patton recalls. *"As I was moving through the line
Montgomery and I had a chance for a short chat. I
would have enjoyed getting to know him."*

Upon graduation from the basic course at Infantry
School Patton went on to take the airborne courses and
received his parachutist badge. The training was tough,
yet exhilarating. Physical training included log-rolling
and lifting logs, throwing them up and down. Patton
also recalls, *"We did a thirty-four-foot tower jump and
slid down a cable into sawdust. Next they hauled us up*

a 250-foot tower. We learned how to perform a parachute landing fall, how to manage the harness and then started jumping. We did five jumps, the final one occurring in the dark of night."

By August 1947, Patton was back in Europe, assigned to a constabulary unit in Augsburg, Germany. Patton remembers the assignment as heavily involved with security and surveillance and says, *"Basically it was a glorified military police unit with much sparkle but no combat ability."* However, during one night everything changed. The squadron duty officer called Patton in the bachelor officers quarters (BOQ) with orders to lead his platoon to Rhine Main Airbase near Frankfurt. When Patton requested more detail, he was informed that no further information was forthcoming. He was simply ordered to report to the first Air Force officer he met inside the gate. He remembers arriving in the early morning hours and being immediately told to dismount his soldiers in order to start loading coal on transport aircraft located at the air field. Patton finally learned the reason for his assignment. The world was once again on the precipice, as Joseph Stalin and the Soviet Union had closed the land routes to Berlin and President Truman had ordered the helpless city to be supplied by airlift from West Germany.

The famous Berlin Airlift of 1948, in which the Soviet Union presented the initial threats of the Cold War, eventually shut down all rail and wheeled vehicle traffic. It was a crippling blow, because the Allies had been running up to fifteen trains daily to the city.

Patton says, *"It must be emphasized that the city of Berlin, like a helpless baby, was incapable of any interior or self-support. The city had been flattened by aerial bombardment and like a mortally wounded animal it was prostrate, with little chance of survival without Western supplies. Thus Berlin was an island of democracy in a Communistic sea."* The Allies, seeking to avoid the strangulation of Berlin, had decided to move quickly, utilizing three twenty-mile air corridors permitted by the Soviets. Doing nothing, perhaps the only other alternative, would have allowed the Soviets simply to fold West Berlin into its area of domination.

The airlift began on June 26, 1948, with an initial load of eighty tons of food delivered in thirty-two flights by C-47 aircraft. Working in concert with the United Kingdom and France, the combined operations eventually provided 4,500 tons of airlift each day, delivering fuel, food and other needed supplies to the 2.5 million people in West Berlin. Patton and the 2nd Platoon of D Troop, 74th Constabulary Squadron, pitched in. Their loading tasks lasted for two weeks, until the local headquarters and the Air Forces Europe contingent were able to hire local nationals to do the job. *"In an odd way these were exciting times,"* says Patton. *"At the same time, however, American forces were so weak that the only alternative open to the National Command Authority was aerial resupply or a nuclear response. Although using nukes was unthinkable, it was an alternative. Ground action was out of the question."*

When the Soviets finally lifted the blockade, Patton and a friend rode the leave train to Berlin in order to acquire a first-hand view of the situation. Entering a bar on the main street of the city, they received several drinks before they could even get settled. When they queried the bartender as to who had bought the drinks, he replied in broken English, "Not important, we like Americans." *"Our nation looked good during those exciting days of the airlift,"* says Patton. *"President Truman's moral courage during those days cannot be criticized."*

As the national leadership of the United States began truly to understand the Soviet threat, the North Atlantic Treaty Organization, or NATO, was born, with World War II hero Dwight D. Eisenhower named as Supreme Allied Commander, Europe (SACEUR). Responding to what was unquestionably a threat to democratic countries in Europe, the United States began to "up-gun,"

Patton recalls, *"The 16th Infantry and the 63rd Heavy Tank Battalion were activated and made organic to the 1st Infantry Division. The constabulary was reorganized into armored cavalry regiments. Several refresher schools were also organized and equipped, and separate artillery battalions were activated and manned."*

All of the changes in the Army caused a degree of turbulence in Patton's professional life and that of his contemporaries. Even as an infantry officer with no armor experience, Patton was assigned to the 7767 European Command (EUCOM) Tank Training Center, located near Grafenwöhr, West Germany. *"My cadre personnel at the center consisted mainly of rejects from other units but did include soldiers who knew something of armor and armor maintenance operations. I expect, however, that officials in the Frankfurt stockade breathed several sighs of relief when the Vilseck personnel requirements appeared,"* he chuckled later.

The types of soldiers Patton contended with are perhaps best exemplified by a story he tells concerning a late-night phone call from the duty sergeant in the MP detachment in Vilseck. He reported to Patton that he had two of his men under arrest and wanted him to come and retrieve them. When Patton arrived at the village there was an MP standing outside a small men's clothing establishment. An M26 tank had been driven through the wall of an adjoining ladies' lingerie store, and the tank driver, his companion, and the tank were covered with ladies' underwear. *"The driver was drunk and looked at me with a little smile as I told him he was going to jail,"* says Patton. *"He said, 'I accept that, sir, but I've had fun. All through World War II I drove an M4 and I always wanted to bust into one of these stores.' "*

While Europe was sorting out the destruction and dislocation caused by the war, Patton found that the Germans, as a people, were deeply depressed. *"They didn't realize what had happened to them. They were bewildered by the fact that we were there and they had lost. They were trying to survive with substitute items, such as wood-burning cars. There was also a thriving black market. As an army of occupation, it was demilitarization, deindustrialization, and denazification. This was known as the '3 D's'. The rules were strict and we were not permitted to fraternize with Germans. Officers, for instance, couldn't date German women, although the enlisted guys went out plenty."*

During his tour with the 2nd Cavalry before being transferred to Vilseck, Patton, because of his ability to speak French, was directed to attend the French School of High Mountain Warfare at St. Anton, Austria. On arrival he was assigned to the 11th Alpine Battalion in Innsbruck. *"We drew our equipment and proceeded to the top of a rather large and threatening hill with orders to form a line. We were then informed that we were being segregated according to our ability. If we fell before reaching a line of red flags, we were beginners. Yellow—intermediate. Blue—advanced. The selection process was typically French and we got a big kick out of it. I got to be pretty good friends with the fellow who ran the ski equipment supply room. He told me during the war he was in the SS. He wasn't particularly proud of it and was working in the supply room at no salary, just board and room, because he was being 'denazified' by the French Army. He had such a good deal that every time he would be called before a board of officers to see if he had been cleansed from his SS and Nazi beliefs he would say something that would cause the board to decide he needed more reeducation. He said, 'I run the ski room and I have a girlfriend living nearby. I also go hunting on a regular basis and enjoy my job, so I keep failing the interviews.' The French knew he was failing the interviews, but he was considered a fine worker and apparently loyal to the French leadership so they kept him on."*

To highlight how chaotic things were after the war, Patton tells the story of going to Augsburg and passing the huge Nuremburg airfield. *"On the tarmac,"* says

Patton, *"were literally hundreds of B-17s wing to wing and nose to tail. Over in the corner of the airfield some Germans were starting a large fire, so I drove over to check them out. I learned they were going to burn Air Corps field jackets with fleece-lined collars. I said 'Wait a minute, I'll take two hundred for my men.' The man in charge said I could have them for two cartons of Chesterfields. I immediately arranged for a truck and cigarettes. With literally thousands of Germans needing warm clothing for a hard winter, it seemed criminal to destroy those valuable and unique Air Force bomber jackets. In all candor that was government waste of the first degree."*

Before reassignment to Vilseck, Patton also had an opportunity to gain first-hand knowledge of long-standing Arab-Jewish animosities. *"My troop, 'D,' was dispatched to the little town of Neu Ulm to take control of a displaced persons [DP] camp in which two persons had been killed that afternoon. The Muslim contingent at the camp was primarily Turkish personnel who had been assigned to the Wehrmacht during World War II. The terrible hatred that existed between the two groups was understandable, yet it presented problems for us,"* says Patton. *"We worked to quiet the situation, which was one more example of the problems which existed in postwar Europe in the late 40s. Notwithstanding all of the treaties activated during the endless strife between these two races, the totally tragic murder and killing, Arab against Jew, continued unabated."*

During Patton's tour at the 7767 EUCOM Tank Training Center, the arming of U.S. Army Europe (USAREUR) and later the 7th U.S. Army continued. The 63rd Heavy Tank Battalion was activated and stationed at Grafenwöhr. The 63rd was a big battalion: three companies of twenty-two tanks each, a sizable maintenance section at company level, and a direct-support ordnance maintenance company. *"But the most attractive news,"* says Patton, *"was the incoming commander, who had been very carefully selected by*

USAREUR, Creighton W. Abrams." Whereas the Tank Training Center was a fine experience for Patton, the thought of serving with the finest armor commander, by reputation, currently serving in the United States Army became Patton's immediate goal.

Patton remembers how he hooked up with Abrams. *"I requested a meeting with Colonel Marshall Wallach, the commander of the training center, and explained my desire to become more involved with the armor branch. Realizing that I wanted to serve with an active duty tank unit, he, like the great gentleman he was, approved my request."* Shortly thereafter, Patton moved to Grafenwöhr and was assigned as a platoon leader and executive officer to Company C, 63rd Heavy Tank Battalion, a unit organic to Headquarters, 1st Infantry Division, the only major combat unit in Germany at that time. Little did Patton realize that he would serve with the 1st Division later in his career, in Vietnam, while commanding the Blackhorse Regiment.

"My initial impressions of the 63rd were really quite negative. Abrams had just arrived and in my view was unhappy with the fact that he would be placed in command of yet another tank battalion at the lieutenant colonel level, especially given the fact that he had successfully led the 37th Tank Battalion throughout World War II.

"What Creighton Abrams found within his new command was beyond description, in both the officer corps and the enlisted side of the unit, to include the very senior noncommissioned officers." Patton goes on to explain, *"These soldiers, just as they were with the 7767 Tank Training Center, were literally pulled out of the bottom of the Army. Several were deserters, people of very questionable moral character, and a few who had done some time in the Frankfurt stockade."*

Within hours of Patton's joining the battalion at Grafenwöhr he decided to inspect his platoon. As he entered his command tank Patton could not even locate the breech block for the 90mm gun. He asked a soldier the obvious question and was told that "this tank never had one as long as I have been here." *"The next surprise,"* Patton remembers, *"was that the SCR 508 radio was tuned to the Armed Forces Network radio station in Frankfurt, talking about a barbecue in Berlin, instead of the company command net which provided orders and general information to the tank commander."* Patton also found a host of other problems, including soldiers facing discharge sitting in the barracks away from training, and other deficiencies, as he says, *"too numerous to mention."*

Abrams took command, and the changes and challenges came like a thunderbolt from the man who had earned that nickname during World War II. *"Within about thirty to forty days all ranks could both feel and see the change,"* says Patton. *"Soon after he arrived the 63rd Tank Battalion could not be beaten as a combat unit. Abrams had transformed it to the top of the mark. In so doing, it became a model unit to which many VIPs were tempted and encouraged to visit."* Patton would later say that the Abrams battalion soon became the best unit he served with in his thirty-four years of service. *"With Abe's leadership and sense of discipline, we led the way."*

Toward the end of his USAREUR assignment under Lieutenant Colonel Abrams, Patton was relieved as the C Company commander, turning it over to Lieutenant Thomas Tyree, who had been his executive officer for almost the entire time. Patton was then assigned to Headquarters of the 63rd, in the S-3 (plans, operations, and training) area and informed that he would perform the remainder of his service with a comparable unit of the British Army of the Rhine. Patton's specific duty was to coordinate with the British gunnery and maneuver training section at the Bergen-Belsen training area located a few miles south of Hamburg. Assigned as a range officer on the staff of the 2nd Dragoon Guards, Patton was stationed at the Bergen Hohne reservation. The assignment required that Patton schedule each

63rd tank company for rigorous tactical and gunnery training during a period of four weeks. *"Due to the paucity of good ranges in the U.S. zone of Germany,"* says Patton, *"Abrams and literally all members of the 63rd jumped at the opportunity to move to Bergen Hohne, under a combination of wheel and troop train."*

Taking advantage of some free time, Patton decided to visit the infamous death camp of Belsen, located a short distance from the barracks that the British had assigned to its U.S. "guest" tank battalion. There Patton witnessed firsthand the horror of Belsen. *"The furnaces remained, along with horrible sights such as false teeth and hair. The Germans responsible for the atrocities, meanwhile, had been rounded up and were being held for war crimes. But as we went through the camp I saw mounds like bunkers on a golf course with signs saying eight hundred bodies, two thousand bodies, seven hundred bodies, and these were all around the camp. While I was stationed in the area I became friendly with the janitor of our BOQ, a World War I veteran with one arm. He had similar duty when the Wehrmacht panzer divisions were training near the camp. He said he and his friend used to sit out at night and hear blood-curdling screams from the camp nearby. One evening, overcome by curiosity, they decided to investigate, and started crawling toward the fence, when they were illuminated by a spotlight and told they would be shot if they came any closer. The guard chased them off after telling them the camp was a secret weapons location."* Patton asked him to explain the screaming and the furnaces and he replied, *"We always had our doubts about it, but there just wasn't anything we could do at our level."* Patton believes he had no reason to lie to him. *"He was just an old man hired to look after the barracks."*

Patton shakes his head in dismay, *"How the leaders of the Wehrmacht mechanized and armor units were able to train in the close vicinity of this unbelievable installation devoted to the total elimination of the Jewish race, without question or examination, will always be a question to me. Literally thousands of German soldiers had trained for almost six years in preparation for the Russian campaign. How was the secret of this wholesale slaughter kept from these German soldiers? There is no satisfactory answer."*

At the Bergen-Belsen training area Patton was considered one of the "Bloody Blokes," and while he was there he met a British fellow, *"a superb-looking soldier who wore an unauthorized, long coonskin coat,"* Patton recalls. *"He was also a World War II veteran who had been through Crete and North Africa. He told me a story about El Alamein, which best exemplifies the British attitude in war. He said he had been in the rear when he got word his unit was in heavy combat. So he moved forward and found the first squadron asleep, the next having tea, and the next fighting like hell. I said that for a fierce fight that sounded pretty casual. He said, 'Oh yes, we had been at it a long time. We learned the hard way how to fight a protracted battle.'"*

Patton also remembers getting into trouble, as well. Numerous groups were using the tank facility, and after each group finished their firing Patton would proceed down-range to make sure it was clear. At the end of the range he would call back to the British that it was ready for the next arriving tank group. It was about a twenty-five-mile drive to the end of the range, and as Patton was driving along one day he came upon a herd of flat-horned Dom Hirsh deer. *"The driver said not to shoot any, as they were protected,"* says Patton. *"But I had a carbine in my jeep and the do's simply won out over the don'ts. Luckily I thought to myself the jeep was pulling a trailer with a canvas cover. So I shot and gutted the deer and put it in the trailer, but didn't realize one leg worked out from under the canvas. We stopped at a butcher shop and I paid to have the deer cut up."* Unfortunately for Patton a British major from the Provost Marshal's office saw the leg sticking out of the cover and followed the group into the butcher's shop. Patton received a reprimand from the British for "unsportsmanlike conduct by an American officer," and Abrams himself presented Patton with the citation. *"It was a little touchy for a while,"* says Patton, *"but I went and apologized and put $50.00 in the British troop fund."*

In 1951 the United States Army, and indeed the American people, received shocking, though not totally unexpected, news when General Douglas MacArthur was relieved by President Truman for insubordination as commander in Korea. *"I was still in Europe at that time,"* says Patton. *"Truman said he had the authority to relieve him and he did it. I have never made up my mind whether he was right or not, but I happened to be with a British unit the night we learned of MacArthur's dismissal. The British had a brigade in Korea at the time and the British officers in the Mess were very anti-MacArthur and celebrating his demise.*

"I think MacArthur was a magnificent general, but he became more and more insulated from the world by his staff, many of whom had been with him since the Bataan days. I think that was part of the problem. He was not a young man at the time of Korea. I think, perhaps, he got too dependent on his staff officers and certain things happened which were not in MacArthur's best interest."

Patton, looking back, says, *"Even after MacArthur was relieved by the President of the United States he had a tickertape parade in New York City and he made two great speeches, one to Congress and one about Duty, Honor, Country. The Duty, Honor, Country speech is one of the greatest ever made by a military man, and he made it without a note at the age of seventy-five. I believe Douglas MacArthur in 1945 could have come home and run for president and won going away. He was worshipped at the end of the war."*

. . .

Returning to the States in 1951, Patton was assigned to the advanced class at Fort Knox in 1952. He also met Joanne Holbrook, whom he would later marry. *"I recall almost killing myself driving to Washington almost every weekend to see her. I drove my sister crazy staying with her, when she didn't really have space for me."*

Joanne Holbrook came from another distinguished military family. Like Patton's, her family also traced its roots to the Revolutionary War. "My mother's original ancestor came into the Army setting with the name of DeRussy," explains Joanne. "His father had been a French naval officer who served at sea with John Paul Jones. After the war, President Washington, in gratitude for the allied help, invited several of them to send their sons to the brand-new military academy at West Point. One of those who took advantage of the offer was Thomas DeRussy, and one of the two sons he sent, Rene DeRussy, was my ancestor. By one of his four marriages our family tree was established.

"DeRussy is also the subject of a legendary family story," says Joanne. "When he was stationed at Fort Monroe he called every Sunday afternoon on the widow of an old friend of his, Mrs. Maxwell. One day he told her he would like to discuss a matter close to his heart. He said, 'Mrs. Maxwell, I have come to ask for your daughter's hand in marriage.' He was sixty at the time and her daughter was sixteen. Mrs. Maxwell agreed on one condition, that he take her along to manage the household, as her daughter knew none of those tasks. He took them both, and even at his age he decided to start a family and they had children. Both ladies outlived him and continued to stay in their quarters at Fort Monroe. People were upset by this special treatment and finally, since General DeRussy was so well regarded, Congress authorized a house be built for them outside the gate. One of the daughters from this marriage married a Lieutenant Hoyle and in turn the Hoyle daughters also married into the military. One became my grandmother, Helen Hoyle Herr."

The Holbrook part of the family line began its military role in the Civil War. General David S. Stanley, who was Joanne's great-grandfather, was well known in his time. He was a corps commander under U.S. Grant and was George Custer's superior in the Washita River campaign. One of his daughters, Anna, had a great deal of artistic talent and went to study in Europe, rather unheard-of for young women at that time. When she returned home she met her father's aide, Willard Holbrook, fell in love and married him. "As he moved from post to post in his military career she carried her paints, and there is every reason to believe she had the quality to have been one of America's major women artists of the time, had she not died so early," observes Joanne. "One of their two sons, my father, was only eight years old when his mother died of pneumonia. Willard Holbrook felt he couldn't take the family with him on assignments so he farmed the boys out to his siblings. My father went to his physician uncle in Wisconsin, where he grew up with a loving family of girls. He later followed his father's example and attended West Point, with a class originally slated to graduate in November 1920. However, they were rushed through so they could go off into the Great War. Ironically, they were graduated on the first day of November 1918, and the Armistice was signed on November 11th."

Joanne's father, Lieutenant Willard A. Holbrook, Jr., was assigned to the Army of Occupation in Germany, where he met her mother in Koblenz. "Helen Herr had gone there with her family and was part of the young Army social set. When he proposed she turned him down. She was sixteen and he was six years older. She said he was too old and she wanted to have a career. She returned later to the States and had many careers, including working as a missionary for the Episcopal Church, and for a time working as a songwriter, and then as a reporter for the *Kansas City Star*. She was quite a freewheeling gal. They met again ten years later when he was a White House aide and she was a young career woman. When he asked her again to marry him, she said yes, and that brought all the lines together."

Joanne Holbrook first met George Patton when she was between her junior and senior years in college. "My ambition at that time was to get on the final college board of *Mademoiselle* magazine. I had been one of their college reporters for three years and had real hopes of being selected as one of a dozen college representatives to go to New York to work on an issue of the magazine. At about the same time my mother and father announced plans to have a wedding anniversary party at Fort Lesley J. McNair, where they had their original wedding reception. They decided to invite the people who had been at the original wedding, and if they weren't around, their sons and daughters. On this basis Ruth Ellen Patton Totten and Jim Totten decided to come and they brought her bachelor brother George. Amusingly, Ruth Ellen had called a couple of months before and tried to set me up with her adopted cousin, Peter Patton. She had invited us to have dinner together and I guess she was match-making. Nothing ever came of it. Meanwhile, she had invited other girls to meet George, but I guess she hadn't thought of George and me as a pair."

Joanne still remembers her mother talking to her cousin Bob, who had been a beau of Ruth Ellen. "My mother said, 'Bob, one of your old girlfriends is coming this afternoon and she is bringing her little brother.' Bob said, 'What! That brat. I haven't seen him since he used to hold me up for fifty cents every time I came to see his sister. He wouldn't leave the room until I paid. He was the most awful kid.' He went on and on and I was thinking what an unattractive fellow this is going to be and when he arrived I absolutely did not go out of my way to be pleasant to Captain Patton."

Nonetheless, the next morning George gave Joanne a call and asked her to play tennis the following day. "When I appeared at the breakfast table in my tennis clothes," says Joanne, "my father and mother said,

'What are you doing up at this hour?' I replied I was playing tennis and they laughed, 'It must be somebody very special, because you never get up this early.' I said it isn't anybody special, it's that awful Captain Patton. Now, my idea of tennis was dressing the part and playing as sort of a social thing. Well, George and I played about ten minutes when he threw his racket down on the ground and shouted, 'You are the laziest player I've ever been obliged to stand on the other side from. You pick up your racket and play.' I was furious and told my parents I had never been out with anybody who swore and I thought he was awful. They chuckled and said, 'Swearing is sort of in his family.' "

Patton later went to Fort Knox, and Joanne stayed in the Washington area, but as she says, "My scheming mother turned the tide. She and my dad had rented a house at Gibson Island, Maryland, for the summer and we used to go up there on weekends. One weekend there was a telegram from George, saying he was arriving on the three o'clock plane. I remember thinking, the nerve of that fellow, just showing up here and expecting us to receive him. So I ignored him and finally at the end of the long weekend he stopped me and said, 'Look, I don't know what kind of a game you're playing, but I accepted your invitation in good faith.' I was dumbfounded and asked, 'What invitation are you talking about?' He replied, 'I got a telegram that said come for the weekend, Gibson Island, signed Joanne.' My mother played absolutely dumb innocent, but she'd done it. I felt so sorry for him because I really had been hard on him. I began to be nice and found he was really a great fellow."

Later, Joanne was invited to Green Meadows to meet George's mother and "passed the acid test." Joanne says, "His mother took me out on the boat and waited until the weather was really choppy. Then she asked if there was a volunteer to go down below and fix lunch. I learned later everybody was supposed to keep quiet and the visiting girl, whoever she was, would usually say, 'I'll help you, Mrs. Patton.' Then the girl would go down below to the galley and get sick and humiliated and flunk the test. I happened to have an iron stomach and didn't know any better, so I made sandwiches and brought them up. I am told at that point I got the family seal of approval. It was on that particular trip that George announced his intentions to me, although it wasn't a formal proposal. During our discussion we had forgotten Mrs. Patton's stateroom window was right below us and she heard everything, but later told George she was delighted."

George finally proposed officially to Joanne in the Palladian Room of the Shoreham Hotel in Washington. They had met in June and formally announced their engagement on the 11th of November, his father's birthday. Patton went back to Fort Knox to finish his advanced class, and Joanne finished her senior year at Sweet Briar College. One week after both of their graduations, in June 1952, they were married in Washington, D.C.

In addition to the marriage of George Patton to Joanne Holbrook, 1952 was also the year that George's sister, "Little Bee" Patton Waters, passed away. Her husband, John K. Waters, the former Commandant of Cadets at West Point, was stationed in Korea at the time. *"The entire family gathered,"* remembers Patton, *"and we were all tremendously saddened by the loss, coming only seven years after my dad's passing."*

Patton believes the early years of his military career, and particularly his first tours in the active Army, were most worthwhile. For the young officer the learning experience was invaluable, and working under Creighton Abrams was a stroke of great fortune. It was an important beginning to a lifetime in Army service. Patton is of the belief that the influence of his new wife, Joanne, was also a key to his success, for it provided the necessary balance in his life. Patton was off to a flying start, but the Land of the Morning Calm was beginning to loom on the horizon.

7

LAND OF THE MORNING CALM

In retrospect, some have and will continue to criticize me for eternally seeking service in the combat zone. The counterargument is, how does one teach or practice war without having known war at firsthand?

—George S. Patton

The Korean War, a precursor to the Vietnam experience still years away, began on June 25, 1950, when North Korean forces invaded the Republic of Korea. President Truman, reacting to the invasion of the South by the Soviet-sponsored aggressor, declared the invasion would not stand. Soon United States military forces and military contingents from twenty other governments were brought to bear against the invaders. They were unable at first to stop the North Koreans, but resistance soon stiffened, and by early August 1950 the Communist offensive had ground to a halt.

Over the course of the Korean conflict, which lasted slightly more than three years until an armistice was signed at Panmunjom on July 27, 1953, it is estimated that over a million people died. In injuries and deaths attributed to the war it is reported that 542,000 North

Koreans and 900,000 Chinese died as a result of combat or disease related to the war. South Korean military personnel killed in action topped 47,000, and American battle deaths totaled 33,629. The Korean War will always be remembered as an especially brutal war fought in treacherous terrain, at times in horrendous weather conditions.

When the war commenced in Korea, Patton was still in Europe working for Abrams in the 63rd Heavy Tank Battalion, 1st Infantry Division, then based at Sullivan Barracks, Mannheim, Germany. Due to return to CONUS (the continental United States) in the summer of 1950, George Patton, much to his chagrin, learned that instead of reassignment his tour in Europe had been extended arbitrarily for an extra year. *"This change I would not have minded had there been no war,"* he says, *"as I was learning much from Abe. However, there was now a war, and since I had never been in a war I felt strongly that I should be allowed to go to the only war we had at the time. My request, which had been submitted in writing through channels, was disapproved."*

Patton's rotation date was reset for spring 1951, with an assignment to Fort Knox, Kentucky, "the Home of Armor." He was scheduled to attend the advance class of the Armor School in the fall, to graduate the following June. Perhaps then, if the conflict was still going on, Patton could fulfill his deep-seated desire to *"at least be in a war of some sort." "In retrospect,"* he says, *"some have and will continue to criticize me for eternally seeking service in the combat zone. The counterargument to this remark is, how does one teach or practice war without having known war at firsthand?"*

As George Patton continued to request that he be allowed to serve in Korea, others, including a senior colonel, were telling him that he would be greatly disappointed by the Eighth Army's armor employment in Korea, because tanks were being used there as pillboxes in a Maginot Line configuration. Still others, if one listened closely, were painting a picture of a Korean conflict that lacked the essentials for success.

At a classic press conference held on April 22, 1951, General James Van Fleet, a highly decorated veteran of both World War I and II, and commander of the Eighth U.S. Army in Korea, was asked by a correspondent,

> "General, what is our goal in Korea?"
>
> "I don't know, the answer must come from higher authority," Van Fleet responded.
>
> "How may we know, General, when and if we achieve victory?" another reporter inquired.
>
> "I don't know, except that somebody higher up will have to tell us," Van Fleet concluded.
>
> And so it went.

Following graduation from the advanced class in mid-'52, Patton was assigned to the tank offense section of the G-3 division of the Armor School's Command and Staff Department, under Colonel Alvin Irzyk, who had been a tank battalion commander with Abrams in the 4th Armored Division in World War II. *"I was teaching basic and OCS armor officer classes at that time,"* says Patton, *"and I was the only instructor in the Command and Staff Department who had never been in combat. Many of the personnel we were teaching, both commissioned and enlisted, were Korean returnees who had been in battle. I was somewhat embarrassed, mounting the platform to teach veterans how to do it when they already had done it. When evaluations were filled out by the students, questions were asked about Captain George Patton teaching things about which he had no personal knowledge. The simple answer was to send Captain George Patton to Korea."*

Patton's application for transfer to Korea was disapproved on two separate occasions. He was told his contribution at the Armor School was essential. *"I finally*

went to Colonel Irzyk shortly after Christmas, 1952,"
says Patton, *"and told him I just had to go to Korea. I
just had to see if I could handle a combat situation. He
said there wasn't a whole hell of a lot of combat in
Korea at that time, as the war was winding down. My
answer was that some combat was better than none and
I just needed an opportunity to prove myself. I said,
'Sir, I've got to go. I'll do whatever it takes, but I must
get into the war.' Finally, he said, 'You feel that strongly
about it?' I said, 'I sure do.' I had been raised in the
environment of the gallantry and the glory of war. The
first memory I have ever had of my father was in his
talk of war, of how he, as a man and more than that, a
soldier, reacted to war and the other things that are
related to war. I was suckled and weaned on this
theme. I reached adolescence through the same endless
diet and as I approached manhood, the talk of war was
so ingrained on my subconscious mind that when Pearl
Harbor occurred, I could think of nothing else.*

*"Irzyk thought about it and smiling said, 'Well, if I
were in your shoes I'd do exactly the same thing.' He
then approved my request."*

Patton left for Korea in February of 1953, while Joanne was pregnant with Margaret, who was born in
July 1953. Patton arrived in Seoul, Korea, via Flying
Tigers Airlines, on a wintry cold day and immediately
went to a replacement detachment at Yong Dong Po,
near Seoul. He was there the night of very intense fighting with the Chinese for a piece of key terrain known as
"Pork Chop Hill." *"I'll never forget it because they had
a graves registration point just outside the building
where I was sleeping,"* he says. *"All night long I heard
the graves registration people trying to identify bodies
just outside my window. The Army should never do
something like that, locate a replacement detachment
near a graves registration unit. After all, the people in
the replacement detachment become quite nervous
when you hear people talking about whether this body
is a sergeant or a lieutenant, and 'where is an arm for*

*the lieutenant before you put him in a sack?' and that
kind of thing. It was unnerving. I marked it as a lesson
learned which should never be repeated."*

After getting settled during the first few days in-
country, Patton was met by representatives of the armor staff of HQ Eighth Army, and there was talk of
assigning him to the Eighth Army general staff. Patton
protested, saying that he wanted a combat company.
Patton felt he would be wasted in a staff capacity.
While at Fort Knox Patton had been involved with the
development of the M47 tank, which had begun deployment to Korea and had recently been provided to
the 89th Tank Battalion of the 25th Infantry Division.
Because of his technical knowledge of the M47, Patton
proceeded to apply to the 25th Infantry Division, which
was commanded by Major General Sam Williams.
*"That was the only time my possible assignment to a
battalion was turned down,"* recalls Patton, *"and the
reason was simple. It turned out Williams, as a colonel
at the time, had somehow 'cross-threaded' with my father during World War II. It was also the only time in
my career that I had an incident of that nature related
to my dad.*

*"Williams, to his credit, was afraid prejudice might
overpower his mind with regard to my assignment and
so he turned down my request. I wrote him later and
told him I understood why he turned me down and in a
general way I agreed with him, but I was sorry not to
be able to serve with the 89th since I knew something
about that recently developed tank which might have
been useful to the division."*

Not long after the Williams incident, Patton was assigned to the 40th Infantry Division in the X Corps
area, located slightly east of the famous "Punch Bowl."
"Luckily for me," says Patton, *"the assistant division
commander of the 40th Division was Brigadier General, later Lieutenant General, Gordon V. Rogers, who
had known my family for years. I went to see him and
said, 'General Rogers, I'm not asking for any favors,*

and please understand that I'll do exactly as I'm told. If you really want me on the division staff, I'm a good soldier, I'll salute; I'll go to division staff, write papers, send messages and do my duty. On the other hand I came to Korea to fight and I hope you will give that chance.' He said, 'I understand. Give me half a day and I'll look into it.' Shortly thereafter he let me know that I had been assigned to the 140th Tank Battalion under Major Joseph W. Pezdirtz, and that I would eventually take command of A Company."

Patton recalls going by air to the 40th Infantry Division and being interviewed by General "Jumping Joe" Cleland, a famous airborne officer. Cleland, the division commander, welcomed Patton aboard and gave him an orientation and confirmed he would be assigned to the 140th Tank Battalion. During the briefing Patton learned that his main adversary was the 45th North Korean Division and that while shots were frequently traded, action was light.

Patton's company was under the operational control of the 12th ROK (Republic of Korea) Division and had 142 men in four and sometimes five platoons, each with five tanks. The breadth of Patton's sector caused the battalion to take a platoon from either B or C Company in order to cover the required frontage. The platoons were rotated so the company always had one in maintenance and one on rest and rehabilitation at the company CP (command post). Specific duties were fairly routine, although A Company's job was to reinforce the ROK, if necessary. Occasionally the company would get into running battles, yet Patton remembers losing only two men in the whole time he had that unit. *"We had several wounded, but it was a good company which fought well,"* says Patton.

A Company was generally dispersed along the northern side of a huge prehistoric volcano site, fifteen to twenty miles across. The weather was a constant factor, as the Siberian winds came down through the passes. *"It was bitterly cold,"* recalls Patton, *"and along with the weather the terrain was highly mountainous and not particularly conducive to armored warfare. In any case, we maintained static positions because of the ongoing negotiations at Panmunjom. The 40th Division and others remained in those holding positions worrying more about survival than victory."*

When Patton arrived he observed and was not happy with what he saw. *"For me the soldier has always been my number-one priority and concern. After a certain number of years soldiering in the Army you can recognize soft points in a unit,"* he says. While there were not too many problems in A Company, 140th Tank Battalion, that could not be corrected, Patton did note that each officer had a young Korean who would bring him coffee in the morning, an orderly of sorts who was paid with cigarettes and candy. *"Meanwhile,"* he comments, *"the troops were being largely ignored."*

Patton's role in supporting the 12th ROK Division was clear. *"I knew the type of target I was assigned and we had the proper ammunition for that target,"* he recalls. *"We had to carry the ammunition and fuel up the hill to the tanks, which was very difficult and time-consuming, since the road was terrible and we were getting vehicles stuck daily. Some days would go by without a round being fired, yet we remained on alert, always looking for enemy infiltration or movement. The simple requirements of living were a problem. One had to keep dry and warm, and keep the equipment maintained. Occasionally, as if sending notice, the enemy would send a few rounds our way."*

When Patton assumed command of A Company, he believes, the troops at first resented him. *"I remember thinking,"* says Patton, *"that they were probably saying, 'Who is this SOB coming in here? He is going to get us all killed, he's ambitious, young and a West Point hotshot from the Armor School.' One could sniff the resentment in the air, after having been around awhile. They don't have to tell you, you can just sense that* tension. Yet a lot of people didn't understand the position I was in. Here I was the son of a very famous general, a graduate of West Point, which to some immediately meant I was a 'spitshine' type. I could tell from the way they acted that my presence wasn't exactly a popular one. Some also felt I was there in order to get credit or get a medal or something and then as soon as I did I would leave for some hotshot staff job back at Corps or even higher."

Patton really felt left out and knew he had to do something. "Remembering the motto that God gave a person two ears and one mouth and to use them in that proportion, I just went about the business of talking to people concerning what was both right and wrong," he remembered. "You have to know a situation before you start charging around making changes and that's what I have always tried to do. I made the rounds and it took me all day. I had three platoons on line and one platoon in reserve located at the company CP, which was back about a mile or two away on the Soyang River. I was checking the tank crews, looking over their maintenance and their positions.

"The only way I could describe these positions would be to refer someone to the World War I films where tanks were totally dug in. All that was showing as far as the enemy was concerned were the turrets and the .50–caliber machine guns, with an observer sitting on top of, or in, the tank, with a set of binoculars looking out to see what was going on." In touring the platoons, Patton asked the usual questions that any soldier would recognize. How is the mail? How is the food? Have you seen any Chinese or North Koreans lately? What's your relationship with the South Korean infantry? Have you coordinated with its commander?

Most of the answers Patton received were positive; however, the troops did not look good. They were short of water for shaving and needed clean fatigues. Although Korean women would come down and wash the uniforms in the stream near the CP, that was occurring infrequently. Mainly Patton observed they were bored and tired and not particularly interested in his presence. In the World War I–type trenches along the ridge, the main job of the soldier was to observe to the front and fire when he saw enemy movement. Patton looked at the company for three or four days and figured one way to relieve some of the tenseness was to start doing things for the troops that they deserved but had not been done. He saw there were opportunities to make major improvements.

Patton listed the problems. There was no mess tent, mail service was very poor, the soldiers were not receiving hot meals when deployed on the line, and, as Patton says, *"the officers were sitting on their asses in the CP. They all had their Korean servants and the troops were eating in the rain."* Of all the immediate administrative problems Patton observed, the issue of hot meals was probably the most important. Patton found out that the troops' rations were being sent up cold and that the tank crews would then cook their own meals in position. After an in-depth look at the subject, Patton returned to the A Company CP and pondered the situation. Remembering that Napoleon had once said, "The army travels on its stomach," Patton resolved he would fix the food situation first.

> Patton called in his "exec," or executive officer, a Lieutenant Stilson, and said, "I want these people fed a hot meal."
> Stilson said, "Sir, I think that's impossible; there's too much exposure."

Patton was given every reason in the book not to do it, then said, "I appreciate your comments, but I'm going to do it personally, with a jeep and a trailer. Not only are we going to do it but I will be there personally. We'll start in the morning with the lunch meal and we'll finish when we finish."

Patton years later recalled that he could tell by looking in the eyes of the tank crews in the company that what he was doing hit the mark. Starting out for the luncheon meal around 9:30 in the morning, they finished at 4:00 that afternoon. The symbol of the hot meal being served by the commanding officer was what counted most. *"The message was, here was a CO that was interested in serving a hot meal for his troops,"* says Patton. *"The principle was that a new company commander was dishing out this food at risk to himself because he felt it was important. We finally got to the last tank crew on the line and I said, 'I'm sorry this is so late, it's not very hot, but it is from the heart.' And he said, 'Captain, this is the first hot meal I have had in three weeks. I understand it's not very good and I understand it is cold, but I appreciate what you are doing.' And those soldiers shoveled it down.*

"That was the type of thing I did because it was the right thing to do. I don't brag a lot about my service; I had some good times and some bad times and I made some mistakes. I'm sure I did. But I can say that care of the soldier was always one of my strong points and after that hot meal was served there was a change in attitude and those tankers responded to me in an exceptional way."

Every day in Korea produced new sights and sounds for Patton. Cultural and religious practices and differences intrigued him. Patton remembers one afternoon when he was driving along in the valley behind the front getting ready to move to the right flank of his position. He glanced over and noticed two Korean soldiers bringing down a body on a stretcher. *"The body lying on top of a blanket was that of a South Korean soldier,"* says Patton. *"I told my driver to stop the jeep, because I wanted to watch what went on. When they got to the bottom of the hill they stopped alongside two fifty-five-gallon oil drums that had been welded together, and carefully laid the stretcher down. They very gingerly took the blanket off the body, stripped the body of anything that would be of any use to them, including the shoes, hat and wallet and then very carefully put the body into the oil drums, poured some used crankcase oil on top of the body and lit it."*

When the corpse had been consumed by the fire, Patton remembers, the Koreans took a scoop and removed some of the residue and stuffed it into a beer bottle. Then he watched as they made out a card with the name of the man for his next of kin, took the blanket, shook it free of dust, folded it, and drove off. Patton was left with the impression that the blanket exceeded the importance of the dead soldier. *"I was shocked that they did not have some sort of graves registration operation which would be a little more reverent toward the remains of a soldier killed defending his country. Yet this Korean casualty from the 12th ROK, who it turned out had been killed by mortar fire earlier that day, was laid to rest without so much as a moment of silence."*

For Patton, in addition to the culture, the area took some getting used to. *"Between the weather and the terrain, that part of Korea was bleak,"* says Patton. *"The local citizens, who lived in tiny villages, were very poor. Because of the high, steep mountains and precipitous roads, constructed mostly by our engineers, riding around on those mountainous roads was extremely hazardous. If it was icy you could quickly lose a tank, and we did. One particularly bitter day one of my tanks went off the side of a mountain and, luckily, the crew rode it all the way down. When I raced to the bottom I expected to find five dead bodies, but we found everyone okay. What the driver had done, and it was real fast thinking, was put the transmission in reverse as they were going down the hill which decreased the rate of descent. It must have been a harrowing ride and I'm quite certain the five men inside were sure that they were heading to meet their maker."*

In late May 1953, A Company of the 140th was directed to move to the Dodge Range, an X Corps–

operated tank and artillery range, for maintenance, rehabilitation, and orientation training for newly assigned personnel. Shortly after arriving Patton was notified that he was to return with his company immediately to the 140th area, to conduct a relief-in-place of B Company 140th, which had been partly overrun. B Company had sustained sufficient losses and battle damage to warrant its withdrawal into a reserve location.

Upon arrival at a designated assembly area, A Company was refueled and resupplied and visited by the division commander, Major General Ridgley Gaither, and his G-3, Major Charlie Jackson, in preparation for the relief-in-place and the night withdrawal of B Company 140th, commanded by a Captain Doherty. At this point, no one was sure how much enemy penetration had occurred, and there was practically no intelligence available, as communication with Captain Doherty was spotty at best.

The division staff was also aware that there had been quite a bit of fighting and that elements of ROK were withdrawing from their established positions without clearing their movements with X Corps. The relief operation started with instructing each A Company platoon carefully and meticulously on its mission and deployment position, i.e., a classic relief-in-place during darkness with totally inadequate enemy information. As Patton explains, *"The nature of the 12th ROK commander, confronted with the possibility of losing face, [was that he] would not report bad news. This was a Korean characteristic. Because of language barriers between the ROK and the U.S. Military Assistance Advisory Group [MAAG] personnel, little help from them would be expected. The situation was terribly unclear and filled to the brim with unknowns and questions for which answers were not available. At any rate, we resolved to do our best, with the tremendous efforts of the reconnaissance platoon of HQ 140th, commanded by Lieutenant Barney Buist, plus that of Lieutenant*

Chuck Madsen [who later received a Distinguished Service Cross for this action] *and several liaison personnel from Division and Corps artillery staffs. The operation was accomplished properly, with full blackout discipline and with great tactical awareness and skill."* This action, later called Phase II of the Luke's Castle battle of late May and early June 1953, prompts Patton to say, *"I don't know to this day how in the hell we did it, but we did it with no enemy contact over a period of approximately twenty-four hours of continuous movement. As we deployed these platoons into the B Company recently evacuated positions, we were* [working] *mostly by guess, since higher headquarters maps were almost totally incorrect, and yet by God we were able to assess the ROK infantry activities and positions and, thankfully, report their actions and locations to higher headquarters."*

As Patton recalls, findings indicated that for the most part, the ROK regiments were holding fairly well and that the enemy penetrators were being contained. About twenty-four hours after the meeting with the Commanding General, Patton was able to report, much to the relief of his battalion commander, Colonel William Fondren, and the division staff, that A Company had accomplished the relief operation and was in position as directed. As he reflects on the action, Patton says, *"My thoughts remain with the officers and men of my company who from the lowest private performed at the heights of professionalism. The difficulties were the very mountainous terrain which had to be traversed, the lack of intelligence, and the ingrained problems precipitated by the language barrier and potential loss of face by the ROK commanders. My respect for the American soldier was once again confirmed."*

The battle experience George Patton looked for came time and again during the lengthy Luke's Castle engagement, especially 4 to 8 June 1953. During one particular engagement A Company 140th was in direct support of the 12th ROK Division in the Soyang Valley area, deployed on Hills 758 and 777, slightly east of the Punch Bowl. Patton's tanks were located in their protected firing positions, generally not vulnerable except to a direct hit. The action, however, was intense, with heavy incoming artillery and 120mm mortar fire literally raining on Patton's positions, which stretched across the hilltop for perhaps one-half mile. There were moderate-to-heavy casualties on both sides, and the immediate task at hand was to resupply all twenty-two tanks with ammunition, consisting of tank-gun and .50– and .30–caliber automatic weapons rounds. All of the vehicles assigned to A Company were dedicated to this mission.

As an indication of the intensity of the action, one platoon sergeant, Harold Potter, announced that "he had been killing enemy soldiers all day, but they keep coming back!" *"The bitter truth,"* intones Patton, *"was that there were a lot of Chinese who were being fed into the meat grinder which A Company and the quad-50 platoon under my direction had set up."* During the engagement, Patton found it necessary to confer with the commander, Colonel Chu, of the ROK A Infantry Regiment, within whose position Patton was located. Parking his jeep and driver behind a mound of dirt across from the well-dug-in Korean regimental CP, Patton coordinated with both his U.S. advisory staff and Colonel Chu himself. As artillery exploded all around, Patton turned to depart and remount his jeep when the MAAG advisor, Major Pete Seminoff, stopped him. "George, don't go! Wait here for the incoming [artillery fire] to cease or at least slow down." It was a very tempting offer for Patton, as the enemy artillery continued at an unending pace. Patton said that he agreed but it was imperative to get to his jeep and issue instructions for Colonel Chu. Seminoff answered, "If that's what you must do, go ahead. But the odds are heavily against you!" He finished his warning to Patton by saying something about fertilizing the trees in Arlington Cemetery.

Patton says, "*I had no choice but to get to that jeep-mounted radio in order to provide my commanders with important changes in the defensive battle plan. The distance from my location in Chu's CP was about a hundred yards. Decision! At the moment, I literally prayed for safety from this intense bombardment.*" During that prayer, Patton looked up into the sky and saw his father and several of his Confederate ancestors looking down at him and smiling. "*They seemed to say, go ahead Georgie, we are watching and you will be okay. With that ghostly encouragement, and breaking, I am certain, all speed records, I ran to my vehicle. In fact, as I exited the safety of the bunker and started across the road, the incoming artillery abated slightly, allowing me to receive no wounds worse than a tiny fragment which hit and cut my left ring finger and cracked my USMA class ring. I had received enough ghostly protection allowing me to reach my jeep and transmit Chu's orders to my platoon leaders. Mission accomplished! This experience has remained with me for all my subsequent years as an Army officer. Someone was watching and helping.*"

During the most intense day of the Luke's Castle combat action (31 May–1 June 1953), George Patton was informed that Lieutenant General I. D. White, commanding general of X Corps, and a well respected officer who had served under General George S. Patton, Jr., for many years, would land at his CP. When White arrived, Patton recalls, "*I immediately briefed him on what was going on. He said that he wanted to talk to me privately. He grabbed me by the arm and we moved away from the crowd. You know wherever there is a general there is a crowd. He said, 'George, I've known you since you were a little boy seven years old. You are in a very key location. Your orders are to protect the X Corps artillery and 40th Division artillery in the valley directly behind you. The enemy is very aggressive and we are having problems finding out exactly where our Korean units are, especially those U.S. units under*

ROK control. I want to impress upon you that you are in a very critical position.' Then he looked me right in the eye and said, 'Do you need anything? Because if you do, speak up.' I said, 'Sir, other than some improvement in the intelligence situation, and the front line trace [i.e., location] of the friendly units, I have only one request—radio repairmen. Our communications are down because we have no repair capabilities for the company radios. We lost two repairmen wounded in action and evacuated them yesterday and today.' The corps commander called his aide and said, 'Get in your helicopter and go up to an altitude where you can talk back to my CP. You tell them Patton needs a radio repairman up here with A company, 140th Tank Battalion, NOW.' He turned to me and said, 'Is that all you need?' I said, 'That's it, sir.' Then he departed."

Patton says the incident was minor in the bigger picture, but it demonstrated effective leadership. "White didn't study the problem, he didn't have a staff meeting, he didn't have a conference, he said, 'Get 'em!' Within the hour two repairmen came in by helicopter to my CP and started repairing radios. He trusted me and was acutely aware that I was in a difficult position and wouldn't overload the bidding. He simply responded to my request and made a terrific impression on me at the time."

Although Patton experienced many incidents during the Korean War, he cannot forget the cruelty of the enemy forces, both Chinese and North Korean, with whom he came in contact. He says, "As one example during the nights of 31 May, 1 June 1953, in the Luke's Castle area we piled up between six and seven hundred enemy dead and wounded on the forward slope of our defensive position. One of my platoon leaders called and asked if he could send our medics forward under a flag of truce and pick up or treat the Chinese wounded." Patton quickly approved and dispatched the medics to the casualty area. It was daylight, and the medics moved with a white flag of truce on a stick in full view of the Chinese across the valley. When the unarmed medics went down on the forward slope of the hill searching for the wounded, the Chinese started shooting at them. *"I immediately withdrew the medics,"* says Patton, *"procured some gasoline and used oil and dumped it down the hill and ignited it with tracer ammo. For health reasons we simply couldn't have rotting bodies around. And if there were some wounded on that slope, it was unfortunate. I had done all I could from a humanitarian point of view, and that gesture was met with hostile fire. Although I did receive some criticism for my actions, in this case my conscience was clear and continues today in that condition. A medical corpsman, unarmed and wearing the correct insignia, is not a target."*

Shortly after the Luke's Castle action, A Company, 140th Tank Battalion, was extracted from the Soyang Valley positions and placed in support of the 20th ROK Division, in the Punch Bowl. This volcanic land mass fit its nickname. It was, Patton recalls, an extinct volcano site with the highest elevations, over three-thousand meters, facing north toward the enemy. The northern slopes of the massive area were nearly straight down, making it almost totally defensible from ground attack. A Company was deployed, again in tank-firing positions along the northern rim of this terrain. The hostile situation facing the 20th ROK was unusually quiet, limited in general terms to reconnaissance patrol contacts between ROK and North Korean elements, together with a few probing attacks generally well handled by the ROK infantry units positioned there.

Not long after Patton's outfit had been moved out from under the operational control of the 12th ROK, he was informed that the Army commander, General Maxwell D. Taylor, would be visiting the sector. *"I was also told that my tanks looked terrible on their exteriors, covered with mud and dirt, and was asked to put a light coat of diesel oil on the tanks and turrets so that*

they would shine and stand out," remembers Patton.
*"Well, it was known to all of us that the Chinese were
using large quantities of white phosphorous in our area,
both by their mortar and artillery. White phosphorous
was designed to cause fires. So I told a colonel, a staff
officer from Seoul who made the request, that I could
not comply. I told him my tanks would be maintained
and clean inside, but outside, except for certain grease
fittings and couplings, there was no way we could wash
them on the hill. First, we had very little water, certainly not enough to wash tanks. One of my positions
was above the clouds! The colonel thought about it and
said, 'I'm ordering you to put on a diesel coat.' I replied, 'Sir, I can't take that order.' The colonel said,
'Well I'm going to the division commander and request
that you be relieved.' I told him that was certainly his
privilege but that I too would take my case to Major
General Gaither, the division commander, as well. He
was furious and shouted, 'You better not go down
there!' I replied, 'I'm going, sir, and I'm leaving now.' "*

Patton called his battalion commander on the radio,
described the incident, and announced he was proceeding to headquarters of the 40th Division to discuss the
matter personally with Gaither. He left immediately in
a jeep and traveled to headquarters, a drive of nearly
two hours. When Patton arrived at Division Headquarters, he called on the Chief of Staff, Colonel Bethune,
and the G-3, Colonel Jackson. He related the story, and
Bethune told him, "Go back to the unit; don't worry
about it." For Patton this was a turning point, because
it is the only time in his life he had ever refused to obey
an order from a superior. *"On reflection,"* he says, *"I
suppose that I've taken some shortcuts on certain orders, as have we all, but in this case, I felt I had to dig in
my heels for my troops. If a phosphorous round landed
near a tank that had been sloshed in diesel oil we would
have had an inferno. But I'll admit to thinking that this
may be where George Patton becomes a businessman*

*or a druggist or a doctor or something, since I was not
sure I could refuse an order and survive in the Army."*

At the time, within Eighth Army at all levels, rumors
were circulating that truce documents had been signed
by both sides and that hostilities would soon terminate.
And so it happened that an uneasy truce began July 27,
1953, but not for A Company, 140th Tank Battalion.
The following night Patton was informed that the 3rd
Infantry Division in the Kumwha area had been attacked and was requesting reinforcements, specifically
tanks. After receipt of road clearance and a message on
road conditions, Patton moved out in a westerly direction over a very mountainous highway. Since hostilities
were officially terminated, Patton's convoy moved with
their lights on, arriving at the designated assembly area
near the 3rd Division, 64th Tank Battalion, at about
3:00 A.M. Patton told Staff Sergeant Polk, his mess sergeant, that he wanted to feed the troops soup, coffee,
and sandwiches after refueling and have a weapons
check before they went to sleep. After finishing refueling, a chow line was established. To make it a little
easier for the two hundred or more troops trying to eat
in the dark, Patton had trucks pull up and shine their
headlights on the chow line so the soldiers could see
what they were doing.

Patton vividly remembers standing with Sergeant
Vaillancourt, his first sergeant, on a slope about one
hundred feet away from the chow line watching the
troops being served. *"It was raining hard, a cold wind
was blowing and it was just a lousy night,"* says Patton.
*"All of a sudden I heard this voice booming out over
the chow line, 'What are you doing here, motherfucker?' And then down comes a cleaver on a poor guy,
wielded by the mess sergeant, who was almost a giant.
It entered the left collarbone of a Chinese soldier who
had infiltrated the chow line. The blow was so hard
that the cleaver rested about eighteen inches above his
right hip. The Chinese soldier died instantly. I took off
running down the hill with Vaillancourt at my side.*

When I got to the mess sergeant I screamed, 'What in the hell are you doing? The war's over!' He looked at me and said, 'My war ain't over.' I'll never forget it as long as I live."

After the incident Patton immediately called Colonel Francis X. O'Leary, the battalion commander, and told him what happened.

> O'Leary said to Patton, "Well, I'll tell you what you do. You just dig a hole and you bury him on the banks of the Pukhan River and you put a little stick up there with any kind of identification he's got and somebody'll pick him up some day."
>
> Patton nodded, "Yes sir. I've done what I'm required to do by reporting the incident."
>
> "I'm not even going to tell Division. We'll just leave it," concluded O'Leary.

While stationed as a 3rd Infantry Division reserve battalion, Patton received word that he was being transferred to I Corps under the command of Lieutenant General Bruce C. Clarke. Chief of Staff of I Corps U.S. Army, was Colonel Creighton Abrams. It was the westernmost of the three corps within the Eighth Army, stationed near a small village north of Seoul. At that time truce negotiators were conferring almost daily at Panmunjom, attempting to resolve problems connected with the cessation of hostilities.

"This transfer came posthostilities," says Patton, *"and although it did not involve combat, it was of interest and useful since some Chinese prisoners of war refused repatriation to Red China and alternatively opted to join Chiang Kai-shek in Taiwan. Although I do not recall the total number of POWs who opted for Taiwan via mainland China, there were literally thousands needing processing and evacuation through Seoul to Taiwan. Thus my assignment, called 'Big Switch,' was a major segregation effort."*

Not having been able to take earlier advantage of the

Eighth Army rest and recreation program, Patton flew to Japan in late September 1953, accompanied by his great friend, Colonel Leonard D. Holder, later killed in action in Vietnam, at that time a member of the I Corps staff. They had been in Japan only a few days, staying at the Ohi-Date Hotel in downtown Tokyo, when Patton received word that his mother Beatrice had been killed in a horse accident not far from the family property in Massachusetts. As Patton says, *"I will always remember the date, 30 September 1953. I was finally located at the hotel and, under Colonel Abrams' direction, I received a priority pass to return to the U.S. I departed Japan via Fleet Air Wing and gradually made it to the East Coast.*

"On my arrival, many of our relatives were at Green Meadows, including my sister and brothers-in-law. We held a memorial service at St. John's Episcopal Church in Beverly Farms, where my mother and father were married forty-three years before. Things were pretty tough for a while, as I literally worshiped the ground on which my mother walked." A bright spot for Patton, if one could be found under the circumstances, was that he met his baby daughter, Margaret. Margaret was nearly three months old and had been brought to Massachusetts from Washington, D.C., so that her father could see and hold her for the first time.

Patton's belief since childhood of life after death was reinforced by an incident that was of great importance to him. Beatrice Patton always told her children that after her death she would return as a dolphin. She loved the affectionate mammal and hoped to come back in that image. While on a short sail a couple of days following the memorial service, Patton recalls two dolphins surfacing slightly aft of the *When and If,* and remaining in its wake for nearly an hour. *"I believe she was sending a message,"* says Patton. *"There are forces at work in this universe about which we know very little. Perhaps that is the best way to look at the tragedy of my mother's death."*

Ruth Ellen explained the accident further. "It happened at my uncle Frederick Ayer's place, about five miles from Green Meadows, while she was fox hunting. She was sixty-seven and died from an aneurysm that burst in or near her heart, something she knew about, because when I was going through her desk, I found a letter from Dr. White, the guy that took care of General Eisenhower, saying 'Dear Beatrice: You have this condition and you've asked me what to do and my advice to you is to do everything you want except drive a car. Because something might happen to you while you are driving and you might hurt someone.' She told us that she'd quit driving because her eyesight had gotten so poor. She never told us that she'd had palpitations, or tachycardia, all her life."

Although informed that he did not have to return to Korea following the brief period of emergency leave caused by the death of his mother, Patton elected to complete his tour with the reconnaissance squadron at I Corps. Returning to Korea just prior to Christmas, 1953, Patton, in a sad, if not cruel, irony, received several letters from his mother, together with a Christmas stocking that she had carefully filled. They had finally arrived after weeks in transit. Patton was brokenhearted, but he steeled himself to carry on.

Shortly before Patton returned to the United States, he was informed that one of the squadron's five-ton trucks had run over and killed a Korean villager. *"Because we were very concerned about getting along with the village where the accident occurred, there was some panic in my mind,"* says Patton. *"I knew we had to go and smooth things over and investigate this driver, and perhaps take some disciplinary action and probably pay compensation to the family. As I was receiving the report, the driver showed up with his truck.*

"He came in and I said, 'What happened?' He replied, 'It was unbelievable. The man jumped right in

*front of the truck. I saw him looking at the truck and I
knew he was going to cross the road, but as I came
closer he jumped right in front of it.' The driver was
very emotionally upset and I told him to remain silent
on the accident since whatever he said could possibly be
used against him. I told him to go to his quarters and
stay there."*

Patton went to the scene and looked around. The I
Corps MPs were investigating the accident, and the
body was still lying in the road. Soon a contingent of
Koreans, all quite old, came to see Patton with an interpreter. They said, "We want to talk about the fatality."
So they all sat to discuss the incident and asked Patton
if he knew about demonism. *"Apparently this was an
offbeat religion somewhat common in that part of the
world,"* says Patton. *"It was explained to me that followers of the religion believe that a demon followed
them constantly, and one of the things they eventually
must do is to eliminate the demon. That's why this individual stepped in front of the truck, hopefully to kill the
demon, and not himself. I appreciated the explanation
and quickly reached agreement with the village elders
with regard to the incident. The truck driver was released and returned to full duty. The circumstances of
the accident, however, similar to other incidents in Korea, provided a perspective of the country and how
much we all had to learn of our surrounding cultures."*

In March 1954, Patton returned to the United States
with a full tour of duty in Korea under his belt. He had
received orders assigning him to the Department of Tactics, United States Military Academy, at West Point. He
believed his service in the Land of the Morning Calm
had matured him greatly, making him into a more effective soldier and combat leader. He knew, however,
that he still had a long way to go, but he had learned
that he improved rapidly as the days went on and that
he was capable of making a proper decision under the
pressure of hostile attack.

Patton, reviewing his service in Korea, felt that his

methods of leadership at that point were about 90 percent correct and *"you can't expect more than that."* Patton also learned that he was instinctively correct when he walked into his first combat unit and took no more than seventy-two hours to observe that things were not being run right and to start thinking about how he would change the outfit. *"Initially,"* Patton says, *"I allowed some petty amateurs to gorge me with tales of 'It can't be done'; 'When you come to Korea, you throw the book away'; 'It's on requisition'; 'You're not at Knox now'; 'Battalion will just laugh at you'; 'Ha, ha, ha, listen to him—he's not a combat man, let him rave for a week or two and he'll settle down like all the others.' But I hung in there and my changes worked and worked quickly."*

In addition to Patton receiving the Silver Star, he earned rave reviews from his superiors. Major Allen Weinfield, his rating officer, wrote, "He is aggressive, persistent, and possesses that undefinable thing called 'color.' He has great ability and succeeds in instilling confidence, pride and skill into the officers and men under his command." Patton's commanding officer, Colonel O'Leary, concurred, calling Patton "brave almost to the point of rashness. This officer is a splendid combat officer."

On November 10, 1953, Patton, finally having time to reflect on his service in Korea, wrote in his diary, *"It is almost 11 November. Pop would have been 68. Casablanca surrendered 11 years ago tomorrow; 35 years ago tomorrow, a stillness fell over the skies of France as the guns ceased firing and both sides laid down their arms to retire and lick their wounds for a few years. Now, on the other side of the world, we are in another armistice, another ersatz peace, waiting, watching, warning and politicking, and growing militarily weaker year by year. West Point here I come."*

8

PEACEFUL INTERMISSION

I worked very hard during that period. I knew that in each assignment I had to do a little better.

—George S. Patton

Following his return from Korea in March 1954, Patton reported to the United States Military Academy as a member of the Department of Tactics, under the command of the Commandant of Cadets, and was appointed the interim tactical officer of Company G, 2nd Regiment, U.S. Corps of Cadets. Later Patton would move to A-2 Company. *"At that time in the history of West Point, a company tactical officer, or 'Tac,' was principally involved with character building—some might say leadership development—perhaps a better definition,"* Patton explained later. *"The Tac was the monitor of the Corps of Cadets aptitude system in his company, which in turn produced some order of merit indicators. This document usually led to selection of cadet leaders in the command and staff positions within the Corps."*

Generally speaking, the Tac officers sought among their cadets individuals who could, as the saying goes, "get the job done." Appearance, the ability to take the initiative, motivation, participation in sports—both varsity and intercompany rivalry—all of these characteristics and, of course, academic standing and more were carefully considered and evaluated under the aptitude system. This system was designed to identify leaders, and West Point has produced many military leaders. MacArthur and Pershing, as two examples, were both First Captains at the academy.

However, no system is infallible, and Patton, after taking over as Tac of A-2 Company, was reminded of that. He had a cadet who was not doing well under the aptitude system and was being considered for elimination from the Corps as unsuitable officer material. One day Patton was attending an intercompany soccer game during which the cadet was injured and hobbled to the sidelines. Patton suggested medical attention. The injured cadet talked Patton out of calling an ambulance and, after a brief rest, returned to the game. At the end of the game the cadet walked toward the sidelines and passed out; Patton learned later that he had sustained a fractured ankle. *"His tenacity in staying in the game, although in great pain, sent a message to me as his Tac,"* says Patton. *"Accordingly, I appeared before the aptitude board strongly recommending that he be retained in the Corps. The board supported my recommendation. To my great sorrow this fine soldier was later killed in Vietnam at the head of his battalion in a very hot firefight. He was awarded the Silver Star posthumously."*

Working at West Point was a plus for an officer's career advancement. There were twelve cadet companies in the two regiments at West Point, and among the officers assigned to them when Patton was there four became general officers and one, Alexander Haig, achieved four stars. The Tactical Department, which dealt with the students, was well selected and highly regarded. *"We were each responsible for about 120 people, so one had to be pretty good at his job,"* says Patton. *"I had to check the files of each cadet at least*

every two weeks. If believed necessary, we would coun-
sel each cadet and inform him of comments on his per-
formance and see what could be done to make him
more productive. I was fairly hard-nosed with them."
Patton and the other Tac officers believed that the
young men who attended West Point were outstanding,
although *"we still had to mold them,"* he says. *"For*
some the experience of West Point came easy, whereas
others never made it. One could not write a description
for a Tac officer's job if his life depended on it. General
supervision and character building is about what it
came down to."

Patton had one student in particular who told him he
did not want to be there but he felt he had to stay,
because his parents had forced West Point upon him.
Patton finally called the parents and told them the
Academy was simply not the place for him, since what
he really wanted to be was a Catholic priest. *"The par-*
ents told me the military was a family tradition and that
they had worked hard to get him to West Point," Patton recalls. *"I responded saying you should want your*
boy to be happy and he isn't happy here. Finally after a
lot of persuasion they authorized his release."

While Patton was a Tac officer he got a chance to try his
hand in the movies, during the filming of *The Long*
Grey Line, starring Tyrone Power, Maureen O'Hara,
and Ward Bond. *"I had a bit part,"* says Patton. *"How-*
ever, what I really enjoyed about the filming was the
work of director John Ford. He was one hell of a histo-
rian. I remember we were out on the parade grounds in
a formation and standing next to me was a guy who
was dressed as a French colonel. Ford walked up to the
'colonel' and looked him over and yelled, 'Prop man,
get your ass over here.' A little old guy came running
over and said, 'Yes, Mr. Ford?' Ford said, 'God damn it,
this SOB is wearing a medal that wasn't approved in
the time frame of this film. You're supposed to know

*your job better.' Ford turned to me and said, 'George,
I'll tell you, if I ever let that medal get in the movie I
would have received forty letters from all over the
world asking me what in the hell I was doing.' I said,
'Mr. Ford, I'm impressed.' He replied that he considered historical accuracy one of his hallmarks and recounted the story of a John Wayne picture where he
had a pistol from the wrong era on one of the actors
and received hundreds of letters from weapons clubs
from all over the world telling him so. He felt obligated
to write them back and agree that he had made a mistake."*

After spending two years at West Point, during which
his first son, named, in family tradition, George Smith
Patton, Junior, was born, a vacancy opened up for an
exchange assignment to the Naval Academy, at Annapolis, Maryland, in the spring of 1957. As was the custom each year, tactical officers could apply to be part of
a program in which they would serve at Annapolis
while selected counterpart Navy personnel would come
to West Point. For Patton it was an opportunity to learn
first-hand about the Naval Academy, but, as he would
comment later, *"I also enjoyed it very much because I
love the sea and the Chesapeake Bay area."* Patton, in
turn, was replaced at West Point by a naval aviator.

In preparation for his new duties, Patton arrived in
time to observe the Naval Academy's equivalent of basic training and "beast barracks." Patton had been in
Annapolis for about three days when his commander
called him in. He had a stack of manuals on his desk
and asked Patton what he knew about naval leadership.
"Nothing," was his response. He then told Patton that
the Marine captain who was scheduled to teach the naval leadership course had broken his leg and that Patton
had been selected to take his place, with class commencing the next day. Patton took the books home and

started to work. Soon a young, recently graduated en-
sign came to his quarters, knocked on the door, and
said, "I'm here to help the Army officer on Naval leadership." The young officer had been a brigade commander and tactically at the top of the Class of 1956.
*"The academy kept certain midshipmen just after grad-
uation to help with the new plebes,"* explains Patton.
*"This man knew naval leadership and we worked to-
gether and under the circumstances he became indis-
pensable to me."* Patton is convinced the young man
would have had a great naval career, but unfortunately
he died on the submarine *Thresher* when it sank with
its entire crew in 1963.

At Annapolis Patton's duties and mission as a company officer were about the same as his as a tactical
officer at West Point. One was expected to get to know
every midshipman in the company, so Patton carried a
notebook with a page for each person and added notes
as necessary. As rule infractions were noted they were
written up.

Patton believed, inherently, that the Navy view of
service differed somewhat from that of the Army.
*"When a naval officer was assigned to 'shore duty' he
considered himself 'on the beach,' paying close attention, for example, to time off with his family,"* explained Patton. *"When at sea, the twenty-four-hour
sense of duty applied. Asleep or awake, reading in the
wardroom or whatever, he is responsible. His ship is an
ever-present duty challenge. With the Army, most of the
time, unless you are in combat duty, you're with your
family. Navy personnel are absent for long periods. De-
stroyer sailors are absent even longer than submarine
personnel. Aviators were around their families on a
more regular basis, yet they would come and go on a
carrier for six months at a time. While their jobs
weren't as demanding on a day-to-day basis, it was an
extremely demanding job from the point of view of
risk."*

The opportunity to serve at both military academies

gave Patton greater insight into other differences in the military services as well. For instance, while at the Naval Academy Patton once went on a midshipman cruise on an aircraft carrier and was a passenger on a couple of takeoffs and landings. Those experiences, along with many others, helped Patton's understanding of the different pressures that affect Army and Navy personnel.

"I have fond memories of Annapolis," Patton comments. "As company officer of 4th Company, 1st Battalion, the Brigade of Midshipmen, I worked with first-rate individuals including several varsity football players assigned to my company." When the Army-Navy game weekend approached, Patton watched as the Navy team trained hard to win this very important football contest. Two days before the game Patton received a call from Coach Eddie Erdelatz inviting him to observe the Navy practice. As he arrived at the field, Rear Admiral William R. Smedberg III, the Naval Academy Superintendent, who was also observing the practice, turned to Erdelatz and said, "What's Patton doing here? He is a damn spy. How do we know that he might not call the West Point coach [Red Blaik] and inform him of our secret plays?"

"Erdelatz's answer was," says Patton, "the simple statement, 'I invited him, Admiral. He will inform no one of our plays because he is a gentleman.' I considered his comments a wonderful compliment. Erdelatz knew that I would keep the faith, and I did."

The night before the Army-Navy game of 1956, Patton was selected for officer of the watch duty in Bancroft Hall, the largest dormitory in the world. The executive department had been denuded of any naval or Marine officers; they were either in Philadelphia, where the game would be played, or partying in an off-duty status. Patton recalls that an officer of the watch had a plebe, or fourth classman, assigned to him as "messenger of the watch." Basically, his job was to take notes or do whatever the officer of the watch required. At about 9:30 P.M., as Patton walked down the main corridor of Bancroft Hall, his plebe shouted, "Look out, sir!" Patton turned around and spotted two bowling balls coming toward him with speed and accuracy. The plebe jumped to the left into a room, and Patton went to the right, as the two balls passed by. Evening the score, Patton wrote up two midshipmen in the room he jumped into for smoking in their beds. As a postscript, the game ended in a 7–7 tie and, as Patton recalls, was a "bone-bruising" contest.

Reviewing the West Point–Annapolis exchange program, sending a Naval officer to West Point and vice versa, Patton wrote in a report dated 4 June 1957, "I have heard that the program has been under fire from some quarters as being a useless and expensive operation. I feel that the entire program is very worthwhile; [it] assists, and will assist, materially in promoting mutual understanding, cooperation and the professional exchange of ideas which will be invaluable to the success of combined-arms teams in future war." Patton also wrote, "We owe our cooperation to the nation that pays our salary, and those who wish to argue with that point are fools. We must understand each other, and these exchange programs provide that kind of relationship, which in all candor, eventually wins battles."

When Patton joined the Executive Department at Navy, he followed Alexander Haig, who had preceded him. Patton had known Haig since 1954, when both officers served in similar duties at West Point. Haig's performance, according to those who worked with him at Annapolis, was outstanding. Haig's company won the colors for best performance in 1955–1956, and Patton's 4th Company came in at the number-two slot the following year. Patton was very fond of Al Haig and joins those who feel that he would have made a good president. "I was saddened that he ran into so much adversity in Washington in later years," remarks Patton. "He has been criticized for his actions after President Ronald Reagan was shot, but he had no plan to *take over the White House, he was simply trying to stabilize a situation. I didn't look at it as Al Haig grabbing for power. It resembled a military mind saying, 'The command structure is now in adversity. I must go in there.' Haig later admitted he made a mistake and that he hadn't done his homework on procedure, and I look at it as an honest mistake made by a person trying to do what he thought was his duty."*

It has also been said that Haig came up the ranks too quickly near the end of his career and that he was not following military channels as much as he was using his political connections. Patton believes he was just lucky. *"He was Supreme Allied Commander Europe, and I believe truly that he was one of the best ever in a terribly complex station, and a demanding one. I really didn't sense a lot of jealousy over that appointment and his successive ones. We all knew Al Haig was a very able officer and we wished him luck. Personally, I was never jealous. I wouldn't have wanted those jobs, even if I had been selected for them. But Haig got them mainly through his relationship with Cyrus Vance* [Secretary of the Army, 1962–1963; Deputy Secretary of Defense, 1964–1967; Secretary of State, 1977–1980], *who pushed him, and that was his privilege to do so. From a political perspective my only problem with Al Haig is that sometimes I don't understand him. I've told him that to his face. I just have a problem understanding what he's really saying and I think others do too."*

After Annapolis, Patton, accompanied by his family, now including a second son, Robert, born in 1957, attended the Army's Command and General Staff College at Fort Leavenworth, Kansas. Following graduation, in the summer of 1958 he travelled to Stuttgart, Germany, for assignment as the senior aide-de-camp to General Clyde D. Eddleman, who had been selected as commanding general of the Seventh Army. *"I was personally picked by General Eddleman,"* says Patton. *"He had a very fine reputation and I was happy to have a new learning experience at a very high level of the Army.*"

Among Patton's tasks as General Eddleman's aide was handling his itinerary and the General's contingency fund, including money the Department of the Army provided for social activities. "*I also accompanied him on trips and submitted reports concerning what and who he saw. Those reports and accompanying comments were sent to him for review and then on to the Seventh Army chief of staff. Eddleman, in his free time, loved to hunt and fish and I would go with him on many of these occasions as well.*"

During his tour as aide, which lasted from July 1958 through December 1959, part of Patton's job was to escort many VIPs to the Daimler-Benz factory in Stuttgart. During one such visit Patton attended a meeting with the chief executive officer of Benz, who spoke perfect English, and the Chief of Staff of the Swedish Army. The CEO took a glass of champagne, raised it, and said he'd like to propose a toast to the United States Eighth Air Force. "*Now of course the Eighth had literally destroyed much of Germany from the air,*" says Patton. "*There was a pause and kind of an uneasy moment of bewilderment. Then he said, 'They forced us to modernize and gave us a place to park.' I'll tell you the house nearly collapsed in laughter.*"

While Patton was in Europe as Eddleman's aide they would often visit the border camps. On one occasion the group took the train to Hersfeld, the furthest-north unit on the southern flank of the British Army of the Rhine. Eddleman was promoting *Army* magazine subscriptions at that time, so Patton knew what would happen when Eddleman decided to tour a recreation hall where the troops relaxed. He made a beeline for the service magazine rack and was looking for *Army* magazine; and there were none on the shelf.

Eddleman turned to the resident First Sergeant and said, "I don't see *Army* magazine. Where is it?"

The sergeant, thinking on his feet, replied, "General, the troops loved it so much it got worn out and I had to throw it away."

When they finished the visit, Eddleman looked at Patton and said, "Do you believe that story?"

"Well, no sir," Patton responded.

"I don't think I do either," Eddleman huffed. "Well, let it go for now, but next time . . . !"

Patton also worked on itineraries with the secretary of the general staff, the SGS, who handled the VIPs. The office billeted them and developed their itineraries with Patton's assistance and support. Patton's lasting memory is of the string of people, the Department of the Army, Secretary of Defense, and others, coming through all the time. *"For some reason, our heaviest load of visitors came just before the Octoberfest in Munich."* When a VIP visit was pending, the SGS would tell Patton what the individual wanted to see, and Patton would suggest appropriate places where that activity or troop placement could be found. Patton would arrange or personally provide a briefing and a tour or luncheon.

Many of the guests during Patton's time as an aide to General Eddleman travelled by a special train the Army operated. The train cars had once belonged to Reichsmarshall Herman Goering, who had used it to travel throughout Nazi Germany. During the war the train had been scheduled by the German railroad authorities and it was a valuable asset, since Goering stayed on the train at night. Clothing, food, everything he needed was on board. *"The train also had a mess area and an excellent lounge,"* says Patton. *"The compartments all enjoyed toilet facilities."* After the war the Americans modified the train slightly and put the SGS in charge of the details concerning personnel and logistics. Onboard assistance included a sergeant who was the NCO in charge, along with a cook, maid, and a waiter—the last three all civilians paid for by the Army. Many of the American VIPs stayed on board the train as a billet, and part of Patton's job was to keep the train's schedule straight. It was not demanding work, but it had to be done correctly. One time Patton woke up very early in the morning, looked out the window, and saw the sign for the wrong town: the train had ended up in Würzberg instead of Koblenz. *"The railroad had made a mistake and my boss was late for an appointment. I died a thousand deaths at that moment."*

Patton also recalls meeting many important people in the job. *"I was impressed with one thing. The more senior they were, the easier they were to work with,"* he says. *"They were not as demanding. Some of the Assistant Secretaries of the Army, on the other hand, were hard to work with. I was not impressed by the civilian managers from either the Department of the Army or the Department of Defense. They, too, would always manage to visit us about the time of the Octoberfest, the Oberammergau Passion Play, or pheasant hunting season."*

During this particular assignment in Europe, Patton learned a great deal more about the suffering and hardships endured by the European people in World War II. While he had certainly been exposed to much deprivation during his trip through Europe in 1946, he was now reminded again that the war had affected not only property, but people as well. *"On one occasion I was invited to lunch by a German colonel who had been captured in the Stalingrad campaign,"* he says. *"He never was able to receive or send mail to his family in Hamburg. After about five or six years of POW time he was repatriated. He had had no connection with Germany for years so he decided to have a look around, before making himself known. He grew a beard and put on old clothing and travelled. He learned that his wife had assumed he was dead and after many years had been remarried happily to a veteran officer. One day the colonel occupied a park bench in order to see her come and go with her children, including his son. He*

*called the boy over one day and became acquainted. 'I
decided they were doing so well I just walked away
forever,' the colonel sadly announced. I said, 'This must
have been terribly hard on you,' and he nodded, 'More
than you will ever know, but it was the honorable thing
for me to do.' "*

Such stories were not unusual, and the difficulties of
the postwar years were etched in the faces of the population. Patton learned that jobs were not plentiful and
life produced tough choices. When Patton was with the
2nd Cavalry in Augsburg, he and his soldiers used to
patrol at night, arresting prostitutes and taking them to
the clinic for medical checks to curtail the spread of
sexually transmitted diseases. One evening Patton and
his men encountered a very attractive, well dressed
thirty-five-year-old prostitute. The medics checked her,
and Patton, speaking with her, found out that her husband had been an infantry commander in Russia. He
had been killed, but his body had not been returned.
She told Patton, "I have no skills, and I so detest what I
am doing." Patton realized she was a *"high-type"* German woman and got her a job as a typist in Headquarters, 2nd Cavalry. *"She was grateful someone finally
gave her a break so that she could have a second chance
at a decent life,"* he says.

While in Europe, Patton also met several associates
of a famous German military commander who figured
prominently in his father's career—General Erwin
Rommel. One of the German liaison officers from the
peacetime German Army to General Eddleman's staff
had been on Rommel's staff in Normandy. He came to
see Patton one day and said, "I know your father was
General Patton and was very respected by General
Rommel, and we would like to arrange to have you
meet Frau Rommel." Patton said he too would enjoy a
meeting and within a few days went with Joanne and
the eldest Patton child, five-year-old Margaret, to call at
her home in Stuttgart. *"She was most cordial,"* says
Patton. *"The house looked like any military home with*

the artifacts collected as they travelled about the world. She told me the story of his death, which has been well recorded, and also offered to show me his death mask.

"We also talked of the African campaign. Frau Rommel said one of the things her husband just couldn't understand was why Hitler wouldn't reinforce the Wehrmacht effort in Africa in order to cut the Suez Canal, which would have caused major problems for the British and American forces. However, Hitler got involved in Russia at the time, directing huge resources in support of the Russian campaign, which left Rommel hanging out on a limb. Basically, der Führer failed to reinforce success."

Patton also met Manfred Rommel, son of the Field Marshal. He was working in a government job in Stuttgart at the time and was later elected lord mayor of the city. He also talked about his father in great detail. Patton remembers one event with Rommel in particular. "*I had been visiting him and when I was leaving he went to get my coat in the closet. I noticed a large package of military-type maps on a shelf and asked Manfred about them. He said they were some of his father's maps. He brought them out and they were all dogeared and torn, really in terrible shape. He said, 'I haven't had a chance to do anything with them.' So, I purchased some rolls of sticky acetate used by the Army as a preservative and we spent some time saving those maps. He gave one battle map to me, which is now on display in the Patton museum at Fort Knox, Kentucky.*"

Manfred Rommel and George Patton soon became close friends and compared notes concerning the representation of their fathers in movies and on television. Patton says Manfred Rommel felt the portrayal of his father by James Mason in the movie *The Desert Fox* was quite accurate. At great length one day Manfred also described the end of his father's career and how he had been forced by Hitler and others to commit suicide or face a public trial. Rommel told Patton that if his father had been found guilty, he would have lost all his entitlements, and his family would have suffered even more. On another occasion, Frau Rommel told Patton that her husband requested that she have an autopsy done on him after his death. History records such an autopsy was not permitted. *"The stories I was told by the Rommels represented a significant piece of German military history, and some of what they shared with me from a military family perspective often sounded very familiar,"* Patton says.

In 1959, while serving as aide-de-camp to Eddleman, who by then had been selected as Commander in Chief, or CINC, of USAREUR, Patton encountered a tradition that called for each new commander in chief to visit his counterpart east of the Iron Curtain. In this case, that was the Commander in Chief, Group of Soviet Forces, Germany, or CINC GSFG. Patton recalls, *"I made the first visit in my aide capacity. We exited through Hof, a border town at that time in the 2nd Cavalry sector, and then on to Leipzig and to GSFG headquarters only a few miles south of Berlin, spending one night there and the final night in the city of Dresden, East Germany."*

Patton had an interesting experience staying at Dresden's Metropole Hotel. *"We had been wined and dined for hours and attended a couple of hosted events. Although we were tired we still hoped to go out on the town and 'show the flag,' as the saying goes. Because this area was strictly controlled by the Soviet occupying force, we had an escort of sorts who claimed he was a lieutenant but certainly was not. Rather, he was most likely an agent of the KGB. Well, we washed up and put on green uniforms and all went downstairs. The lieutenant, named Viturin, who spoke excellent English, was sitting in the lobby. He said, 'Where are you going?' We said we were going out on the town, intending to see some sites and enjoy a relaxing evening. He said, 'Aren't you guys tired?' We said we were a little tired, but we wanted to go out and look around. He said, 'I wish you wouldn't go. I'm supposed to go with you, but I want to go to bed. I've had a hard day.' We said, look, fella, if you're supposed to go with us, you're welcome. We'll even pay for the drinks, but we are going out. He said, 'I don't want to go, and I don't want you to go.'*

"*With the word that we were going out anyway, the lieutenant arose, reached into his briefcase and pulled out a map of the town. He looked around to see if anyone was observing and handed me the map. The shaded areas on the map indicated restricted areas where we were not to go. He whispered to me, 'Please just stay out of the areas marked on this map and everything will be fine.' With that we left and I assume he went to bed or found something else to do. That was, however, an example of the cat-and-mouse game going on at the time.*" In effect, Patton remembers, "*the distinguished Lieutenant Viturin provided the United States with a piece of intelligence about Soviet military units in the famous city of Dresden.*"

During the trip into the Red Army world in East Germany, Patton concluded that the occupying forces had their shortcomings. On the approach to Zossen-Munsdorf, otherwise HQ GSFG, he saw that a few villagers were present but mostly Red Army personnel. Only at the main headquarters did Patton see anything that resembled barracks, and they were very austere. On the surface Patton could easily sense a very powerful and brutally disciplined force with little respect for the local people. Such a force, Patton learned time and again, had trouble holding power.

Also during that particular visit Patton witnessed an interesting exchange between his boss, General Eddleman, and the CINC GSFG. "*At the start of the day an honor guard was present, and I must add, a more impressive group of seventy to one hundred soldiers I've never seen before or since. The Soviet guard of honor was clothed in the uniform of the guard of honor of Peter the Great, a leading eighteenth-century despot. Eddleman asked the Russian about the choice of clothing. The CINC answered, 'Yes, General, we realized that you would find it strange, but we like the uniform and decided to clothe the guard of honor in that fashion.' Whether or not the Soviets were using a little subtle psychological warfare I don't know, but we learned not to put anything past them,"* Patton says.

After working as an aide to Eddleman, Patton changed assignments. *"He didn't like to keep an aide over eighteen months so he transferred me to the G-3 section of the U.S. Army Europe. I was in the operations division until I went to the 11th Cavalry as executive officer of the 1st Squadron at Straubing, Germany, a truly magnificent assignment.*

"The 11th Armored Cavalry Regiment was straight troop duty on the Czech border. My job was to do things that were not important enough for the squadron commander to do personally but needed to be done for the squadron. I was responsible for mess halls, maintenance and numerous other areas including supervising the staff who worked for me. The squadron commander rated the troop commanders and me and I rated the squadron staff." For Patton this was one of the most enjoyable times in his career. It was a beautiful area, the Pattons had good quarters, and there was great hunting and fishing nearby. The squadron always had a troop on the border and he inspected them regularly, as did the squadron commander. It was typical peacetime duty, but very sensitive in the bigger picture, given the continuing Cold War.

Patton's interest in military history was expanded by many onsite tours of historic places in the area. *"The visits confirmed that history, in a military sense, does indeed repeat itself,"* says Patton. *"When I was stationed near the Czech border we used to hunt with Herr Hans Schneltzer, who was a professional guide under the German system. Hans had been wounded in both arms in Russia during World War II. He shot a special shotgun with a curved stock so as to permit his crippled arms to handle the weapon. Straubing and nearby Regensburg were areas occupied by the Romans. Regensburg had been one of Caesar's headquarters, so there had been considerable Roman activity in that part of Bavaria."*

Another guide, very often with George Patton, was Herr Willy Huderdt, who, like Hans Schneltzer, was wounded seriously during the Russian campaign. Huderdt once told Patton they could get Hungarian partridges if Patton could figure a way to get Huderdt inside the five-kilometer restricted zone, next to the border. As a German national and nonresident of the zone, Huderdt was not permitted to enter the area without U.S. Army permission. Patton did the necessary paperwork and they hunted and shot birds. On one particular day, having shot their limit of partridge, they stopped for lunch at a local *gasthaus*. After lunch, Huderdt asked Patton if he had time for another short tour. They drove about five or six miles, parked the car on the side of the road, and started walking through the forest in a northeasterly direction, following a slight depression in the ground. If one observed carefully, one could see that, although barely noticeable, the depression was manmade; the border between Czechoslovakia and the Federal Republic of Germany was perhaps no more than a hundred meters further to the east. Overlooking this depression was an 11th Cavalry observation post, manned, armed with the best night-vision equipment available at the time, and supported by a fully operational and half-loaded .50-caliber heavy machine gun. Willy looked at Patton with a big grin, stretching from ear to ear.

"Do you have any idea where we are?"

Patton answered, "Of course. My observation post is right over at the edge of those woods."

Huderdt said, "Of course that's true, but George, I must tell you that you are standing on the front line trace of the occupying Roman legion, circa 44 A.D."

He then queried Patton as to the squadron mission in the event of a Soviet attack. Patton replied that the details of the regimental mission were highly classified but that elements of an armored cavalry regiment had been stationed in Straubing since 1945; it was then 1961. Patton discussed the unclassified mission, which was to provide early warning of an attack; defend as far to the east as possible; and gain, maintain, and execute continuous delay, with passage of lines westward through the main battle positions of Seventh Army and other NATO forces. Finally, if there was anything left of the 11th after combat against what was expected to be a heavily superior force, it was to go into reserve, reconstitute as well as could be expected, and prepare to counterattack to the east under Seventh Army operational control, on order.

Huderdt nodded knowingly, then said that he had a very interesting document he would like to share with Patton. Withdrawing a large notebook from his backpack, he read the mission of the Italio Legion stationed in that location in about 40–50 A.D. The mission was almost 100 percent the same as that of the 11th Cavalry mission of 1961—early warning, gain contact, continuous delay. Then Huderdt brought up the logistics side of the equation. He said he knew that some of Patton's barrier material, including wire, mines, obstacles and other necessary items, was stored in Ingolstadt, a small town to the west of Straubing.

"Why do you store it there?" he asked.

Patton explained that if the main supply routes forward were interdicted by enemy forces, this material could be loaded on barges and floated up the Danube, ensuring timely resupply.

Huderdt said to Patton, "Let me show you another paper." This was a letter from a Roman centurion to his superior saying he recommended extra supplies be kept in Ingolstadt, because they could be moved up the Danube in case of attack by the barbarians. He looked at Patton with a smile of satisfaction and said that which Patton already knew: "George, there is nothing new under the sun." *"The story was incredible,"* recalls Patton, *"and as I toured the area I could just smell those legion personnel. The Roman lines were barely a hundred feet from my machine guns. Decisions made hundreds and thousands of years ago, and in some cases much earlier, were based then as now on terrain and political necessity."*

Patton also enjoyed visiting the Regensburg area, where the 3rd Squadron of the 11th Cavalry was stationed. Regensburg was famous as a Napoleonic battle site and had been referred to in a Robert Browning poem (as Ratisbon). It was also Caesar's advance headquarters and the seat of one of the early leaders of Bavaria. Regensburg has the remains of a Roman amphitheater that once held over twenty-five thousand people, along with a complex of Roman baths. Ruth Ellen, who also admired Regensburg, once visited the Pattons in Straubing and toured the underground tunnels where slaves built fires to heat water for the baths above them. *"Ruth Ellen, who always had a sharp eye for artifacts, reached down and picked up a bronze earring on the dirt floor of the tunnel,"* says Patton. *"As many as two thousand tourists walked through these same tunnels in one week and had missed the earring: an amazing find. It was authentic third century, according to the Straubing historical authorities."*

Patton has always held an affinity for Napoleon and, in addition to Regensburg, spent time at many other Napoleonic battle sites, including Waterloo. *"There were two sharp fights at Abensberg and Eggmuhl, precursors to the Regensburg campaign. I remember being in Abensberg on night duty with the First Squadron one evening. As I sat on a rock in the dead of night observing the squadron, I sensed the Napoleonic cavalry go by me, actually sensed it, clattering by, real quiet and ghostly in the dark. I know for a fact the town had not changed very much since those days: the same manure piles outside the same houses and the same old honeywagons, that kind of thing. The feeling I got that evening was a sense I had from time to time, like my father, [that] I had been there before."*

While stationed in Straubing, Patton used his knowledge of military history to teach a course as adjunct faculty for the University of Maryland. He would take groups of students on field trips around Regensburg and study the battles very carefully. Later, when he was offered a job teaching history at West Point, he turned it down. *"I just didn't want to go there and teach, but I truly enjoyed the onsite battlefield tours. I would take the appropriate maps and study the positions trying to figure out what went on and whether those ancient commanders had made the correct decisions of the moment."* Patton called the exercises *"terrain appreciation."* *"For example, why did* [Marshal Michel] *Ney attack in one spot instead of another? Where was* [Marshal Jean] *Lannes when the emperor called him to commit his force?"* Patton believes such exercises are invaluable experiences for professional U.S. officers.

In Europe, as was often the case, Patton took time to commit his thoughts to paper, and he became a frequent contributor to military trade journals, including *Armor* magazine. In his many articles one gains insight into Patton's development as an officer and student of history. In an article printed in the May–June 1958 issue of *Armor,* Patton wrote, *"Not since the advent of gunpowder to the fields of armed strife has such an awesome change come to the art of war as the atomic weapon. This mechanism, now being refined to a form of ground tactical employment, is acting to change some of the basic concepts of organization and tactics— even perhaps, to the ageless nine principles of war which have guided our thinking for centuries.*

"It is the solemn duty of the military professional to examine this power closely in the light of the probable

conditions of the next war. The vast destructive potential of atomics in warfare causes one to realize that its skillful employment and accurate application, integrated with the operations of streamlined ground forces, will be the decisive factor in land battle.

"National policy contemplates the use of this weapon. Common sense warns us of its employment against us."

Allowing for healthy disagreement, Patton went on to write, *"The reader may not agree with what is said herein; this condition is not material to the issue. If he does disagree he should do so constructively, and then go one step further in his examination of this approach."*

Discussing the atomic battlefield, a subject often discussed in military circles after the conclusion of World War II, Patton cited leadership as the key. *"On the atomic battlefield leadership must be personal. Troops must be aware of the commander's presence and know that he accepts the same risks of horrible and vaporized death that they do. It is the task of leadership to strengthen the will of the troops."*

Patton returned from Europe during the winter of 1961 and attended the Armed Forces Staff College, at Norfolk, Virginia. The AFSC mission was to train selected members of the officer corps from all the military services in the business of serving in a jointly manned headquarters, up to and including the Joint Chiefs of Staff. Cross-training, including an emphasis on amphibious operations, was the order of the day. Consequently, Patton was able to tour the amphibious base at Little Creek, Virginia. He also visited a nuclear submarine and participated in a short dive.

Time at AFSC was mostly filled with lectures followed by work-group seminars during which the lectures and speakers would be discussed. In addition, the students were also required to group together as a joint staff and plan an amphibious attack by a corps involving both Army and Marine divisions. *"Some of the work at the AFSC was quite sensitive,"* says Patton. *"Early on, I learned that the more 'sensitive' it was, the less people would grade it. That appealed to me. Consequently, I prepared my thesis requirement on the projected role of Sweden in the event of general war."* During the five-month period Patton attended AFSC his family remained in their home in Washington; Patton commuted home on occasional weekends.

As Patton worked through the curricula at the Armed Forces Staff College he made a very good impression on those around him, including the deputy commandant, who would later say in his efficiency report of Patton, "He is a rugged, sinewy officer, erect and correct in bearing, meticulously groomed and the very model of the professional soldier. He appears to have established for himself a private set of professional and personal standards of the very highest order and strives ceaselessly to attain them. This officer is aggressive and forthright by nature, but works well and harmoniously with others. He will function anywhere and in any assignment as a loyal, highly effective and selfless staff officer. He is equable and easy in society, urbane with his contemporaries and deferential in the finest sense of the word to his superiors. He possesses a natural courtliness of manner and is by breeding and cultivation a complete gentleman. He is acutely conscious of, though properly reticent about, the great military traditions of his family and has absolutely dedicated himself to living up to those traditions. Having an ardent thirst for knowledge he is an omnivorous reader for both pleasure and improvement. His mind is incisive, flexible, far-ranging and imaginative and he has acquired the ability to cut through minutia to seize the essence of a problem. Perhaps the most conspicuous single characteristic of this officer is his fierce and burning pride in the honorable profession of arms. He has a lovely and charming wife who is a decided asset to any military or civilian community."

Such a glowing assessment of Patton, extending as well to Joanne, was a source of great pride. *"I worked very hard during that period,"* Patton would say later. *"I knew that in each assignment I had to do a little better."* Indeed he was growing as an officer and man.

9

UNE GUERRE TRÈS DIFFICILE

*Prior to Ap Bac, the Kennedy administration had suc-
ceeded in preventing the American public from being more
than vaguely conscious that the country was involved in a
war in a place called Vietnam.*

—George S. Patton

Patton graduated from the Armed Forces Staff College
early in 1961 and was assigned to the Pentagon in the
Operations and Training branch of Deputy Chief of
Staff of Military Operations, and further assigned to
the so-called "West Point desk," a small office that handled West Point business for the Chief of Staff of the
Army. *"At that time the superintendent of West Point
was William C. Westmoreland and I spent time writing
papers and running around the halls like a crazy man,"*
says Patton. *"In my view I was accomplishing very little. All it did for me was to expose me to and acquaint
me with the Army General Staff, which I would learn
about in spades when I was assigned there during the
Vietnam era."*

Meanwhile, the situation in Vietnam was heating up.
The Joint Chiefs of Staff, or JCS, established a four-star
U.S. Military Assistance Command Vietnam (MACV),

with General Paul D. Harkins, USA, selected as commander. Patton, not wanting to miss another war, contacted Harkins, volunteering to serve. Harkins answered, with a "come ahead." *"General Harkins served under my dad and was very close to him during World War II and I will freely admit that I took advantage of that prior friendship in order to serve in what was rapidly becoming an active combat zone,"* Patton says. *"Nevertheless, I felt no guilt with this request, since I was hopefully headed for some strange form of warfare about which I had no background, although in preparation for this war, I had read many books on guerilla warfare, especially some of T. E. Lawrence's works."*

The reasons Patton requested to go to Vietnam were simple and historical. As in the past, he would recite the Patton family response: "Why does a surgeon want to operate or an author write a book?" *"My entire family going back generations all understood the reasons,"* Patton explains. *"I asked to go early since my participation in the Korean War came in the waning years of the conflict. In that regard, I felt that my education in terms of possible combat was wanting. Finally, I felt that the best course of action available to me at the time was to serve in Vietnam and see what 'counterinsurgency,' a new buzzword, was all about."* Patton's experience and lessons learned in Vietnam would serve him extraordinarily well in later years. Perhaps his only concern about volunteering was that his daughter Helen had been born in March, and there was some trauma with his departure toward what was then the unknown. *"However, on reflection, it was expected that I would go,"* he concludes.

Patton deployed to Vietnam in April 1962 aboard a commercial aircraft under contract with the Department of Defense. When he arrived in Vietnam it was obvious that the HQ MACV was in no way ready to receive the large influx of advisory personnel and staff people it had requested. There were almost no quarters available, and the conditions were poor. After two or three unpleasant days, Patton moved into the Majestic Hotel on the Saigon River, remaining there for about a month. He was later billeted in the Ham Nghi Hotel in downtown Saigon. At that time Saigon was still known as the Paris of the East; there were beautiful shops, several fabulous restaurants, and the Street of Flowers, of international renown. It was a lovely, colonial-type city, with a large Chinese suburb, Cholon. *"Unfortunately, the American role in Vietnam over the years changed all of that,"* says Patton.

After being in the country a few days Patton was directed to report to General Harkins. *"He greeted me with a cup of coffee and said, 'I've got a job for you. I'm going to assign you in a CIA liaison slot. You will be working in an outfit known as Combined Studies.'"* The office was located at the Military Assistance Advisory Group (MAAG), which was some distance from Headquarters, Military Assistance Command. It was about a twenty-five-minute drive from Saigon. When Patton reported, he found that he would actually be working in three locations: the American Embassy, at MACV J-3 [joint operations] (under Colonel George Morton), and Combined Studies. While in the embassy Patton would spend a great deal of time with John Richardson, the CIA chief in Saigon, Colonel Gilbert B. Layton of Combined Studies, and Lucien Conein, *"a very knowledgeable but controversial person who had spent many years in Southeast Asia and was married to a Vietnamese woman."*

The role of the CIA was principally gathering and processing information into intelligence, but Patton's particular assignment had very little to do with that function. He did receive some intelligence-related tasks, such as finding out if a certain village had a new village chief, or other similar types of information; however, his main job was to assist in coordinating the transition of the few Special Forces detachments in the country, which had been funded and supported by the CIA, to

MACV control. This effort found Patton travelling the entire peninsula to become familiar with the South Vietnamese armed forces. Patton recalls learning soon after his arrival in Vietnam that there were five Special Forces detachments in the country. By the time of his departure a year later, MACV had between thirty and forty detachments deployed. Generally the units were assigned on a six-month temporary-duty basis from a Special Forces Group HQ on Okinawa. Eventually, the original group was unable to support the expanding MACV Combined Studies requirements, so additional detachments were deployed from the United States.

When Patton joined Combined Studies, he found that though his supervisor, Layton, wore a uniform with a colonel's insignia—he had a fine combat record with the 10th Armored Division in World War II—he was now actually in the CIA. *"Layton was a superior caring, patriotic individual who always kept the needs of America foremost in his mind. Summarily, he was my boss and my teacher,"* explains Patton. *"Layton supervised the Special Forces program for the* [Central Intelligence] *Agency, which was then coordinated through the joint MACV staff in Saigon. The evolving concept was that if the Special Forces program was to expand, which everyone thought it would in view of* [President] *Kennedy's great respect for the concept, then eventually the transfer of funding, logistics, and operations would come under MACV control. The Layton concept for Vietnam was a fascinating one, yet underfunded, and called for Special Forces detachments positioned along the entire, tri-zonal Laos, Vietnam, Cambodia border."*

The detachments, according to Patton, had the mission of organizing, supplying, and equipping paramilitary forces, mostly Montagnards. The CIDGs (Civilian Irregular Defense Groups), Patton recalls Layton saying, were "a fence of people hostile to the Viet Cong and North Vietnamese trained and armed to delay, prevent or finally defeat infiltration" as the supreme goal.

In retrospect, while there were many benefits to the "fence of people" concept, the obvious disadvantages involved tension and hostility between numerous tribes and the problems associated with the varying dialects of the Montagnard border people.

Patton would eventually spend much of his first tour in Vietnam concentrating on the organization of the paramilitary forces, their ranks filled primarily by the Montagnard tribes. *"We were running some experiments to determine how we would organize a village and what our relationship would be with the aboriginal tribes,"* he explains. *"While there were ten or eleven different tribes, we were mainly working with the Rhade tribe which was centered around Pleiku and other small villages in the area. Our job included arming the men and training them to fight with the mission of eliminating infiltration. Working closely with the Montagnards, we were able to form units paid and equipped by the United States. In turn, their mission was simply to resist incursions by the Viet Cong. The results of these particular missions were spotty at best."*

Patton found that the Montagnards had many unusual customs. For instance, because of the matriarchal structure of certain tribes, if a man was killed, a wedding was held within twenty-four hours in order to marry off the widow. *"Additionally,"* says Patton, *"they are animists, in other words they believe in special powers of the sun and the moon and often had their daily activities directed by dreams. We studied their society very closely. Since their dreams directed their actions, we studied what various dreams meant to them. For instance, if one dreamed of a deer in the jungle, he would have a good day. After a short time we learned how to influence the tribe by meeting with the village chief and describing our own 'personal dreams.' It allowed us to relate to the chief and helped us gain and improve the confidence of the villagers."*

The Montagnards were an extremely superstitious people. They lived in long, thatched-roof houses on stilts, some as much as a hundred feet long, each containing three or four families, and their pigs and chickens lived underneath the structure. Building these houses required much work. Nevertheless, if a crow, considered a bad omen, landed on the ridgepole of a longhouse still under construction, they would tear the house down. *"They kept little boys up there with long sticks to keep the crows off,"* says Patton. *"It was okay if another type of bird landed, but no crows."*

In the final analysis, the organization and implementation of paramilitary forces, Patton remembers, was a concept agreed to by MACV and by those in the know. Yet he laments today, *"Somehow, somewhere, similar to many other initiatives later adopted by the United States during the Vietnam War, the mission fell of its own weight into the rubbish pile of history."*

During his first tour in Vietnam, Patton worked closely with the CIA and enjoyed the experience. He felt that they were interested, motivated, and did their job in a professional manner. *"Importantly, they were also very focused on victory in Vietnam,"* Patton says. *"What should be understood by the American people concerning the CIA in a war such as Vietnam is the immense amount of work required in order to bring about either a paramilitary force, one agent, or a cluster of agents. These were very delicate operations and many times one realized that the chances of success were perhaps 50 percent or less."*

Soon after going to work at his office in Combined Studies, Patton began looking around and asking questions. One fellow in particular piqued his curiosity, since he sat at an adjoining desk and never once told Patton his mission. Finally, Patton asked him. His reply was, "Major, I can't tell you. But if it ever comes to a point where you need to know what I do, you will be assisted either by me or someone else who is specializing in our area of expertise." Later that year Patton did indeed develop a "need to know," and his request for assistance was satisfied immediately.

Patton also met another man in the Agency who was an expert on religions, especially offbeat religions throughout the world. *"For instance he studied people who threw bones which would tell them what to do that day,"* says Patton. *"Any time an embassy person was being deployed to someplace where there were unusual beliefs this agent would brief the employee on the understanding of that particular religion and culture. His input to agents was invaluable."* Patton so strongly believed that one must understand the culture with which one is working that he considered cultural awareness his own tenth Principle of War. *"I firmly believe it should be added to the nine provided by Clausewitz and now considered sacred by the United States Army."*

In his role with Combined Studies, Patton was actually carried on the MACV J-3 roster and therefore spent at least a third of his time in that office. What he found there was disturbing. *"Parochialism was rampant. All four services, the Marines included, wanted more than their share of the pie, and with a Marine chief of staff, reporting directly to Harkins, it was quite easy to see who was being stroked at the moment. The awful truth is that very early in this terribly important conflict, we did not yet have a clear picture of the battlefield and environs. The national leadership together with the operational capabilities of the Republic of Vietnam armed forces, especially with regard to their loyalties, were unclear. In a word, we faced an increasingly foggy battlefield. The interservice rivalries ongoing at the time were no help to the U.S. leadership which, quite frankly, was attempting to operate in a war that was totally foreign to its experience and understanding."*

During the early months of Patton's first tour in Southeast Asia, he was profoundly affected in his attitude and understanding of Vietnam by an incident of blatant terrorism. At the time, Patton was on a Combined Studies staff orientation visit to a unit of Vietnamese irregulars in the southern Delta. The area was a flat and unattractive region of the country where the principal activities of the people were limited to harvesting rice and fishing. Shortly after Patton's arrival at a village, he received a radio message that the Viet Cong had raided one of the smaller villages within Combined Studies jurisdiction, about ten miles to the east; the request was, "Come at once." Patton's group scrounged up some small boats and headed out. The instructions were to search and secure the village the best they could.

The reconnaissance group, including Patton and a senior South Vietnamese noncommissioned officer by the name of Hu, arrived within walking distance of the village; cautiously, weapons at the ready, they moved toward the village chief's residence. There was no sign of either enemy or friendly forces. Not even civilians were to be seen. As the group approached the house Patton was shocked to see a man's head mounted on a stake; Hu identified him as the village chief. His dismembered and headless body lay nearby. Patton entered the chief's house, where the sight that greeted him will forever live in his memory. The chief's wife was hanging by her wrists from a beam in the ceiling. She had been raped repeatedly and much of her skin had been removed from her body. Her child, a girl, perhaps six months in age, had been placed in boiling water on the stove.

The woman, who was barely alive, whispered something to Hu, who in turn requested that Patton and the others step outside. *"We did so,"* says Patton. *"I was about to vomit; it was the worst scene I have ever witnessed."* A second later a shot was fired. Hu came out of the house reholstering his pistol. *"Tears were streaming down his face and an expression of hate and pity dominated his countenance,"* says Patton. *"I will always remember the words that he spoke at that tragic moment:* 'Mon Commandant, c'est une guerre très difficile'—*or translated into English, 'Major, this a most difficult war.'* " Indeed, "difficult" was an understatement, as America was beginning to learn.

In addition to his many other duties, Patton was often called upon to handle unique situations. He received a message one day that the National Aeronautics and Space Administration was sending astronaut Gordon Cooper on a space mission. *"NASA was adamant that if Cooper was forced to abort his flight, they did not want the capsule or its pilot at the mercy of the Viet Cong,"* explains Patton. *"We were ordered to coordinate some sort of rescue plan in the event Cooper went down. I was directed to divide the country into sectors of responsibility for various organizations—special forces, helicopter groups and others—to pick him up so as to avoid any chance of capture."*

Patton visited each helicopter company in the country at the time and gave the commander an area of responsibility and information concerning the orbit time. Each aviation unit was to be on alert and ready to pick Cooper up if necessary. *"The amusing aspect of the story is that I assigned a certain sector to an Army major and helicopter unit commander who replied, 'Sir, I've got a problem. I don't have as many helicopters as I should have. I have two that are down for repair.' I said, 'Are you requesting a narrower sector?' He said, 'Perhaps you should as I don't have much chance of getting these two aircraft going before the orbit.' He then escorted me to his 'problem.' We walked over to the helicopter pads and observed that both aircraft had arrows sticking out of shattered windshield bubbles, obviously delivered by some enraged Montagnard. I got to thinking, on one hand here we are with the most sophisticated device ever devised by man carrying an Air Force lieutenant colonel circling the earth. On the other hand, I'm in Vietnam with two helicopters, also fairly sophisticated, grounded because of arrows shot by local aborigine tribesmen."*

Vietnam was a study in contrasts for Patton, and understanding the customs was important especially for newcomers. *"At one point I was working with an Air Force brigadier general, a well known fighter pilot and a wonderful officer,"* relates Patton, *"but who knew nothing about the country. One day, after work, he came into my office and said, 'Hey, let's go down and find a nice restaurant for supper.' As we walked along the street seeking a restaurant we passed two Vietnamese Rangers who were in fatigues with ribbons from the French colonial period on their uniforms. You could tell these noncommissioned officers had seen a great deal of service. They were walking along the street holding hands. The general looked at me and said in a loud voice, 'Look, George, look what we're doing here, we're supporting a nation of homosexuals.' The reality was that holding hands in Vietnam was a custom when two good friends were walking together. It had nothing to do with homosexuality. That was the type of thing one learns on almost a daily basis. One must always remember to dig below the first coat of varnish in order to understand what makes a society tick. I recall a statement made by a friend of mine who had been with the OSS [Office of Strategic Services] during World War II. He said, 'It is not necessary to agree with what they do, or what they believe in, but it is necessary to understand what they do and why.'"*

Early on, Patton, involved with the possible expansion of the Special Forces program, needed to go out and see what they were up to. He was not trained in Special Forces operations but knew how they were organized and came away impressed. *"They were first-class people, obviously mission-oriented and extremely conscientious. It was a pleasure to be associated with them."*

At one point Patton was on an operation with the

Special Forces in the Da Nang area as they were attempting to locate enemy personnel who had killed two Americans, Specialist 5 James R. Gabriel, Jr. and Staff Sergeant Wayne Marchand, the first Special Forces people to be killed in the war. *"Today, these men are memorialized at Fort Bragg in the Special Warfare School and Center,"* says Patton. *"But we went out with mercenary tribesmen of Chinese background, trying to find the people responsible, and were unsuccessful. The enemy was elusive and that, too, was a clear lesson from my earliest days in Vietnam."*

Patton's experiences in his first tour of duty in Vietnam included an airplane crash in the highlands while flying aboard an Air America plane on New Year's Eve, 1962. *"We took off and were up about a hundred feet off the ground and gaining altitude, when our single engine failed. We landed in a mahogany forest. Our Turkish pilot did a super job of saving our lives. He brought the plane in and managed to somehow drag the tail on the ground to slow it down. He found a spot between two gigantic trees and ripped the wings off while landing. Everybody climbed out and we moved rapidly to some distance from the aircraft. We had no idea if there were VC [Viet Cong] in our area. I had left a sawed-off shotgun in the airplane but all the others had pistols."*

Patton remembers that one of the passengers, the CIA station chief and the only one with a serious injury, looked at him and said, "George, I think I saw a sawed-off shotgun in the aircraft before we took off. Do you have it?"

"No," said Patton.

"I think you ought to get it."

Patton, his clothes soaked with fuel and worrying that the plane could blow up at any minute, ran to the wreckage, rummaged around, found the shotgun, and returned to the huddle about a hundred yards away.

"I'm glad you found it," said the CIA chief. "Didn't I see a box of shells in there?"

"Yes sir, you did see a box of shells," confirmed Patton.

"Do you have that?"

"No, sir, I don't have it," Patton sighed.

"Well, I think we ought to have it."

Patton once again returned to retrieve the shells. *"As it turned out we were on the ground about an hour or so waiting for a VC attack that never came,"* says Patton. *"Soon a rescue crew found us and returned us to the air strip where we boarded another plane back to Saigon. The situation was scary and I could have done without running back and forth to the plane. I think it took years off my life."*

In any wartime situation, humor provides a needed release. Patton recalls that one of the Special Forces detachments, near Dalat, was staffed with an experienced medical NCO who delivered babies as a specialty. This U.S. soldier had delivered several hundred with no fatalities, and the Montagnards loved him. *"I was working in Saigon when a letter came from the American Medical Association complaining about an unqualified Special Forces Medic NCO practicing obstetrics,"* says Patton. *"The letter was to General Harkins who passed it to me to prepare a response. In my answer I said we would be delighted to have the American Medical Association deploy some doctors and we would at once attach them to the Special Forces detachment. I went on to say they would probably learn a great deal concerning the control of disease and prenatal and postnatal care in the jungles of Southeast Asia. We never received an answer."*

In addition to the Montagnards, Combined Studies worked with many other aboriginal tribes. *"What one has to remember when discussing the Vietnamese aboriginal tribes,"* explains Patton, *"Is that these tribes were settled in long before the Vietnamese immigration south from China. They were of Malayan-Polynesian extraction. They do not resemble Vietnamese, but more closely resemble Polynesians. One of our missions was to improve the relationship between the tribes and the lowland, generally farm-oriented, Vietnamese. The farmers raised rice, cattle, coffee, tea, and citrus fruit in the low country of Vietnam. They considered the aboriginal tribesman savage, quite similar to our vision of the American Indian in the past century."*

Patton remembers going to a supper party in Da Nang with a couple of Vietnamese intellectuals, professors at the university in Hue, the former, traditional capital in central South Vietnam. They were talking after supper and asked Patton about the Indian wars. *"I said, I guess in ignorance, that the Indian wars were somewhat similar to what you've got going on now between your lowland people and the Montagnards,"* recalls Patton. *"The conversation was in French and one of the other guests said, 'I fully understand what both sides are trying to do here in this tortured land. I concur with that, but at least we have never resorted to gunfire between the South Vietnamese and the Montagnards as America did during its western expansion, when the cavalry and the Indians often fought.' That stopped me because he was totally correct in his analysis. The story of the tribes in Vietnam and especially, the Montagnard story,"* Patton concludes, *"is wrapped in sadness from beginning to end."*

Patton's duties in Vietnam did not always involve military activities. At one point a small research institute was sent to Saigon by a U.S. medical school. Its mission was to perform research on amoebic dysentery; a particular requirement was the collection of fecal samples from the personnel who had deployed to Vietnam and were now preparing to return to Okinawa. One of Patton's specific responsibilities was to see that samples were turned over to the designated medical research team. Therefore, he assigned an enlisted medic to assist with the details. As Patton says, laughing, today,

"I had targeted two noncoms who had experienced a big night in Saigon the evening before departure. They had forgotten to provide their sample so the medic was chasing them down and finally was able to hold them at the airport. They were told to leave a stool sample with my medical NCO. So these guys disappeared for a few minutes and returned with their samples in separate containers. About a month later we received a letter from the research outfit: 'Dear General Harkins: We've heard of the toughness of Special Forces and how they can eat anything and exist in the jungle. We have two unusual specimens here and we'd like to ask you to arrange to have the two donors returned to Vietnam soon so that we can meet with them.' We sent the letter on to Colonel Woody Garrett, a relative by marriage and a close friend, and the commanding officer of the group in Okinawa. Well, there was hell to pay. They called in the noncoms who finally, with their heads bowed, confessed. They had gone out to the street and picked up some dog droppings and thought their problem was solved. But the stray dogs, half-starved most of the time, ate whatever they could find. We got quite a chuckle out of that, but of course a lieutenant general in Okinawa wanted to courtmartial our two soldiers for misleading the authorities. I got that word and visited the CIA station chief in Saigon. I told him the story and he nearly fell out of his chair laughing. He said he would take care of it. I suspect that one of those poor old research guys saw those dog turds under the microscope and just about jumped off the hinges."

While dealing with a variety of missions during his first tour, Patton says he found the idea and setting for the escalation of American involvement palpable. "This became very evident after the battle at Ap Bac, a significant turning point which directly oriented the United States toward greatly increased involvement in Southeast Asia. This action of the 7th Division of the ARVN [Army of the Republic of Vietnam] occurred on 1 January 1963 when MAAG personnel, whose mission it was *to advise and support that division, found it necessary to take over the ARVN unit which was not doing well in the battle. John Vann, a close friend since we were students at the Command and General Staff College together, was 7th ARVN Division Advisor. Vann got into very hot water resulting from the Ap Bac post mortem briefing at which, apparently unknown to him, media personnel were present. It is important to realize that there were practically no controls or censorship on or against the many media representatives in the country at that time. They ran free. They had observed the 'miserable damn performance,' as John P. Vann called it, by elements of the 7th ARVN Division, and basically informed the public of that performance. This conference or briefing by Vann was not at all appreciated by Harkins, who called for his immediate relief.*

"Prior to Ap Bac, the Kennedy administration had succeeded in preventing the American public from being more than vaguely conscious that the country was involved in a war in a place called Vietnam. The public had been focused on Berlin, Cuba, Laos, and the Congo as the scenes of the nation's foreign policy crises. Ap Bac was now putting Vietnam on the front pages and on the television evening news shows," says Patton. General Harkins was reportedly embarrassed and enraged by the stories from Ap Bac. The dispatches, replete with details of cowardice and bungling and salty quotations like Vann's remark, were describing the battle as the worst and most humiliating of all the failures in the South Vietnamese armed forces. President Kennedy and Secretary of Defense Robert McNamara ordered an explanation. Harkins was also under pressure from the regime to make Vann a scapegoat. Meanwhile, the president of Vietnam and high-ranking military officers were in fury over their perceived "loss of face."

"I happened to be the J-3 MACV duty officer when we put together the operational summary of the Ap Bac affair," says Patton. *"As I recall, a couple of Vann's U.S. advisory group members had been killed. In those*

days of Vietnam contacts, whenever U.S. personnel got injured in any way, a major investigation was ordered. I cannot recall the identity of the briefing officer but the important point was that the incident report was heavily modified and was a watered-down version which in no way reflected actual happenings."

To Patton the mistake was critical, leaving the MACV staff in an untenable position that the press had been present throughout the action, witnessed the poor performance of the 7th ARVN Division, and finally had attended Colonel Vann's after-action briefing. *"We were never totally trusted by the media following the Ap Bac affair,"* Patton remarks today. *"That lack of trust was significant and contributed heavily, in my view, to the disastrous events which hastened the U.S. withdrawal from the war in Vietnam. In sum, we lost the media at Ap Bac."* Patton also saves criticism for Harkins as well. *"I hate to say it because he was one of my dad's closest friends, but he desperately wanted to depict success during his time in Vietnam, which was difficult, if not impossible, to do."*

Following his tour in-country, during which he was promoted to lieutenant colonel, Patton returned to the United States in April 1963, to assignment as commanding officer of the 2nd Medium Tank Battalion, 81st Armor, 1st Armored Division, stationed at Fort Hood, Texas. *"Although I was delighted to take command of a tank battalion,"* says Patton, *"I could not help feeling badly that no one thought to use my experience in Vietnam during the early days."* Patton remembers that while the CIA debriefed him for a full day, he was never debriefed by military personnel, either formally or informally.

On November 22, 1963, Patton and the preponderance of his battalion were attending a National Day of Prayer midday service at Fort Hood when a soldier came running in and whispered to the chaplain. The chaplain then said, "Please bow your heads. President Kennedy has been shot. The report is that he has been grievously injured, so let us pray for his life." About ten minutes later another soldier came in, looked around, found Patton, and said, "Sir, your battalion has been put on alert to go to Dallas." Patton left to join his troops and begin assembling certain equipment and moving it to the railhead. *"We spent whole next day getting ready and loading tanks. Supper was brought to us as we worked until the whole battalion was loaded. About ten o'clock that evening we were told to stand down. We left the equipment under guard and went home, returning the next day to unload when it was determined that there would be no need for our protective services in Dallas,"* says Patton.

Looking back on it now, Patton believes the murder of our president was an event of great significance to the government of the United States for more than the obvious reasons. *"As the Vietnam conflict gained in importance to the new president, Lyndon B. Johnson, the projected operations of Task Force X-Ray* [the Cuban invasionary force] *began to fade in importance. Thus Fidel Castro was home free, at least for awhile,"* says Patton. *"Therefore, a case can be made that the Cuban leader was somewhat rewarded for the terrible events in Dallas on that tragic November day."*

The whole Patton family liked central Texas, and George Patton came to love the post like no other, with the possible exception of the Armor Center at Fort Knox, Kentucky. It was the first major command of Patton's career, and he enjoyed not only his assignment but also diversity of his mission. In addition to his regular tasks, the 2nd Battalion, Patton's unit, was a member of Task Force X-Ray. *"It was a brigade task force and my battalion was part of the brigade."* Patton explains, *"We trained at Camp Pendleton, a Marine base in California. At that time I was briefed on the war plan. It was highly classified, but I was intimately familiar with my mission, the area where I was going in and the units with and against whom I would fight. This*

was two years after the Bay of Pigs. We were still mak-
ing contingency plans and in reflection, I continue to
wish we had carried out the plan."

While at Fort Hood Patton's lifelong dedication to
educating and motivating those under his command inspired him in September 1963 to issue Letter of Instruction Number 1, wherein he wrote: *"In so far as*
personal characteristics are concerned, the most im-
portant of all is Loyalty . . . Secondly, Pride in the
Profession of Arms and Self-Confidence born of dem-
onstrated ability to do a particular job well. . . .
Thirdly, I seek the competitor who absolutely refuses to
give up, who, for example, beset with the many prob-
lems of personnel, equipment, higher headquarters and
the like, 'continues to march' and delivers results. . . .
Of course it follows that all of these so-called character-
istics fall under the simple word 'duty.' " In the margin
Patton would later pen the words, *"Have fun, too!"*

The Patton family departed Fort Hood during the late
spring of 1964 with Carlisle Barracks, Pennsylvania,
and the Army War College as their destination. The
senior educational course of the Army was a great stepping-stone for Patton and his fellow students, especially
for those who hoped to become general officers during
the last years of their service to the nation. Patton enjoyed a high degree of academic freedom, while learning much about the top levels of the Department of
Defense. Each student officer had an advisor; Patton's
was Colonel, later Lieutenant General, George Gordon
Cantlay, whom Patton remembered well from his first
tour at the Armored School and with whom he was
destined to serve again in Vietnam. Cantlay shared an
office with Colonel William R. Desobry, also later promoted to lieutenant general, and for whom Patton later
would serve when Desobry was the Armor Center commander. Patton has said time and again that these two

distinguished soldiers were among the best in his memory.

Patton's major obstacle before graduation from the Army War College was a thesis requirement set by the Commanding General and Commandant, Major General Eugene Salet. *"Quality work was the name of the game,"* says Patton, *"and it was stated that a passing grade on your thesis on a military subject of your choice, approved by your faculty adviser, was the single requirement for graduation."* Patton's chosen subject was a study of the motivation of the Viet Cong warrior-guerrilla, from whom he had learned a great deal during his 1962–1963 tour in Southeast Asia. Patton received an A on the paper, a voluminous report that, to his disgust, was neither referred to nor ever used by the Department of Defense. Ironically, he was prohibited from retrieving it from the archives years later, because his security clearance was not high enough to gain him access to his own work.

The Pattons loved their Army War College tour. Along with their three children, Margaret, Robert and Helen, they lived in College Arms housing. George, Jr., having been identified over the years as being mentally challenged, was in residence at the Devereux Foundation, in another part of Pennsylvania, coming home for vacations. Joanne was pregnant with their fifth child, due the following summer.

The War College student body, representing all services, together with professional civilians from many branches of government, was brimming with talent. They were experienced soldiers, sailors, airmen, and Marines who, as Patton says, *"in many cases were more qualified to address the subjects and discussion periods than the classroom monitors whose duty it was to lead the particular discussions."* Patton recalls there was a feeling, at least during his class, that if one paid attention he could learn more from his classmates than from the faculty members. This seemed true more often than not.

The War College day usually started with a lecture, which lasted about forty minutes, from a senior member of the U.S. government. It might be the chief of staff of one of the services, a cabinet member, or someone of equally high stature who could make an impact on the student officer's education. After a short question-and-answer period in the auditorium, the class would be dismissed to the study rooms. Certain officers, however, those engaged in studies that were related to the expertise of the guest speaker, would be invited to meet with the VIP for a no-holds-barred, no-notes-taken discussion. *"These sessions were remarkable,"* recalls Patton. *"They provided background which would have been unattainable under normal circumstances. They were invaluable to our education."*

At the conclusion of the academic year Patton attended graduation ceremonies at which the speaker was former President Dwight Eisenhower, who was retired and residing about thirty miles away in the Gettysburg area. *"He was on the platform and the graduates were assembled on the lawn on a lovely spring day. Following his introduction by the Commandant, President Eisenhower spoke briefly to the AWC Class of 1965. When it was my turn to receive the diploma the announcer stated my name. As I moved forward for the familiar routine—shake with the right and take with the left—he exclaimed, 'God almighty, what are you doing here?' I responded that I, too, was graduating. He patted me on the shoulder and handed me the much-sought-after diploma."*

The War College is designed to help prepare officers for high-level staff and command duty. Thus it did not surprise Patton when he received word that he was being transferred to the Office of the Deputy Chief of Staff for Operations, Department of the Army, Washington, D.C. *"Specifically I was assigned to the Far East Pacific Division [FEPAC], or in short, the Vietnam Desk. With the 1965 buildup commencing, all that I can say is, What a desk!"* says Patton. In preparation for their

Washington, D.C., assignment, the Pattons purchased a home in Bethesda, Maryland. For the older children excellent schools were available, and Joanne, a District of Columbia native, had many relatives nearby to help with the new baby, Benjamin, who arrived in late July, on George Patton's first day of work at the Pentagon. The neighbors were helpful and friendly, but, except on a few weekends during that period, *"the owner seldom saw the house in the daylight."*

Although Patton was acutely aware that this duty was looked upon as a reward for successfully moving through the Army school system, he dreaded the assignment. Most of what he had heard about Army Staff duty, especially with the Vietnam buildup in full swing, was not good. Nonetheless, he accepted his assignment to FEPAC, under the direction of Lieutenant General Vernon Mock.

Patton's office reacted to requirements of MACV, which were considerable and, as Patton says, *"came upon us like snowflakes in a storm. FEPAC's work was voluminous,"* he recalls. *"What seemed to be the foremost questions in the minds of the JCS and all its components were, 'Where do we go from here and why?' and, 'What is the strategy and how do we fabricate and implement it?' Bottom line, FEPAC was in the numbers game."* Specifically, as a strategy was approved, FEPAC would activate and deactivate units so as to allow the military to pursue that particular aim. Divisions were brought on line to the highest readiness conditions possible and marked for deployment to the combat zone. *"All of our major actions were reported through JCS channels to the president, who often announced that he would not approve a major deployment until he was provided more detailed justification supporting it,"* says Patton.

For Patton, tenure with the Army Staff in the Pentagon was unpleasant at times, but it did teach him to prepare and staff a paper. He also learned that lieutenant colonels and colonels run the Army. *"The generals*

*are so busy going to meetings that they seldom have
time to look into most subjects with a fair amount of
detail. Suffice it to say, I frequently remained at my
desk until 1:00 A.M. or 2:00 A.M.,"* he says. *"There were
many nights when I would return to the house and see a
sign which said, 'Your dinner is in the oven.' "* Patton's
basic objection to the Pentagon was really based on his
feeling that there are those who like to be out in the
field and those who like staff duty. *"I always knew the
field was where I wanted to be."*

One of Patton's first projects after his arrival at the
Pentagon concerned the overall Vietnam strategy. In
late November 1965 he was part of a team that was
ordered to explore a range of possible courses of action
in Southeast Asia. The alternatives were few and self-
evident. *"One was to pull out, another was to continue
what we were doing,"* says Patton, *"another was to
apply graduated military pressure on the enemy, and
one more was to adopt intensive military pressure and
do it fast. My memory tells me the JCS recommended
the intensive military pressure immediately because it
seemed to offer the best probability of success, yet history shows we ended up initiating graduated military
pressure."*

The selected course of action, according to Patton,
was doomed to fail since it was adopted without real
determination to see things through. He felt that build-
ups encouraged the enemy to respond accordingly. The
graduated course of action entailed the highest military
risk, in Patton's view, because the resolve of the United
States was then in question. *"It brought about all kinds
of political pressure not only from within the United
States, but internationally, as well. I have every reason
to believe that the Joint Chiefs of Staff felt the same
way. I think they were following orders, but the decisions were made politically."*

Patton believes those stuck in the Pentagon were all
victims of the bureaucracy, running in place day and
night. *"It was drudgery and in a JCS planners' meeting*

where we were putting together the final words, we might argue for fifteen or twenty minutes whether the lead to a paragraph should say 'whereas' or 'moreover.' "

To say Patton was uncomfortable in a staff job in the Pentagon would be an understatement. *"I can't begin to count how many times a senior officer would bypass a general, for instance, in favor of wanting to speak with the guy who prepared a report, the action officer, as he was called. To do so was wise, but the process got old in a hurry. You would walk into a meeting with a group of generals or officer levels several echelons between me and the Chief of Staff, and questions would be asked such as 'What is the organization of this company?' and I'd say, 'Sir, I don't have the specific details, but I'll find out.' Meanwhile all the other guys are sitting around looking down at you like you're a shit. But they don't know the answers either. Then you might be given ten minutes to find out answers before the big man had to leave in order to attend some other meeting."*

On the plus side, Patton says one of the advantages of the Pentagon is the presence of experts on any subject. You just had to know where they were; hence, a small telephone book never left his pocket. *"You would call some guy in another part of the building because he was an expert on your problem,"* Patton explains. *"I'd say, 'I need an answer in ten minutes!' Everyone knew the drill. When they knew that you were 'hot,' meaning you needed answers immediately, those soldiers would stop everything to help you."* The search for answers in a hurry was known as 'crashing,' and Patton many times briefed the Chief of Staff of the Army literally as he was walking into a meeting of the Joint Chiefs. *"Perhaps I had received the answer to a question just moments before, and he'd say, 'You think we ought to do it,' and I'd say 'Yes sir, we should,' or 'No, sir, I don't think we ought to do it.' That was the influence you had."*

Patton also describes an interesting relationship between President Johnson and the Pentagon. "*We would get questions from President Johnson which came down through the bureaucracy,*" says Patton. "*Usually, the questions were nothing more significant than 'How's the war going?' The questions would normally be asked on a Friday afternoon, when Pentagon staff officers sort of sat at their desks in the readiness position waiting for the bell to ring to depart.*" However, late one Friday Patton received a call asking him to see the DCSOPS [Deputy Chief of Staff for Operations], Major General Elmer H. Almquist, known as "Hook."

"What are your plans for the weekend?" asked Hook.

"I'm hoping to do a little work at home and play a little tennis," replied Patton.

"Cancel them," said Almquist, handing him a photocopy of a note written by LBJ.

Patton remembers the note saying something to the effect, "To Secretary of Defense: I've just found out that I have to speak to the American Legion next Thursday. I'd like a whole new approach to the Vietnam War. I'd like to see this by Tuesday so my staff can plan it and work on it." "*Soon the Pentagon was crashing on the issue,*" says Patton. "*Everyone canceled weekend plans and began reviewing all the old strategy papers, then cutting and pasting and getting more information. I remember working that whole weekend; I didn't even go home. I called in six people and the JCS colonel who was my counterpart on the Joint Staff. He already knew about the memo and was doing the same thing with his staff. We had the intelligence picture, the logistic picture, the force development picture and dozens of other pieces of information. A lot of the material was highly classified and we were directed to submit the American Legion speech unclassified. We finally had nearly ten pages, with the backup material filling four binders.*"

General George S. Patton, Jr., European Theater, May 1945.
U.S. ARMY PHOTO COURTESY OF THE PATTON MUSEUM, FORT KNOX, KENTUCKY.

General George S. Patton, Jr., Commanding General, U.S. Third Army. 1945.

Beatrice Patton, General George S. Patton, Jr., and West Point cadet George Patton just after General Patton arrived in Boston on his last trip to the United States. June 1945.

Beatrice Patton in front of the George S. Patton, Jr., Monument at West Point. The statue was unveiled by Mrs. Patton in 1950. Melted into the bronze hands of the statue are four silver stars worn by General Patton and one gold cavalry insignia that Mrs. Patton had worn since their marriage. U.S. ARMY PHOTO.

Gravesite of Colonel W. Tazewell Patton and Colonel George S. Patton in Winchester, Virginia. Both were killed in action during the Civil War.

PHOTO BY AUTHOR.

General Creighton Abrams and Colonel George S. Patton with key 11th ACR officers: (left to right) unknown, Colonel James Leach, then Senior Advisor to the 5th ARVN Division, who later would succeed Patton as CO 11th ACR; Lieutenant Colonel John McEnery—CO 3rd Squadron; General Abrams; Lieutenant Colonel Lee Duke—S-3; Colonel George S. Patton; and Vietnamese general commanding 5th Division ARVN. 1968–1969. PHOTO COURTESY OF THE PATTON FAMILY COLLECTION.

Colonel George S. Patton, Commanding Officer, 11th Armored Cavalry Regiment. 1969. PHOTO COURTESY OF THE PATTON FAMILY COLLECTION.

Colonel George S. Patton (left) and General Creighton Abrams (right) share a moment in the field, Vietnam. 1968–1969. PHOTO COURTESY OF THE PATTON FAMILY COLLECTION.

George S. Patton, Jr., and George Patton at the Washington Horse Show. 1930. PHOTO COURTESY OF THE PATTON FAMILY COLLECTION.

Lieutenant General George S. Patton, Jr., and senior staff at
Third Army headquarters awaiting arrival of General Dwight
D. Eisenhower. September 1944. U.S. ARMY PHOTO COURTESY OF THE
PATTON MUSEUM, FORT KNOX, KENTUCKY.

Major General George S. Patton, Commanding General,
2nd Armored Division, Fort Hood, Texas. 1975–1977.
PHOTO COURTESY OF THE PATTON FAMILY COLLECTION.

Patton got the report to his immediate superior that Monday evening around 5 P.M., and the Chief of Staff looked at it about 9 P.M. *"Changes and additions were ordered and of course we had no word processors in those days. At this point I had over thirty people working on the report, which after its completion was then routed through an Air Force section, a Navy section and Marine section. Then the report had to be brought to a joint level where they dovetailed the information from the Air Force and the Marines, and so on. Following that review, then the State Department and CIA had to take a hard look at the report."*

Patton remembers getting the report to the White House on Tuesday. What happened next causes him to shake his head at the irony. *"On Wednesday, we received word from the White House that something else was breaking on the Hill and the president had called the American Legion national commander and canceled. I don't know where that report is today, but I'll tell you there was some blood spilled on it. My blood. All over the pages of it. It was the damnedest thing I ever went through in the Pentagon."*

While he was on what Patton calls *"the Joint Chiefs of Staff circuit"* in 1966 and 1967, protest against the war was heating up on the streets of America. Most of the animus was focused on the military, and protests began occurring around the Pentagon. Patton remembers one particular Sunday in January 1967, because the Joint Chiefs were going to meet on Monday morning at 9:00 A.M. and he was still working on a report, at home. Patton was getting set to leave for the Pentagon when he received a call from the duty officer passing along an order to the staff telling them not to come in unless they were working on a high-priority item. The duty officer explained to Patton that protesters were around the Pentagon but that if he had to come, he should arrive in civilian clothes at the parking lot entrance, where an MP would meet him.

"I put on a sport shirt and was there about 7:00 A.M.

*in the north parking lot," says Patton. "An armed MP
corporal and an escort group came up to me and asked,
'Are you Colonel Patton?' I said 'Yes.' He said, 'Follow
me.' We went up the stairs to the Mall entrance and it
was the goddamndest thing that I've ever seen. There
were longhairs all around carrying buckets of shit and
sticks. They were writing obscenities on the walls of the
Pentagon. There were also some guards outside to put a
cordon around the building and prevent entry. Young
women were busy sticking flowers in their gun barrels.
As I was going through the door my escort pointed to a
figure in a window on the second floor of the Pentagon.
It was Robert McNamara, the Secretary of Defense,
peering through the venetian blinds, watching the protest. My scout's comment was, 'I guess he is afraid to
come down.' "*

Patton remembers reading the book *American Caesar* by William Manchester, particularly a story about
MacArthur's landing in Tokyo. *"The general stepped
off the plane,"* recounts Patton, *"and the Japanese were
all around, yet he walked alone into that crowd. That
was about three days after the surrender document had
been signed. He could easily have been attacked or
killed. With only the courage that MacArthur had, and
he had plenty, he just walked out into that crowd.
What a contrast between MacArthur and McNamara!
There was McNamara looking through the venetian
blinds instead of walking out there and telling that rag-
tag group of bums to leave, or at least trying to better
understand their motivation, or even just showing his
face instead of peeking through the window shades."*

Patton returned to Vietnam for a second tour in 1967,
this time as a member of a study group. *"There were
two studies made at that time with regard to combat
operations in Vietnam which were very important,"*
says Patton. *"They were technical tactical studies concerning 'Army Combat Operations in Vietnam,' and*

'Mechanized Armor Combat Operations in Vietnam.'
The mechanized study was a companion report with
regard to use of tanks, armored personnel carriers, and
air calvary in Vietnam. I was a member of that particu-
lar study group and spent three months in Vietnam col-
lecting data for our project."

During the trip Patton roomed with Ed Smith, a lieutenant colonel, who like Patton had already been in
Vietnam on an earlier tour. He told Patton a story that
for Patton aptly describes the early days of the war.
Smith had arrived at Pleiku in the MAAG detachment
for II Vietnamese Corps.

Smith met the colonel in charge, who said, "I'll bet
you thought you were going to be an advisor, didn't
you?"

"Yes, I thought so," responded Smith.

The colonel said, "Well, maybe you'll be an advisor
sooner or later, but right now you're going to go out
and take charge of a sector as a squad leader, because
we're going to get attacked shortly." And Patton remembers that's the way it was.

Travelling all around the country on the study tour
Patton found an entirely different scene from his tour in
1962–1963. By this time, the United States had several
divisions and separate brigades located strategically
throughout the countryside. While Patton's particular
mission at the time was information-related, seeing the
changes and speaking with the troops gave him an excellent overview that he believes better prepared him for
his later and final tour in Vietnam.

At the same time, Patton was continuing to absorb
many of the war's realities. Reviewing statistics on combat deaths, he saw that it was the young soldier with
little experience who most often paid with his life.
Twenty-year-olds suffered the largest casualty rate, the
Army having the most deaths. The majority of deaths
occurred in the ranks of those with less than two years'
experience in the military, after which the death rate
took a significant downward trend.

Upon considerable reflection Patton feels Vietnam was a *"poor man's war,"* and indeed his thesis is corroborated by statistics. Generally, the death toll was highest in the states that contributed large numbers of volunteers, often linked to high unemployment, or in states where young men did not attempt to go on to college or get other types of draft deferments. As an example, West Virginia suffered high comparative losses per hundred thousand population; by 1972 its rate was 39.8 percent. At the height of war one general was quoted as saying, "The basic price of admission to this war is well over 100 U.S. casualties a week." Patton also points out that West Point contributed its share to the war. *"The class that got hit the hardest in Vietnam was '65. In fact the classes of 1963–1965 were all hit hard because they were junior officers,"* he says.

Patton, along with many of his counterparts, questions the military strategy employed in the war. He agrees with those who feel the United States should have cut South Vietnam off from the North by stopping all supply routes, setting up infiltration barriers, and forcing the South Vietnamese military to take care of the Viet Cong guerrilla factions: in other words, as Patton explains, *"Letting the U.S. handle the external and the South Vietnamese the internal.*

"The military also made a big mistake by remaining silent through the debate about the war," says Patton. *"By choosing not to say anything and by not attacking our critics we were left exposed. And because Johnson did not go to the Congress and say, 'Hey, is this a war or isn't it?' he could never get a full backing of the American people. Because we did not mobilize, we also had a segment of our population marching off to war and it tended to be those individuals who couldn't figure a way to get out of the draft."*

Patton agreed from the early days with the concept of putting in conventional U.S. forces in Vietnam, provided the mission was clear. *"However, after the buildup in the late winter of '65 it became evident, even to me, that we were in violation of the time-honored nine principles of war,"* he says today. *"We were in total violation of surprise, simplicity, command and objective. I used to teach the principles of war. Objective is known as the fundamental military principle of war. I think that somewhere someone made the statement that we would not go above the seventeenth parallel with land forces. We never should have told them that, we should have let them worry. Most importantly, we should have taken Vietnam on as a theater of war—just exactly like the Italian theater of the Mediterranean or South Pacific or Central Pacific theaters. We should have drawn a circle around Southeast Asia, perhaps even to include parts of Thailand. I also believe that the commander, such as Westmoreland, should have been reporting directly to the Joint Chiefs of Staff and not to a regional command structure, which was* CINCPAC [Commander in Chief of the Pacific Command] *at the time."*

Only later, however, would Patton have time for reflections about the lessons of Vietnam, for in 1967, after a two-year tour with the Army General staff, his expertise and combat skills would once again call him to the war in Southeast Asia.

Because he believed that all professional soldiers must ride to the sound of the guns, Patton's Vietnam tours, including 1968–1969, were voluntary. *"Although this resulted in considerable personal turbulence and family separation, I know that my actions were correct,"* says Patton. *"When I left for my final tour in Vietnam my family was well situated in the D.C. area and the environment for them was generally wholesome. Besides, I would leave the Army Staff and the Pentagon pandemonium, hopefully never to return."*

10

A RETURN TO WAR

He just had an instinct for doing the right thing at the right time in combat and many American soldiers are alive today because George Patton was their boss.

—James Dozier

A comment made by General Harkins, MACV commander, to Patton back in early 1963 was to prove prophetic as events unfolded in Southeast Asia. Harkins had said, "George, without doubt, the Army will be blamed for any failures in the Vietnam war." At the time, Patton nodded, perhaps thinking of the Army's minimal involvement to date, but nevertheless he mentally filed the comment away. It certainly did not affect his volunteering to return to Vietnam once again, which he did in early 1967. Patton felt his place was to be with troops, and, he hoped, in command. In view of his earlier tour and experience gained at that time, he knew that he could contribute.

Orders were officially issued in December 1967, and Lieutenant Colonel George S. Patton, a veteran of both Korea and Vietnam, was slated to return once again to Southeast Asia. This time Patton was to become Chief of Force Development Division, reporting to the Assistant Chief of Staff, as G-3 at Headquarters, U.S. Army, Vietnam (USARV). Patton hoped that the position was short-term, as he was interested in a field command, certainly not a desk job in a war zone.

Patton felt that the coming challenge would be the biggest test of his military career, and diary notations of the period reflect feelings of anticipation and excitement about returning to war. Patton's commentaries written in early January 1968, as he was in transit to Vietnam, are particularly revealing. One in particular may be the most introspective of his time in the Army. Patton wrote, "We Americans are so lucky. Therefore why not pay back a bit more? Southeast Asia, Vietnam, what about it. Can I help? Can I carry the load? Will my deceased ancestors and parents be proud of me? What really is my destiny? This tour will answer all of the above and more besides. It will determine whether or not I'll be selected to flag rank. It will determine whether or not I'll stay in the Regular Army. It will influence the futures of those I command. There has not been nor will there be a more important year in my army life. I must prepare well. And in a sense, I must be about my father's business. I took a long hard look at him just before I left this morning. His portrait gave me confidence. So did Ma's. They were all sort of smiling to themselves; perhaps I sensed they were proud. To be a member of that group, the Pattons, is a proud honor. To be a part of them is a privilege. To hold up your end is a duty but it is hard work."

Upon arrival in Vietnam, Patton went to his staff position in the Force Development office, located in Long Binh, a huge base near Bien Hoa and about fifteen miles northeast of Saigon on the Bien Hoa–Saigon highway. Long Binh, as did a few other bases, housed large ammunition dumps and also served as a processing center for incoming troops or those redeploying to the so-called "land of the big PX [Post Exchange]." Activity on the base was almost nonstop, due to the wide range of missions. When Patton arrived he replaced Colonel, later Lieutenant General, Eugene Forrester, an old friend. Patton's job consisted of manpower and organizational analysis, which basically called for looking at organizations and recommending troop reductions, increases, or at times creation of new units.

Patton found Saigon a city teeming with Americans, many of whom were involved in the various facets of the war. However, those working in Saigon represented but a tiny portion of a U.S. military force, which was burgeoning at more than 536,000 soldiers and would increase to a peak of 543,000 by 30 April 1969.

The Vietnam War, by the time Patton arrived in 1968, had escalated beyond almost any early prediction. Hundreds of thousands of Americans were fighting a protracted war, which was clearly far from settlement. American forces were doing well in the field yet losing the war on American television, in the newspapers, and most importantly in the hearts and minds of their fellow citizens. The political process in the United States had polarized, which in turn sent confusing signals to military leaders in the field. Names once foreign to the American public were becoming common-place: battles, cities, and regions like the Ia Drang Valley, LZ [Landing Zone]-XRay, Tet '68, My Lai, Da Nang, Long Binh, Hué, and Khe Sanh were featured daily in the American media.

The general public soon began to believe the role of American troops in Vietnam lacked purpose, and these feelings were only fortified by comments such as that of an Army officer at the town of Ben Tre, in the Mekong Delta, who was quoted by an Associated Press reporter as saying, "It became necessary to destroy the town to save it." Then too, America was perplexed by the semantics of the conflict in Vietnam; catchwords and phrases seemed to direct the war effort. "Vietnamization," "pacification," "war of attrition," "clearing operations," "search and destroy," "counterinsurgency," "winning the hearts and minds"—the list was nearly endless.

"Pacification," as one example, was defined officially as the establishment or reestablishment of the military, political, and social aspects of local government. This would mean guaranteeing that local people were allowed to participate in a government responsible for their needs. "Pacification" was dependent on the ability to keep VC and NVA (the North Vietnamese Army) out of a specific area to allow the process of trust and security to build amongst the locals. The program had its noble successes, especially where the villagers were armed for their united security; however, after friendly forces left the villages they often quickly reverted.

"Clear and hold" was another term heard by the American public, as was "search and destroy," which superseded "search and kill" and was superseded in turn by "reconnaissance in force." "Clear and hold" missions were offensive operations designed to move enemy forces from a sector and secure it against their return. "Search and destroy" used a surrounding technique, followed by mounted or dismounted sweeps, or combinations of the two, designed to eliminate enemy personnel, mines, and equipment. It also generally included measures to affect the political thinking of the area by reeducation programs designed to show the people benefits of democratic rule.

Over time, as the military continued to implement various battlefield programs, it became apparent that the importance of each new strategy was not being conveyed adequately to the average American.

While America was grappling with the complex question of Vietnam, unrest was increasing on its college campuses and in city streets. Massive protests were occurring in front of government buildings, and in August 1968 bloody riots took place in Chicago, the site of the Democratic National Convention. The subsequent crackdown by the Chicago police, right or wrong, was a gruesome television spectacle. The anti-war movement drew activists, such as Dr. Benjamin Spock and actress Jane Fonda, along with a number of others who took leadership roles in the protest against the war. Some felt the protesters were being duped by the North Vietnamese, and visits to North Vietnam by Americans, including Jane Fonda's to Hanoi, only fueled that perception. Later, Patton would learn first-hand on the battlefield how Jane Fonda, for one, was being exploited by the North Vietnamese.

The South Vietnamese military and political structure was also confusing to Americans. In 1967, in the midst of war, a new constitution was created that called for the establishment of a government with upper and lower legislative houses, plus the offices of president and vice-president. Assuming the job of president was General Nguyen Van Thieu. Under Thieu, the armed forces of South Vietnam would eventually swell to 1.2 million. The air force alone, judging by the numbers of aircraft and personnel, was the third largest in the world. The vice-president of South Vietnam during this period was a flamboyant young air force officer named Nguyen Cao Ky. Ky had been chosen prime minister by the Armed Forces Council in 1965 and served in that capacity until he was elected vice-president in 1967.

Barely settled in new quarters, Patton had been in Vietnam less than a month when the Tet '68 offensive was launched. North Vietnamese regulars and Viet Cong made a desperate attempt to destroy the military capability of the forces in the South. The military thrust was launched against numerous cities and military targets, and it occurred during Tet, which to the people of Vietnam is a time for celebration in honor of the lunar new year. The holiday lasts seven days, and during the war, beginning in 1965, a truce was normally called by agreement with all the warring parties.

In 1968, the Viet Cong called for a full seven-day

truce, with the U.S. declaring a three-day cease-fire. But in a skillfully planned operation, the NVA and Viet Cong used the holiday to their advantage, launching a January 30 attack on seven cities. A little over twenty-four hours later the full blast of the offensive swept over the South. The Communists committed nearly seventy thousand troops in the assault against thirty-nine of the forty-four provincial capitals. Additionally, some seventy-one district capitals came under attack, as did several major cities, including Saigon and Hue. The NVA and VC had been repelled in large part by 3 February, except where some major battles were still being fought. Hue, the third largest city in South Vietnam, located about fifty miles south of the Demilitarized Zone, was under siege for nearly four weeks, well into late February. In Saigon, too, Free World forces were still clearing pockets of resistance until February 9. During the offensive, Communist forces suffered enormous losses, including scores of women and children involved in the fighting. Additionally, vast amounts of material and supplies were expended.

Some estimates place the enemy dead during Tet at from thirty-five to fifty thousand soldiers, though no one can ever be certain. South Vietnamese losses during the offensive numbered over three thousand killed, with several thousand wounded. For the Americans, 1,500 were killed in action, with 7,500 wounded. As was most often the case in Vietnam, the civilian population suffered heavily, and during Tet alone nearly ten thousand were killed, with many others wounded. Still more were murdered by the Communists as they swept through villages and cities.

Patton, not yet in a troop unit because of his position in G-3, could not get into the fight, but he was greatly impressed by the mobility of the enemy. At that time, certainly no one in Vietnam or in the upper reaches of the American political system could have envisioned how great an effect Tet would have on American public opinion. After all, Tet by military standards proved to be an unqualified success for the Free World forces, in terms of its toll on the enemy, who were forced to hide and rebuild for several months following the offensive.

At the start of Tet, in Long Binh, Patton and other officers in the know quickly realized that reports of truce violations actually represented an all-out effort, since intelligence sources were indicating enemy action in and near cities throughout South Vietnam. Within hours of the initial reports, action was furious at Long Binh as well, where Patton was living in a trailer near his office. Nearby, several ammunition compounds were hit early in the offensive, sending thick, black smoke billowing hundreds of feet into the air. The pop of small arms fire could be heard coming from every direction, and troops were running for cover or assembling in groups to head out to the perimeters.

Perhaps the most ironic moment of Tet for Patton occurred when a group of officers went into Saigon for a special briefing at Westmoreland's request and while there caught a glimpse of Ellsworth Bunker, U.S. ambassador to South Vietnam, riding along a downtown street in an armored personnel carrier. Patton recalls, *"I saw Bunker, an elderly gentleman with an extensive business and diplomatic background, peering from the turret opening with his white hair clearly observable. I thought, 'What the hell have we come to when the United States has to protect our ambassador in an APC on the way through Saigon to the embassy.'"*

Tet '68 produced a number of heroes, including a man named George Jacobson. Jacobson, a retired colonel whom Patton had come to know and admire from his first tour, was assigned to the U.S. embassy staff and became intimately involved in the VC attack on the compound. Jacobson, hiding on the grounds in an old French villa, killed with a pistol a VC sapper who was climbing up a flight of stairs leading into the building. The incident, if nothing else, demonstrated how precise the attack was. Yet the bravery of people like Jacobson and others, especially the military police contingent, who fought courageously at the embassy, was able to repel the attack. The fight resulted in fifteen VC killed, along with four Vietnamese employees of the embassy and five Americans. Viet Cong troops were unable to penetrate the main building, and so the whole operation might have been a dismal failure had not American newsmen arrived. Their coverage of the embassy battle encapsulated and dramatized America's vulnerable position in the war.

In spite of the military response to the Tet offensive, which resulted in heavy enemy casualties, there were charges that U.S. and South Vietnamese forces had been taken by surprise. Perhaps supporting that view is a notation in Patton's diary that appears alongside an article quoting General Westmoreland as saying, "I felt that there would be fireworks during Tet and therefore had my command on full alert." Patton wrote, *"Not True, C.W.A.,"* referring to a private comment made by Abrams, who was deputy commander at the time.

In the wake of the Tet offensive, due in large part to the graphic television footage taken during the battles and to the vulnerability of Saigon in general, many people in America came to believe the situation in Vietnam was out of control.

Other television and still pictures taken during Tet also crystallized the attitudes of some Americans. One scene in particular had substantial visual impact; it occurred during the height of battle, when a Viet Cong prisoner was summarily executed by General Nguyen Ngoc Loan. Loan, the national chief of police, was photographed just as the impact of a bullet registered on the prisoner's face. The photo, taken by AP's Eddie Adams, ran in newspapers across America, and film of the execution was played to the country the next night by NBC. Only later would Adams discover the man who was executed had just murdered a police major who was a close friend of Loan's; he had also killed the major's wife and children. Nonetheless, the incident made for frightening television and still photos. Loan had obviously killed his prisoner in the heat of anger, yet Americans in Vietnam who were aware of the execution were to learn only somewhat later how much revulsion it caused Stateside. When Patton heard about the incident, he attempted to look at the shooting from the Vietnamese point of view, which he had come to understand. *"Quite clearly,"* Patton says, *"in a similar situation an American officer would have placed the man under arrest and had him moved out of the area. The Vietnamese approach was to take care of the problem without delay."*

As the confusion surrounding Tet subsided, Patton began his duties as Chief of Force Development Division, USARV. As such, he was responsible for projects in connection with MACV troop needs. A major portion of his time was spent guiding Program 6, designed to provide for balanced deployment of American forces in Vietnam, including assisting the transition of the newly arrived 101st Airborne Division into an airmobile force. During his tenure other high-priority groups, including the Americal Division, were either activated or reorganized. Burning the midnight oil, Patton also concentrated on standardizing combat forces, combat support, and combat service support units.

While Program 6 dealt primarily with military matters, it did have a civilian element as well. In fact, Patton was to spend time in the conversion of military billets, nearly ten thousand, to civilian positions. This resulted in a significant reduction of military manpower. Patton, in Army reports, was later credited with saving nearly $5 million dollars by recommending the elimination of approximately four thousand positions held by local civilians working for thirty-nine different agencies of the United States government. This was accomplished after Patton conducted numerous onsite reviews and appraisals of the services actually being rendered. He also recommended scores of troop reallocations to areas with shortages. Soon Patton was given more responsibility and was named Acting Deputy, Assistant Chief of Staff, G-3, Headquarters, United States Army, Vietnam.

In the early months of Patton's third tour, as a result of Tet '68, troop strength and organizational concerns had the highest priority in MACV; Patton spent most of his time with the Westmoreland plan for significantly increasing troop strength. "Augmentation," as the controversial concept would be called, involved building up manpower in Vietnam at a rate that would require full mobilization in the United States.

While putting together the proposal, Patton, as principal action officer for the plan, often briefed Westmoreland, commander of the U.S. Military Assistance Command Vietnam. He was also called upon to brief a task force visiting Vietnam to evaluate the request. The group included General Earle Wheeler, Chairman of the Joint Chiefs of Staff; then–Major General William De-Puy, a special assistant to the Joint Chiefs; and Robert Komer, who came to Vietnam as deputy to the MACV commander. In his job Komer held the rank of ambassador, but by background he was alleged to be the "counterinsurgency" expert who put together CORDS (Civil Operations and Revolutionary Development Support). According to Patton, it was also accepted among military people that he was an informant for the president.

After a series of briefings and meetings, the task force left Vietnam and returned to the United States, where President Lyndon Johnson formed the Ad Hoc Task Force on Vietnam. The next group included military and diplomatic personnel, who eventually recommended an immediate deployment of 230,000 additional troops. Additionally, they called for increasing the draft numbers, bringing up reserves, and stretching duty tours. Johnson, after military and political consultations, would startle most observers by deciding not only to reject mobilization but actually to begin phasing out American involvement in Southeast Asia. President

Johnson, weary of the war that plagued his administration, had apparently seen and heard enough. Later, under President Richard Nixon, the plans for withdrawal would come to full fruition.

For Patton, the sad part of the discussions on scaling down the war effort was the sense that America was willing to settle for peace at any price. This attitude, in Patton's opinion, put the United States on the road to ruin in Vietnam. A number of other factors also worried Patton. In addition to the political side of the war, he felt the United States had committed numerous mistakes in the way soldiers were sent to the war. Patton says, *"While they were the best soldiers I've ever worked with, in peace or war, they were bound to suffer commitment problems owing to a variety of things, including having only a twelve-month tour of duty. This tour, as an example, gave the soldier a short and difficult learning curve in the beginning which undoubtedly caused friendly casualties, plus an understandable tenuousness near the end because he was heading home."* Those who had just a few short days to go were seldom found *"on point in the thick of the action."* These fundamental but natural problems caused constant concern at all levels.

After working in USARV operations for about six months, Patton would be ordered to take command of the 11th Armored Cavalry Regiment—"The Blackhorse Regiment." In that capacity he would work closely with a number of soldiers in the upper echelon of the war effort, including, once again, his mentor, Creighton W. Abrams.

Patton fought alongside other notable officers as well, including James Dozier, who was on his Blackhorse staff and later made worldwide news as a captive of Italy's infamous Red Brigade terrorist group. Dozier and Patton had met first at West Point, where Captain Patton was a tactical officer and Dozier a cadet, Class of 1956. After serving in Vietnam, Dozier went on to become a major general and in 1981 was serving in Italy as the highest-ranking U.S. Army officer in the NATO southern Europe command when he was the subject of an intense and successful manhunt following his kidnapping.

Patton also worked closely with General Keith L. Ware, commander of the 1st Infantry Division. Ware, to whom Patton and the 11th ACR reported in an operational capacity, eventually became the fourth American general to die in Vietnam as a result of hostile action. A highly respected officer, Ware had a long history of meritorious service. He had been awarded the Medal of Honor while serving with the 3rd Infantry Division in World War II. Ware died when his helicopter, with seven aboard, crashed north of Saigon near the Cambodian border on September 13, 1968.

Throughout his military career, Patton was known to be extremely loyal to those who served under him, and many whom Patton tutored went on to distinguished Army careers. Dozier was a good example, as were Andy O'Meara and John McEnery.

Patton first met Andrew P. O'Meara III, the regimental intelligence officer, S-2, when he took command in July 1968. The new commander was thirteen years senior to O'Meara but valued the younger man's knowledge. First, O'Meara was a student of Vietnam and the war; in addition, he was personable, intelligent, and had a keen sense of humor and dedication, which Patton admired and appreciated. In 1962, O'Meara volunteered for duty in Vietnam as an adviser to the South Vietnamese Army. He spent a year as the only American soldier in a Vietnamese company; by the time it was over he was convinced the South Vietnamese cause was a good one. In 1968 he returned to Vietnam and was assigned to the Blackhorse as the S-2. O'Meara not only worked closely with Patton but also shared his military heritage: O'Meara's father had attended West Point and attained the rank of general. Later, the younger O'Meara was to say of Patton, "Being the son of a famous general is not an advantage because many feel you're the beneficiary of favoritism. Sometimes it's not just peers, but superiors who feel you were born with the silver spoon in your mouth. So there is jealousy which is regrettable and was of no help to either him or me."

John McEnery, meanwhile, had arrived in Vietnam and assumed command of 3d Squadron, 11th ACR, just three days before Patton took command of the regiment. McEnery, like all the senior commanders in the 11th, spent considerable time with Patton. "He has a personality that can fool you," McEnery says of Patton. "He is all gung ho and tried not to be like his father, but the similarities were just immense." McEnery goes on to comment, "I've never known a commander as concerned about his people as Patton and I knew immediately Patton was someone I could work for and who would allow me to get the most out of myself. Patton would give the overall mission and then stand back and allow it to go. He proved to be the smartest tactical commander I ever came into contact with, and of all the people I worked for, pushed me further in my career than anyone else."

McEnery tells a story that depicts Patton's loyalty to his soldiers. "He received a captured VC document detailing how their forces were decimated by the actions of my people," says McEnery. "Patton wanted the message added to my personnel file and as part of my efficiency report. The Army had no rules for this type of request and therefore refused. But, Patton believed it was important for my career and fought for over a year to have it added, and he finally succeeded, much to my benefit and appreciation." About the incident, Patton says, *It is most unusual to have your efficiency report written by the enemy but that was the case for John McEnery.*

O'Meara says Patton fascinated him. "The American senior staff I knew early on were rather timid, and until you fight for a bold man like Patton you really don't know what bold is. The pace at which Patton fought simply overwhelmed the enemy. He would pour in artillery and use every asset at his disposal until the enemy, suffering heavily, would go into a defensive posture.

"I found Patton to be very consistent and principled. The soldiers too, respected Patton and were devoted to him. He always took the time to talk with them and understand what they were going through. When they were at attention he would put them at ease. He'd routinely check on their clothing and food, and when he found something wrong he'd have it fixed immediately."

Most officers who served in Vietnam, including Patton, agree that the American military put some of its finest commanders into the war zone. Patton served under two of the best known, General William C. Westmoreland and General Creighton W. Abrams. In June of 1968, Abrams was named COMUSMACV, succeeding Westmoreland. With Abrams in command, allied strategy picked up steam, and he began pursuing the enemy with vigor. After Tet '68, the advantage was clearly with U.S. and ARVN forces, and Abrams was anxious to capitalize. He acted swiftly to "cut off the enemy's logistic nose," as he phrased it.

The difference between the Abrams war and that of Westmoreland was in both style and substance. In a 1969 *New York Times* article, writer Kevin Buckley called Westmoreland's war "a monolithic, ever-growing, ever confident enterprise filled with optimistic generalities." Abrams, on the other hand, impressed many as a soldier's soldier, realistic in his appraisal of the enemy and not prone to making rash predictions.

Abrams, in addition to shifting strategy, also brought a new sophistication to the war in Vietnam. He knew how to ask the right questions and, more importantly, get the right answers. He knew instinctively that many different wars were being fought in Vietnam and not all occurred on the battlefield. Some were being fought in the villages using not guns but ideas as weapons, and he set out to make headway on all fronts.

Abrams supported the concept of fire support bases, in the hundreds, spread out around the countryside. These camps sent out large numbers of patrols each day and kept the enemy off guard. Additionally, selected areas were continually probed to detect enemy activity. Abrams was also credited with securing Saigon, which had often been the target of rocket attacks, and he used his expertise in and appreciation of B-52 bombing as one of the most important elements of his technical policy.

In addition to his command duties, Abrams became the point man for "Vietnamization." The term, simply defined, was the continuing process of turning the war over to the South Vietnamese. Abrams, along with a number of military experts, helped to develop and plan the details for a phased withdrawal of U.S. troops. In June of 1969, President Nixon met with South Vietnamese President Thieu at Midway and set the stage for the conclusion of wholesale American involvement in the war. The first installment, which numbered some twenty-five thousand soldiers, left Vietnam the following month.

Undoubtedly, particularly because of Abrams, Westmoreland, and others, Patton soon became known as an outstanding battlefield commander. This was confirmed by his later making the promotion list to brigadier general from colonel in a shorter time than anyone else serving in the Vietnam War. Patton, who had been promoted to colonel in April 1968, made brigadier general June 1, 1970.

Westmoreland, who served under Patton's father during World War II, recognized familiar traits which Patton used to help command soldiers in battle. "Patton looked like his father and had similar mannerisms," says General Westmoreland. "Their speech was somewhat alike as well. It was pretty evident that young Patton was the son of the old man. It's that simple. However, the impressive thing about George is that he didn't concern himself with his last name. He went out and made a career, earning everything on his own." Westmoreland remembers keeping track of Patton on the Vietnam battlefield. "He did a very good job in command of the 11th ACR and handled himself professionally. It's quite a burden the son of a senior officer has to carry and I must say, to his credit, he did it well. Because down through history, when you look at the sons of famous people, they were not all winners."

Working for Patton in a battlefield environment was a test of endurance. As Dozier says, "Patton would drive himself all day long, then work well into the night. He didn't get much sleep." Typically, in the field during a battle, Patton made a point of not interfering with his subordinate commanders if they had things under control. "He was aggressive, but his finest attribute was his battle sense," Dozier explains. "He just had an instinct for doing the right thing at the right time in combat and many American soldiers are alive today because George Patton was their boss."

Commanding officers, peers, and subordinates were not the only ones in Vietnam to recognize Patton's ability as a combat soldier; the media were taking notice of his prowess as well. Because of his reputation as a fighting officer and, as Patton acknowledges, undoubtedly in part because of his last name, he attracted the attention of the media, who often sought to make comparisons between father and son. Patton proved to be a good copy, and articles talked about his tough demeanor, professionalism, and connection with military history. A good example of the type of story, which appeared during Patton's last tour in Vietnam, was one that ran under a headline proclaiming, "The Son Also Rises." The article, about Patton's taking command of the 11th ACR, in part said, "The general they called 'Old Blood and Guts' would have been proud of his boy—who admitted feeling kind of proud himself. At its headquarters northeast of Saigon, the Eleventh Armored Cavalry Regiment, a tank outfit, last week came under the command of Colonel George S. Patton, 43, son and namesake of the flamboyant World War II tank commander." It went on to describe Patton's introductory address to his troops wherein he said, "Soldiers, together, you and I will continue to maintain the high standards of the Eleventh Armored Cavalry Regiment. Good Luck and good fighting." It concluded by saying, "Then Young Blood and Guts led his men into action in a five-hour battle with North Vietnamese regulars near the Cambodian border."

Another article from 1968 describes Patton as "a big, amiable man with straw-colored hair and booming voice." The story speaks of Patton stepping past rows of tanks waiting to move out, and it quotes him as saying, "In World War II these tanks were spearheads, the ground-gainers. Here it's a hell of a lot different. The helicopter lets the infantry do the exploiting while the armor more or less supports or fills in the gaps."

While often getting what one might describe as positive press, Patton at times also received less than favorable reviews in connection with actions or comments that somehow found a path to the media. Patton's candor produced a number of controversial quotes, and this style is even reflected in his diary. In May 1968, for example, he wrote, "Engineers are all over the place. Building useless crap, overhead covers, courts, clubs, etc. And yet, the road to Saigon is not open. Closed by the VC last night. I wonder how good these generals really are." Similar straightforward comments and actions in public caused Patton considerable problems at times, as was evidenced in December 1968, when Patton incurred the wrath of the media and others for a Christmas card sent to close military friends. Patton mailed less than a dozen cards with a color picture of several dismembered VC and a greeting reading, "Peace on Earth," signed "Col. G.S. Patton, Commanding, 11 ACR, Viet Nam." Patton meant the card as a satirical statement. *"I intended to highlight the irony of war, yet it appeared I was actually glorifying it,"* says Patton in retrospect. Word leaked of the card's existence, and soon it was reported in a *New York Times* article. The story containing the Christmas card episode as well as a couple of other Patton stories upset some people Stateside, including New York congressman Richard D. McCarthy, who demanded an explanation. Patton provided one in a letter to his superior shortly thereafter in which he pointed out the reasoning behind his sending the card. Contrary to the article, the card was not signed by Patton and his wife Joanne, since, as he said in his letter of explanation, *"Following long custom, a typical family group photograph (less the absent undersigned) was mailed in quantity by my wife as our seasonal greeting to the many persons with whom the Pattons correspond at Christmas."*

The article that raised questions about the Christmas card also said, "Patton likes to say he doesn't hate the enemy, but 'I do like to see the arms and legs fly.' At his farewell party before leaving Vietnam, he frolicked with a peace medallion around his neck while he cradled the polished skull of a Vietcong with a bullet hole above the left eye in his arms." Answering the congressman's salvo about his comments and skull episode, Patton wrote, *"I departed Vietnam for CONUS [Continental United States] on 7 April 1969. On 5 April, at a party in my honor, I received several gifts from both U.S. and ARVN units which had operated under my control. These consisted of a photo album, a captured weapon (completely disarmed), and other mementoes of sentimental, not commercial, value. One of the gifts was a peace symbol mentioned in the article. This item was given to me by the enlisted men of the aero-rifle platoon of the Air Cavalry Troop, which enjoyed the highest kill-ratio of any ground unit under my command (280 VC/NVA to 1 U.S.). Practically all of the soldiers in this platoon wore the peace symbol under their fatigues. They gave one to me simply as a token of remembrance. I treasure it today as a symbol of what they fought and died for—honorable peace. The skull, an old one, obviously retrieved from the jungle, was presented to me on the same evening, 5 April 1969. On a base beneath it was inscribed, 'We found this bastard and piled on.' The slogan, 'Find the Bastards and Pile On,' was the regiment's motto prior to my arrival at the unit in July of 1968."*

Patton, under close scrutiny by the media, also raised some eyebrows after the tough battle in which he had advanced on an enemy position, wounded a VC, and pulled him out of a hole. Later, as the enemy soldier was lying on a stretcher awaiting evacuation, Patton saluted him and in French said, "You put up one hell of a fight!" The soldier returned his salute. Not long after the incident, a story ran in the press reporting that Patton had saluted the enemy. About the incident, O'Meara, who watched the scene unfold, says, "It's not something I would have thought about doing, but Patton was apolitical. To him it came naturally as an extension of his feelings about the profession of arms. Generally, Patton was polished with the press, though at times he would sound very aggressive. And part of the problem is that after fighting in a war for a while you lose your sensitivity, forgetting that someone not involved in the fighting won't understand your emotions."

Patton respected the enemy and at one point, according to Dozier, tried to meet secretly his counterpart in the Dong Nai Regiment. "Patton had high regard for this fellow as a soldier and a fighter," says Dozier, "so we attempted to contact him through a series of complicated message drops at abandoned fire bases. We were unsuccessful in arranging a meeting and later found out he had been killed in a B-52 strike."

Andy O'Meara also remembers an incident concerning Patton and the enemy. "In Chanh Luu, we had a hell of a battle and one of those killed was a North Vietnamese general. We heard about it when Radio Hanoi announced he had been killed in the village and was still there. Immediately, Patton wanted to retrieve the body and so we returned to the village. We started

walking down the main street and everyone disappeared. We decided to check the pagoda and found the
general in a coffin. Nearby, three Buddhist monks were
worshiping the deceased. They looked at Patton and
bowed, and Patton returned their gesture. We then
stood in silence for at least five minutes before Patton
again bowed and we departed, leaving the body with
the monks. I know that we were being observed by the
enemy in the village, who I'm sure were not displeased
by this American commander paying his respects to
their general."

In studying the Vietnam War, one cannot understate
the role of the media. The influence of television in particular was profound, and, along with the American
people, it had a significant influence on the national
leadership and the general conduct of the war. Patton
uses the Normandy invasion as a good example of how
television coverage, if it had been available during
World War II, would have affected morale at home just
as it did during the war in Vietnam. *"Consider the
beachhead scene,"* says Patton, *"with young Americans
pinned down and dying from murderous fire coming
from the Normandy cliffs. The camera is taking color
pictures of our boys crying out for medical assistance,
while the sound of war is all about. Death, and dying
are the realities of war and during Vietnam it was being
broadcasted on the nightly news. It was bound to take
a toll in the living rooms of America.*

"In Normandy," Patton continues, *"as with Tet, in
spite of the losses, the results were the same. In both
cases the enemy was beaten, yet the outcomes were
completely different. One cannot really compare the
two in other than purely military terms; however, it
remains true the media had a significant effect on the
outcome of the conflict in Vietnam since a vocal portion
of the American public reacted in horror and outrage at
the brutality of this particular war. But, any veteran
will tell you death in any war is a horrible sight, yet it
all looks pretty much the same. To me, the influence of*

television in the Vietnam War was similar to that of Mathew Brady to the Civil War. Brady's photographs were very graphic and I am confident that those who first saw them many years ago were greatly moved."

Patton's feelings concerning the reaction to Mathew Brady's photographs during the Civil War are accurate and, indeed, are borne out in a *New York Times* article written in 1862 after Brady opened an exhibition entitled "The Dead of Antietam." The reporter observed, "We see the list [of battlefield casualties] in the morning paper at breakfast, but dismiss its recollection with the coffee. There is a confused mass of names, but they are all strangers; we forget the horrible significance that dwells amid the jumble of type.

"We recognize the battlefield as a reality, but it stands as a remote one. It is like a funeral next door. It attracts your attention, but it does not enlist your sympathy. But it is very different when the hearse stops at your own door and the corpse is carried over your own threshold.

"Mr. Brady has done something to bring to us the terrible reality and earnestness of the war. If he has not brought bodies and laid them in our door-yards and along [our] streets, he has done something very like it."

During Patton's first tour of Vietnam duty, in 1962, he and others observed little attempt at control of the media. This policy meant a member of the media could hear about a fight going on somewhere, jump in the first available helicopter, and head to the scene. Then at the briefing that night, which was referred to as the "dog and pony show," the media representative would usually hear a sanitized version of what had happened that day. Often conflicts between the media and military arose because the media knew what had occurred, having been on the scene and spoken to the participants. Meanwhile, a staff officer would brief the reporters on the fight. Generally, the briefing officer had little actual knowledge of what had really happened and was giving details based on information received in either a message or phone call. In many cases, briefing officers were not attempting to mislead the media; the briefers had no real knowledge of the events.

The result of the difference between what the media saw for themselves and what was relayed in the briefings, such as at Ap Bac, served to destroy military credibility over a period of time. Eventually, and in many ways understandably, a hostility arose between the media and the military that remained throughout the war and still exists to some extent. Patton, looking back, believes the degree of hostility that developed was largely the fault of the MACV staff.

"As events unfolded over the years coverage from Vietnam took on a bleaker and bleaker tone," says Patton. *"Each article and television news report seemed more pessimistic than the last. There was no longer 'a light at the end of the tunnel,' and in spite of success in the field, the die of ultimate defeat was inexorably cast."*

Patton contends the media's erosion of confidence in the military occurred also because they too were confused about the war and how to report it. An episode Patton uses to illustrate the point occurred after one of the 3rd Squadron APCs hit a mine. Patton received word of the action and arrived a few moments later to find the vehicle smoldering, the metal twisted by an explosion. The driver had been blown in two, with the bottom half still in the APC and the upper torso lying on the ground but a few feet away. Patton was surveying the scene when a press photographer came up and started to take pictures of the body.

Patton looked for a long moment at the photographer and with a rage building inside said, "Fella, just hand me your film."

The photographer retorted, "I won't give it to you."

Patton thought it over for a second and said, "Look, there are some dead VC over here which this guy was instrumental in sending to their ancestors. Why don't you take pictures of them?"

"Oh," he said, "that wouldn't sell."

Patton could not believe what he was hearing and demanded the film again. Once more the photographer refused. Patton reached down, pulled his pistol from the holster, and said, "For the last time, hand me that film, now!"

The photographer's jaw dropped, and staring into the barrel of a gun he stammered, "Uh, uh, Colonel, don't get excited!"

He then handed the film to one of Patton's men who dropped it in the mud to destroy it. The incident was never reported by the photographer, although Patton did tell his boss what had happened. *"I don't know what I would have done had he again refused my order to turn over the film,"* says Patton, *"but I was in a foul enough mood to have put a bullet between his feet. All I could imagine at the time was the mother of this soldier seeing her son lying face up in that condition on the front page of some newspaper. Then too, I just couldn't reconcile the attitude of the photographer, who showed a total lack of regard for human decency."*

In contrast to the incident with the photographer, there were several members of the media with whom Patton enjoyed special relations. Don Baker of ABC News was one who Patton felt reported fairly from the scene. Baker hooked himself to Blackhorse and after gaining Patton's confidence began to be tipped off before something was going to occur. *"Not once did he breach my confidence,"* says Patton. *"I felt good about him because he reported accurately, in balance and responsibly. On one of these occasions I might say, Don, you ought to be around here at 3:00 tomorrow afternoon because we have something going on. That was the most information I would ever give since further specifics would have violated orders regarding releasing details of a mission prior to commencement."*

One day Baker came by the regimental CP with a cameraman as ferocious action was being reported in a nearby jungle. Patton decided to fly into the area and asked Baker if he wanted to go along. Baker readily agreed. Patton ordered the chopper down about two hundred yards to the rear of the fight and jumped out and started to move forward. Behind Patton, Baker and his cameraman were also moving up when suddenly small arms fire erupted; a second later Patton heard a crashing sound and someone yell, "Jesus Christ!" He turned around to see the camera blown in a hundred pieces. Baker looked at Patton and, grinning, said, "I guess we'll just have to *write* this story."

Vietnam, before all was said and done, would also be the stage for a number of correspondents who gained notoriety for a variety of reasons. During his first tour Patton became acquainted with David Halberstam of the *New York Times* and Neil Sheehan of United Press International. Halberstam, a thorn in the side of the Kennedy administration due to his reporting an ever-worsening situation in the early years, eventually shared a 1964 Pulitzer Prize for his work. Sheehan, later as the *New York Times* correspondent at the Pentagon, broke the Daniel Ellsberg–*Pentagon Papers* story.

The so-called "Pentagon Papers" constituted a 7,100-page study officially called *The History of the U.S. Decision Making Process on Vietnam*. It contained the history of U.S. involvement up to 1968 and was a highly classified document. Daniel Ellsberg, recruited a number of years before by Robert McNamara, took the highly classified documents and attempted to give them to several outspoken congressional critics of the war. Unsuccessful in the main, Ellsberg then passed them along to Neil Sheehan. The *New York Times* began running excerpts of the report on June 13, 1971. Patton feels Sheehan's actions in accepting classified material and passing it on to be published showed a basic disloyalty to the nation, although *"from a journalist's point of view I can see why he did it and perhaps had I been a member of the press I may have done it too."*

Patton, while concerned about press and electronic coverage, nonetheless enjoyed the immediacy and vibrancy of the media, and while on the Army Command Staff would spend time each day reading newspapers or magazines. He especially enjoyed columnists, including Art Buchwald, who caught his fancy. In the evenings Patton would also take a few minutes to write in his diary. *"I suppose like many other things, it was something my father did which I thought was well worth emulating,"* says Patton, *"so from 1947 on I began recording the day's events and my impressions of the world around me."*

While Patton spent time catching up on reading at night he was also constantly involved in family business Stateside. Any soldier in war devotes a great deal of time to thinking of loved ones and the day-to-day problems they may be having. In Patton's case, though Joanne was at home with the children, family business still needed to be tended to. In that regard Ruth Ellen helped considerably, and in fact alerted George in 1968 about a film being proposed concerning their father. The movie would eventually be called *Patton* and win a number of Academy awards. At the time Patton was concerned about a war being fought a long way from any movie location, but he listened to the details, which early in the planning process worried the family considerably. It appeared the film script contained numerous historical as well as interpretive flaws that combined to distort greatly the elder Patton.

George C. Scott once confirmed the Patton family's worst nightmare about the portrayal of Patton. "I don't think he [Patton] should have been characterized as the insane show-off that 20th Century–Fox wanted to make him—which I resisted down the line." Scott went on to say about Patton, "He had many admirable qualities: duty, honor, country and so forth instilled in those men. The most admirable quality about him was—I have to be so precise in wording this—that he disapproved of taking casualties. Almost fanatical disapproval, and coupled with that, his intense desire to inflict casualties on the enemy."

Juggling disparate duties, from the monitoring of Patton family business to pursuit of the enemy on the battlefield, was stressful, yet exhilarating. Patton was in the thick of action, where he felt at home, fulfilling destiny's call.

11

BLACKHORSE

In retrospect, I did my best.
—George S. Patton

On July 15, 1968, Colonel George S. Patton assumed command of the 11th Armored Cavalry Regiment, succeeding Colonel Charles R. Gorder. The Blackhorse Regiment had its beginnings in 1901 when it was activated as a horse cavalry regiment. In 1902 it was deployed to the Philippines to assist in putting down an insurgent uprising. In 1916, the regiment participated in the Mexican Punitive Expedition led by General John J. "Black Jack" Pershing against the bandit Pancho Villa. Through the years, the regiment made the transformation from horse to armor, and from existence as the 11th Cavalry to the 11th Armored Cavalry Regiment in 1942. In the closing months of World War II, elements of the regiment fought throughout Europe including the Battle of the Bulge. Twenty-one years later, on September 7, 1966, the 11th arrived in Vung Tau, Vietnam, as the only deployed brigade-size armored unit in the MACV force structure.

Patton was especially proud to take command of the 11th for several reasons. Not only had he once served the regiment as executive officer of the 1st Squadron at Straubing, Germany, from 1960 to 1961, but he was also instrumental in helping to design and shape the future mission of the 11th as plans were being made at the Pentagon for the regiment to join the war effort in 1966. Patton firmly believed that the 11th, properly led and deployed, would be a tremendous asset in Vietnam. Two years later, when Patton learned he was to take command of the Blackhorse, he knew that it would be a tough assignment. *"I realized,"* says Patton, *"that I would be subject to media attention and therefore I would have to maintain the highest possible standards in order to keep from getting criticism connected with the achievements of my father and various relatives stretching back through Army history."*

In fact, the pressure on Patton as he prepared for a command position in war is evident in a diary notation made before he took over the 11th. His diary said, *"JHP, BAP, GSP jr* [Joanne Patton, Beatrice Ayer Patton, and George S. Patton Jr.] *are watching. Well, here goes—the whistle has just blown!"*

The regiment Patton commanded was, by now, a veteran of Vietnam, having seen action during Operation Hickory near Phu Hoa Dong in early October 1966, and later having conducted several major search-and-destroy missions through the first five months of 1967. Operation Cedar Falls, which occurred in early January 1967 in the "Iron Triangle" region, was one of successive missions designed to eliminate VC strongholds. This assignment was quickly followed by Operations Junction City I and II in February, and then Operation Manhattan beginning in late April 1968.

When Patton took command, the regimental headquarters and most of the assigned units were under the operational control of the Commanding General, 1st Infantry Division. Patton started working for Major General Keith Ware and, after his death in battle on 13 September 1968, for Major General Orwin C. Talbott, for whom he would work for the balance of his tour.

Andy O'Meara, who was assigned as regimental S-2 at the time, has distinct memories of Patton's first day with Blackhorse. "He joined a unit which had been living in the environment for some time," says O'Meara, "and when you live in that heat you make adjustments quickly, and those of us in the field were outside all the time. When I first saw Patton he was sweating through his uniform because he was undergoing the adjustment from having worked at higher headquarters in air-conditioned buildings."

O'Meara also recalls that Patton's first day was a long one. "After arriving and speaking with the troops he called a staff meeting, and when we got through briefing Patton he pulled out a notebook and shared with us his style of operation. It quickly became clear to me that he had been preparing those notes his entire career. I found that to be a beautiful insight and testimonial of professional competence. He wasn't there to punch his ticket. He was there because he was a professional soldier and a leader who had prepared himself his whole life for that day."

As Patton began operational work in the field, the basic fighting structure in-country was the U.S. Marines in the northern provinces (I Corps), the U.S. Army in the central region (II Corps) and around Saigon (III Corps), and ARVN soldiers fighting in the Mekong Delta (IV Corps). Along with the large number of forces committed by the United States and South Vietnam, Korea had deployed approximately forty-nine thousand soldiers in-country, Australia had contributed 7,672 soldiers, and to a lesser degree other countries contributed soldiers and equipment as well.

Under Patton's command from July 1968 through April 1969, Blackhorse was almost always reinforced with at least one infantry battalion organic to the 1st Division. From time to time Lieutenant General Do Cao Tri, the ARVN III Corps commander in the area, placed one or two ARVN Ranger battalions under Patton's operational control as well. Patton would sometimes assign one of his line troops or a tank company to an ARVN unit, in cross reinforcement. This system was first suggested and later directed by General Abrams, COMUSMACV, and it proved to be an effective arrangement for all concerned. The ARVN units assigned to the Blackhorse responded to the orders of the Blackhorse commander; logistic and administrative support continued to be an ARVN responsibility. Medical evacuation and support were handled by 11th Cavalry headquarters.

With this organization—three squadrons, an infantry battalion, one or two ARVN Ranger units, and a very effective air cavalry troop under the command of Major John C. Bahnsen—Blackhorse participated in a myriad of operations throughout the III Corps Tactical Zone. The regiment also provided ground, rocket, and mortar security for the Saigon area and participated in operations carried out by II FFV/III CTZ (Field Force Vietnam-Designation for U.S. Corps-Level Tactical Control Headquarters, Corps Tactical Zone-Military and Political Subdivision of the Republic of South Vietnam) with the mission of interdicting VC/NVA advances in the Tay Ninh and Binh Long provinces.

By the end of 1968 and well into 1969, the regiment's attention was focused on the Cambodian border. The mission called for destroying enemy staging areas and preventing the massing of forces for eventual advances on the Saigon area. Operations were conducted continuously in the Iron Triangle, the "Catcher's Mitt," and other regions north of Saigon.

Patton's Senior Officer Debriefing Report dated April 7, 1969, described the 11th Armored Cavalry Regiment's area of operation as composed of two types of terrain. The first, a farming region in northern Binh Duong Province, was a horseshoe of local villages that were providing food supplies in support of enemy tactical operations north of Saigon. The supplies were used to support the 5th and 7th NVA Divisions and the very aggressive and elusive Dong Ngai Regiment. The second type of terrain in Patton's sector of responsibility was dense jungle, which provided cover for the Dong Ngai Regiment, the 81st Rear Service Group, and a number of VC elements. The jungle area was located east of Highway 13 and was traversed by trails coming from the western portion of War Zone D.

A primary mission for the regiment during this period was "to secure and pacify Long An Province." The resulting plan, called Operation Kittyhawk, consisted of several specific objectives, including keeping the main roads free of Viet Cong interference and preventing the enemy from launching major offensives. Another part of the mission was to institute MEDCAP (Medical Civil Action Program) and DENTCAP (Dental Civil Action Program) assistance, which was designed to provide free medical and dental help to the local population. Both MEDCAP and DENTCAP were very popular in the villages and hamlets, and in some areas they were critically helpful in achieving and maintaining good relations with the villagers.

Patton knew what he wanted from the 11th when he took command, and in a memo to its executive officer, Lieutenant Colonel Meritte Ireland, dated July 2, 1968, Patton outlined his thoughts about the regiment and fighting in general. Patton said in the memo, *"Actually I consider that the preponderance of operations in this war commence as a reconnaissance. This is followed by a movement to contact and a meeting engagement where the battle is joined. At that time, a force generation exercise takes place which must hold the enemy, compress him, and maintain contact with him until his eventual destruction."* Patton went on to say, *"Now Charlie* [common slang expression for the enemy] *will fight in three instances. He will fight when surprised. He will fight to protect a base camp. He will fight when he has planned it that way, i.e., when he wants to fight. The most demanding task for U.S. units unquestionably is the maintenance of contact with the enemy. Finally, Blackhorse will react to 'good intelligence' as opposed to perfect intelligence, and secondly always will position one unit available within striking distance."* During Patton's command tour, these guidelines formed the bedrock of regimental combat operations.

Patton's command thoughts were further articulated to Ireland: *"I will back you publicly right or wrong and correct you privately if you are wrong, but it has been my experience it is better to have an XO* [Executive Officer] *that will 'move it' than one who will hold everything for the CO and crowd him at night, thus distracting him from the primary mission."* Patton went on to summarize, *"I make these points: First, this is basically a reconnaissance war keyed to the meeting engagement. Second, when joined, the secret is to react promptly with a good plan—not perfect but good; third, all of this takes absolutely flawless administration. Many say that armor is all 'slapdash.' In this connection, I have sometimes been accused as an advocate of this so called 'slapdash' methodology. I deeply resent that criticism. Armor, armored cavalry and air cavalry are logistically highly sensitive and require continued attention."* To illustrate his understanding and appreciation of logistics, Patton would later cite his regimental S-4, Lieutenant Colonel Glenn Finkbiner, as a great example of one who, even under the most difficult circumstances, never let Blackhorse down in obtaining the many classes of supplies required by a highly mobile unit.

In Patton's concluding comments to Ireland, he emphasized a point for which he had already gained a reputation. He said, *"I would like to get plenty of PI* [public information, including news or feature stories in the media] *for this regiment with particular emphasis on the people that nobody ever notices such as mechanics, scouts, code clerks, cooks and the little guy who never gets any glory."*

When Patton took command he began dispensing

many battlefield lessons, and as he did in his memo to Ireland, Patton emphasized the importance of timely intelligence gathering. *"When I took command,"* Patton once said, *"the watchword of the regiment was to react to 'good' intelligence immediately rather than attempt to develop a perfect intelligence fix. A good plan now is better than a perfect plan two hours from now, especially in this type of warfare."*

Prisoners and others of Chieu Hoi (meaning "open arms," an amnesty program designed to induce Viet Cong forces to defect) were normally the best sources of intelligence for the 11th, especially if the information was gathered in the field and exploited immediately. Patton said, *"The nature of this conflict is such that the average local force VC is so compartmented information-wise, that his contribution to the 'big picture' will usually be marginal. However, his knowledge of the local area, coupled with his unexplainable willingness to give information, contributes significantly to the 'little picture.'"*

In fact, Chieu Hoi were so important that such a person, when identified, was quickly moved to the regimental command post. A leaflet could then be prepared and within eight hours dropped on a suspected VC base camp while a message was broadcast over a thousand-watt, helicopter-mounted loudspeaker. During Patton's time forty-three Chieu Hoi came forth, several of whom proved to be important intelligence coups at the province level.

Patton felt that the Blackhorse tactical operations could be characterized by three key words: variety, imagination and boldness. Its tactical missions were varied in nature and on a daily basis might include convoy escort, route and bridge security, counterinfiltration operations, area and zone reconnaissance in force, pacification, mounted and dismounted day and night ambushes, and base camp security.

Patton also made his battlefield philosophy well known throughout his command. He insisted on day and night random armor activity so the enemy would find no particular pattern as a way of predicting future movement. He directed his field commanders to refrain from building permanent positions, stopping only long enough to rest, refuel, and take care of necessary maintenance. He also said, *"No idea, no solution, is discarded out of hand regardless of how unorthodox it may first appear. Typical solutions to problems have included: thunder-running a road at night with six Cobra gunships to stop enemy mining efforts; utilizing air cavalry operations at night to stop snipings from riverbanks, and issuing false radio traffic employed to confuse the enemy radio monitors prior to the start of an operation. The latter also included leaving falsely marked maps where the enemy would find them."*

Patton, upon taking command of the 11th, decided to help shape the doctrine of the war. He acknowledged that weather played a vitally important role. For example, he realized that during the rainy season the medium tank was not effective in his area of operations, due to the ground saturation; thus, alternative battle plans were designed. The dry season, on the other hand, was particularly hot, with temperatures often exceeding one hundred degrees, with heavy humidity. Therefore, during the dry months the 11th would rely heavily on the tank. The usual method called for combining tank platoons with aircraft, using the aero scouts to guide, advise, and generally oversee tank units as they moved about within the area of operation.

During Patton's time in command and during the course of the war in Vietnam, the helicopter played a key role in 90 percent of all engagements. With choppers, the various commanders could reach far-flung battle locations and reinforce them as necessary. However, the helicopter could also be a dangerous mode of transportation. On several occasions Patton's chopper had to land because of mechanical problems, and twice it was knocked from the air by enemy fire. The first incident occurred when Patton was moving into hostile fire;

the aircraft received a direct hit, blowing away a fuel tank. As warning lights flashed, the pilot, Warrant Officer Charlie Watkins, was forced to autorotate (allow the rotor to free-wheel) to a hard but safe landing. Another time the command chopper was accidentally hit by artillery from friendly forces; a round exploded right under it. The helicopter rocked violently, and Charlie Watkins called back on the intercom, saying, "Sir, we've got serious problems." A moment later Watkins frantically reported, "Sir, I've got to take her in." Patton only had time enough to say, "Good luck," as the helicopter entered autorotation. Fortunately, Watkins was able to gain some control and wrestle the chopper down safely near a bridge, which, luckily, was under U.S. control.

Such incidents notwithstanding, time and again the helicopter proved to be a powerful weapon during the Vietnam War, and Patton, with his forty-one choppers distributed among three organic squadrons, the air cavalry troop, and the regimental headquarters troop, took advantage of their mobility to find and engage the enemy whenever possible.

In July of 1968, after considerable thought and debate on the proper organization, Patton reorganized the air cavalry troop from a gunship, or fire-team, group, to employment as *"the eyes and ears"* of his fighting force. The basic organization of the air cavalry troop would consist of "white" (scouts), "blue" (lift-ships), and "red" (aero-weapons platoon) helicopter teams. Therefore, combining a team of (red) Cobra gunships and (white) scouts would form a "pink team." Combination "pink" or "purple" teams then carried out various duties in the field. While the helicopter configuration might be different depending on the mission, the basic fighting doctrine of the air cavalry troop was called "pile-on." Pile-on was a steady buildup based on the receipt of intelligence reports, from the first visual contacts to fighting the enemy, always increasing the amount of force until achieving the hoped-for result:

defeat of the enemy. It usually started with a quick survey of the available facts given by POW, defectors, or captured documents, and was followed by what were known as VRs (visual reconnaissances). At a point when contact with the enemy was made, the aero-rifle platoon (ARP) moved in with Cobra gunship support, tactical air, and artillery to engage the elusive enemy. If the platoon ran into strong resistance, a series of moves began that would bring in an increasing number of elements under the command of the appropriate officers until the enemy was suppressed. This in essence was the pile-on procedure, which, after a short training period, was executed to near perfection by the Blackhorse units.

Other types of operations included "firebug" missions, utilizing incendiary grenades, and CS gas drops (riot control gas often used to clear enemy tunnel systems). Dropped in large quantities the gas, which burned the skin and irritated the eyes and noses of the enemy, would send the foe fleeing into the open, where Cobra gunships could fire.

The aero-scout platoon of the air cavalry troop worked in tandem with the S-2 section to pinpoint B-52 targets and aero-rifle platoon insertions. As Patton once said in a report, "This is an S-2 war. The primary problem facing the commander in Vietnam is locating the enemy. Once located, the concentration of combat power is seldom a problem provided it is executed with some rapidity."

Patton relied heavily on his scouts, who flew in light observation helicopters, usually the Hughes OH-6A. The scouts were probably the most highly decorated aviators in the regiment, and they performed many tasks. They would attempt to find the enemy, develop B-52 targets, assess the success of the bombings (referred to as bomb damage assessment, or BDA), and guide infantry and armored elements on the ground toward various positions. Equipped with miniguns, the pilots had lethal capability but used it mainly in a defensive role. Typically, they would fly at thirty or forty knots and about forty to fifty feet above ground level. Exposed and vulnerable to the enemy, the scouts often found themselves in precarious situations and under heavy fire.

On November 30, 1968, Warrant Officer Justin H. Ballou was flying his normal reconnaissance mission in search of VC or NVA indications. He looked down and observed some fairly large fish swimming in a flooded B-52 bomb crater, perhaps indicating the enemy was using the hole to store fish. He returned to the HQ and reported this observation to his troop commander, Major Bahnsen. The next morning Patton inserted a rifle company into the area and gained immediate contact with the enemy. By the time the battle terminated, a large portion of one 1st Division brigade was heavily engaged. Patton frequently referred to this action to emphasize the complexities and unique character of guerrilla warfare.

"Fellows like Ballou often flew in the face of danger," says Patton. *"Like the scouts of older days, the Hickoks and Codys, and those who served so well as the American West was being opened, our scouts had the same spirit and motivation towards the effort to gather and report information about the enemy. They merely rode a helicopter instead of a horse, and carried a minigun instead of a Winchester 73."*

In the early months of 1969 a new weapon was introduced into the Vietnam War. Called the M551 Sheridan, it was designed as a light tank and antiarmor vehicle. It carried a 152mm main gun, a .50-caliber machine gun, and a 7.62mm co-axial machine gun. Although the Department of the Army had been putting off since 1966 a decision to accept the Sheridan because of various developmental problems, it was nonetheless decided to equip two divisional cavalry squadrons with them on an experimental basis. Both squadrons, the 1st and 3rd of the 4th Cavalry assigned to the 1st and 25th

Divisions, respectively, were highly suspicious of the vehicle. They had heard through the grapevine that the Sheridan was not only penetrable by rocket-propelled grenades but vulnerable to land mines as well.

General Creighton Abrams in a visit to the Blackhorse CP detailed the planned alignment of the Sheridan test, and Patton responded that he thought the Sheridans might get a better evaluation if they were assigned to one divisional squadron and one regimental squadron, since the two units had dissimilar organizations. General Abrams agreed, and as Patton suspected the tests conducted by each group yielded different results.

In the divisional squadron, in its first action with the new vehicle, a Sheridan hit a land mine, igniting the combustible-case ammunition of the big gun. This caused a second explosion, which destroyed the vehicle. Squadron crews were upset, knowing that a similar explosion under an M48A3 tank would not have caused such horrific damage. However, Patton's Blackhorse 1st Squadron, commanded by Lieutenant Colonel Meritte Ireland, had better results. In its first encounter the squadron used the withering firepower of the vehicle to full advantage, killing over eighty VC. In the final analysis it was concluded the Sheridan had superior firepower, range, greater mobility, and better night-fighting capability than the equipment it was sent to replace. By 1970 over two hundred Sheridans were being used on Vietnam battlefields.

Patton as a commander was instrumental in developing solid working relationships between American troops and ARVN units. However, it was important to Patton that the concept of "working with" a Vietnamese unit still allowed the American commander to have operational control. In Vietnam, a unit might be "attached," meaning that the commander to which it now reported was responsible for both operation and logistical support; on the other hand, if the unit was put under "operational control," it responded to operational matters but retained responsibility for its own logistical support. As a prime example, the Blackhorse was under the operational control of the 1st Division but was not attached.

Patton was not enamored of the "working with" doctrine and made arrangements to put ARVN units under operational control of American forces. In doing so, he also had to explain the details of battle plans directly to Vietnamese commanders. The first such situation resulted in a long briefing session, until Patton felt the ARVN had a grasp on the plans. A couple of days later, the ARVN troops were inserted into a small action with elements of the 11th. It was a simple operation, calling for a sweep through a wooded area. The ARVN commander in charge of the Ranger battalion stood just over five feet tall, wearing lines of ribbons, including the U.S. Silver Star, which he had received as a result of action during Tet '68. *"I explained our working relationship,"* says Patton. *"Then I ordered him to move a company across the river to engage the enemy. I had previously run into some problems with this fellow because he didn't know how to direct a combat assault, handle artillery or communicate proper orders to his people."*

Later, during the operation, while flying overhead, Patton observed the entire battalion returning to base camp in total violation of the battle plan. Patton landed immediately and confronted the commander, demanding, "What the hell is going on?"

"My men are tired and hungry and so we're moving out," the commander replied.

"You violated my order," Patton said, lifting his voice.

"No," came the reply. "I don't work for you, I work for the Vietnamese Army."

Patton shoved his face into the commander's and shouted, "You little son of a bitch, you work for me. Now put a halt to this unit now, and I'll tell you

something else, your battalion isn't worth a god
damn!"

The Vietnamese commander jumped to attention,
said, "Yes, sir," and moved his people back into action.

Patton did not report the incident, although the
ARVN officer bitterly complained to his superiors that
Patton had harassed him. About three days later the
unit was again involved in a battle, which ended with
Patton having to extract the commander and his men
from a firefight.

When Patton saw the commander he said, "See, your
battalion is unsatisfactory. I gave you gunships, artillery, U.S. infantry, and you still screwed up!"

"I'm beginning to agree with you. Please give me
one more chance," the commander sheepishly replied.

His last chance came on November 27, 1968, when
his troops literally threw themselves at enemy bunkers
and charged positions with abandon. It was a nearly
flawless operation, and the commander rushed up to
Patton following the battle and said, "I did it!" Patton
responded, "You're goddamn right you did and you
were great!" From that point on Patton found the Vietnamese officer to be an excellent commander whose
men developed into fine, fighting Rangers. On a personal basis it also began a close friendship, which Patton remembers with great fondness.

In addition to battles, Blackhorse also attempted to
destroy, wherever possible, the VC political infrastructure that existed in many villages under U.S. control.
One such operation, called Treasure Isle, occurred in
the village of Tan Binh, which was a few miles east of
Lai Khe, in Binh Duong Province. The majority of the
villagers were very old men or little boys, and women of
various ages. Most of the younger men had already left

the hamlets to either join or avoid the VC. To destroy the VC organization in the village Patton decided to use a technique called a "soft cordon," first suggested by Lieutenant General Walter T. "Dutch" Kerwin, the same officer who had accompanied Beatrice Patton to Europe in 1945 after her husband's accident. Kerwin, Commanding General (CG) II FFV and later Vice Chief of Staff of the U.S. Army, called for a long-term sealing off of a village with the hope of forcing the VC out into the open. The soft cordon of Tan Binh began with U.S. troops moving into positions after dark. To divert attention, a night strike was conducted in an area just north of the village; its artillery, mortar fire, and tank searchlights were designed actually to assist the cordon, yet also work as a deception.

After the ring was set, no one was allowed either to enter or to leave the village. As morning broke, a helicopter with a loudspeaker flew overhead announcing that the village was surrounded by Free World forces. Blackhorse troops then began moving through the village, talking with the people and showing movies that were designed to expose the errors in VC propaganda and the true nature of VC tactics and motives. MEDCAP and DENTCAP programs were initiated.

For the residents of Tan Binh, it was an unusual situation but one that provided services not readily available to the people of that region. For the VC in the village the noose tightened as interrogation personnel set up a central location to process those suspected of either collaboration or direct involvement in VC operations. The list of suspects was long, but at the end of the eight days it was apparent the action had been quite successful. The Blackhorse 3rd Squadron had processed seventy VC supporters and detained an additional thirty-two personnel. Of the 102, twenty-two proved to be VC, forty-six were VC village members, and the remaining thirty-four proved to be either draft dodgers or deserters. The operation not only netted the United

States a number of VC but was pulled off without a shot being fired.

Blackhorse also built schools, constructed playgrounds, and even put together a fifty-foot defense tower for one village. Water pumps were installed for irrigation, and arrangements were made for crop seeds. Medical personnel went so far as to inoculate domestic animals against disease. Clothing was also provided to the village children. *"Our generosity was often overlooked,"* says Patton. *"One time, in a village called Binh Co, elements of the 919th Engineer Company, which was organic to Blackhorse, were laying a foundation for a new school and playground. As a vehicle carrying water and food for American troops approached, it hit a mine buried in the road, wounding two soldiers and destroying the vehicle. The mine location must have been well known to some of the villagers. Yet, within thirty minutes of the incident other dedicated engineers were back onsite to finish the playground job even without orders."* Following the explosion and the almost unbelievable sight of other U.S. engineers completing the unfinished work, Patton remembers, reports began to come in on a regular basis, alerting the American troops as to where additional mines might be located. The reports came almost exclusively from children.

While Patton and his troops attempted to build permanent structures in the midst of war, his own command maintained a very austere forward command post, in the Bien Hoa area. In fact, the main command post was trained to move within two hours, day or night.

Numerous battles were fought under Patton's command, but several found him in the forefront of the fighting. One, at Chanh Luu, occurred in early August 1968. As the battle began to unfold, Patton and others, including General Abrams, moved towards the fight by helicopter. The press also got wind of the action, as did

Major General Tuan, the South Vietnamese 5th Division CG. Just after landing a soldier came running up to Patton saying the ARVN had trapped some VC in a hole. Patton went over with O'Meara and found the situation in pandemonium. Near an area with a long, low warehouse Patton saw a group of ARVN soldiers running around out of control, with little idea of how to get the VC from two long holes under the northwest side of the building.

"*I slowly moved up on one of the holes,*" says Patton. "*I could see from my angle an arm holding a hand grenade. I went back and asked O'Meara to cover me as I grabbed a smoke grenade from an ARVN soldier and went back towards the hole. I crept up and dropped the grenade in. At the same time we had the ARVN yelling for the VC to surrender. The VC, coughing and spitting from the smoke, hollered back, 'I'm not coming out, come and get me!' With that I pulled my pistol and moved to a better position inside a door. O'Meara meanwhile was located directly in front. A moment later the VC came out of the hole with grenades in both hands and O'Meara, with the best angle, shot him and killed him.*"

One of the largest Blackhorse battles began inauspiciously on September 5, 1968, when the 11th received intelligence from a defector that led them into battle against the famed Dong Ngai Regiment. The situation began developing early, when it was learned that an executive officer of the K4 Battalion, Dong Ngai Regiment, was ready to defect. Information had been gathered by an ARVN Major Phouc, District Chief of Chau Thanh District, Binh Duong Province, that the enemy soldier would give himself up in Chanh Luu. Later that day the pickup was completed as planned, and the NVA defector was quickly evacuated.

In such a situation, as always, the key was debriefing the defector and moving troops into the area. Every second counted, since the defector would soon be missed and the best opportunities would pass. The

defector, known as Ka, gave the Blackhorse intelligence
personnel some features to look for; these were accepted at face value. Within thirty minutes the air cavalry troop had inserted two squads of the aero-rifle
platoon into the area he had identified. Ka was able to
give approximate locations of soldiers from the K4 Battalion which were along the northern and western
boundaries of the Blackhorse area of operations.

The squads advanced across a broad hill, devoid of
vegetation, moving towards a line of trees. They quickly
drew fire from the enemy, who upon taking return fire
started withdrawing to the north. The pursuing
Blackhorse troops forced rapid enemy movement.
Meanwhile, overhead, Patton was circling the area in
his helicopter and noticed four enemy going into a ravine, later nicknamed Mulcahey Ravine by Patton in
honor of Daniel Mulcahey, then the regimental sergeant
major, who was awarded a Silver Star for the part he
played in this action.

As Patton's troops were moving into the ravine the
helicopters were ordered to direct massive firepower
into enemy positions from an altitude of one hundred
feet. On the ground, the platoons soon uncovered a
tunnel complex and began dropping concussion and
fragmentation grenades into the holes. As the situation
on the ground was developing Patton sent in the remainder of the aero-rifle platoon and increased the gunship support for protection. Once the gunships lifted,
the ground troops came under heavy enemy fire from
the trees and the same tunnel complex.

Near the ravine, Patton instructed his pilot to land.
He jumped out and crawled into a position which put
the VC between Patton and the aero-rifle platoon. At
the same time infantry arrived on the scene, and Patton
ordered them into the ravine to flush out the enemy.
"The lieutenant in charge was obviously terrified," says
Patton. *"I repeated my order to search the ravine from
north to south. He said he would, but just stood there. I
looked at him and said, 'Are you going to move out?'*

He muttered, 'Well, I want a little more fire support.'
'God damn it, then follow me,'" Patton replied, and
took the lead with O'Meara, the lieutenant and his men
close behind. Patton, with the small column of troops,
moved forward and heard a groan about twenty meters
to the front. Taking no chances, Patton and O'Meara
lobbed four grenades into the area and then advanced
through the creekbed at the bottom of the ravine. Moving cautiously, they came upon a wounded VC; the others had disappeared into the jungle. As in so many
other fights, the enemy had evaporated. Yet Patton once
again had proved a willingness to lead in person when
necessary.

On September 24, 1968, Patton was awakened at
4:00 A.M. with word that B Troop had come under
heavy fire. One vehicle was reported destroyed and a
soldier was dead, with three others wounded. Patton
immediately had the area sealed off awaiting first light,
when troops could effectively get in to find the enemy.
The seal was completed quickly, and a little less than
five hours later Patton had B Troop hook up with the
ARVN 36th Ranger Battalion in a tandem movement.
With the area covered by B Troop, the Rangers began
to take solid positions. As they moved through the
sparse trees and hedgerows, fire erupted from the enemy, hitting an ARVN lieutenant and blowing off both
his legs. Fire and smoke were filling the area as Patton
landed and spotted O'Meara carrying out the wounded
officer.

The ARVN lieutenant was in bad shape, and Patton,
studying the situation, told O'Meara to use his aircraft
if medical support was not available. A moment later
Patton noticed two Rangers escorting a prisoner. The
POW was young, perhaps eighteen years old, and wearing only a pair of trunks. Patton looked at the mutilated
ARVN soldier being moved to the helicopter, and his
anger erupted; he turned to the prisoner and slapped
him across the face. "I was hopping mad," says Patton.

"But the real irony was watching as the wounded soldier and the prisoner shared my chopper on the way out."

Patton stayed on the ground and moved into the contact zone, where the ARVN were disorganized and shaken by the loss of their commander. B Troop meanwhile was doing a good job against the enemy, using .50-caliber machine guns and moving rapidly to engage the enemy. Patton, at the same time, was rounding up the ARVN and starting towards a house from which heavy fire was emanating. The house, as they later learned, helped disguise a tunnel opening. Patton got a good angle on the structure with an M79 grenade launcher and began to fire against the walls with such intensity that one wall gave way completely. Still, to everyone's amazement, fire continued to come from the mass of rubble, including an RPG (rocket-propelled grenade) round which rocked the American position back and forth like a pendulum. Patton called for a helicopter with a loudspeaker to ask for enemy surrender. The VC refused to give up the fight, and Patton, in a move he later called foolish, advanced with a smoke grenade, found the tunnel opening, and dropped it into the hole. *"Nobody was doing anything, and I decided enough was enough,"* said Patton later.

Meanwhile, as the VC withdrew further into the tunnel, Patton's troops were able to throw twenty-four pounds of explosives down the entrance and detonate it. The ground was churned up, yet the VC emerged again to carry on the battle. Patton then ordered another run at the hole, and troops exploded an additional forty pounds of explosives in the tunnel system and silenced the fire. The action resulted in sixteen VC killed and another ninety-nine captured.

In mid-October 1968, Blackhorse began preparations for operation Saginaw Lake. This was a carefully coordinated plan in which the 11th Cavalry, plus two infantry battalions and the air cavalry troop, were to assault an area two miles east of the Song Be River, and

approximately ten miles southeast of Phuoc Vinh. The
mission, highly classified and attended by much covert
deception, was to rescue a small group of American
POWs, some of whom it was said had been held captive
for over three years. The preliminary planning phase
involved the insertion of a Vietnamese Provincial Reconnaissance Unit (PRU), which was supported and
trained by Americans. The PRU consisted of twelve
well-trained soldiers whose mission it was to lie in ambush for two or three days and then try to capture an
enemy soldier. The soldier then would be questioned as
to the existence of American prisoners. The PRU was
dropped in by helicopter at 8:00 A.M. on October 17. By
1:00 P.M. they had gained contact with the enemy and in
a skirmish killed three VC and wounded a few others.
However, the PRU leader was also killed in the fight,
and the PRU immediately called for reinforcements,
which Patton provided by sending in an aero-rifle platoon, plus one company of mechanized infantry.

As the story emerged, it was learned the PRU had
actually engaged rear elements of an NVA company. In
the ambush they had attacked its administrative and
medical personnel, some of whom were not over sixteen
years of age.

Patton was informed about the ambush and quickly
took to the air to help in finding the NVA, now moving
quickly away from the fight. Flying in a chopper close
by, Major John Bahnsen, nicknamed "Doc," quickly
discovered a "Charlie" heading into the underbrush
and opened fire. The enemy soldier jumped into a hole
filled with water, and Bahnsen zeroed in and killed him.
Though it was unknown at the time, the soldier shot by
Bahnsen was actually a point man for a large NVA
force that had been in hiding awaiting possible movement by the 11th. After killing the soldier, Bahnsen
found a spot on which to bring his chopper down and
was walking towards the hole to examine the body
when the NVA sprang a trap of their own. The ambush
caught Bahnsen and a contingent of ARP by surprise,

forcing his pilot to take off immediately to protect the craft from destruction. As gunfire erupted from every direction, Bahnsen and two dozen American troops scattered near the water hole, which afforded only minimal protection.

Bahnsen then started calling for a nearby platoon of mechanized infantry to move up and lend assistance. However, the infantry platoon, now pinned down, could not advance. Under heavy fire the ARP dragged themselves from the edge of the hole and in prone positions began answering the ambush, directing intense fire into the underbrush. Bahnsen, incensed at the momentary inaction by the mechanized infantry, at one point stood up in the middle of the firefight and started yelling at the enemy, shaking his fist at the frozen platoon, and simultaneously urging those near the hole to advance. The ARP had just begun to move forward when Patton landed and grabbed a radio to gain control over the chaotic situation. As the infantry advanced, firing as they ran, the NVA began leaping up from the grass and soon disappeared. For his bravery in the pitched battle Bahnsen would later receive the Silver Star. The sad ending to the story was that the troops searched the entire area and found no trace of American prisoners.

Two days after the action of October 17, the 11th planned to spring another ambush, ideally one more successful than the PRU effort two days previously. Patton landed near the ambush patrol west of Binh My and found the operation not being coordinated to his satisfaction. He went to the front and personally led the patrol into the woods. No sooner were they in a few yards when the terrain became choked with trees and high grass. After a few arduous minutes Patton and his troops came to a stream to be crossed; the water was chest deep, leaving the men extremely vulnerable. While fording the stream, Patton noticed trouble ahead: a few meters away there appeared to be a partially hidden bunker. Taking no chances, troops instinctively opened fire and began racing for the far side of the stream. As

Patton emerged from the water he looked down and saw his hand covered with blood. Then he glanced at his jacket and saw a ragged hole. Feeling a sharp pain in his right side, Patton knew he had been hit, probably by a ricocheting fragment.

As American troops continued searching, again finding no evidence of POWs, Patton was evacuated. At a division aid station in Lai Khe medical personnel made a decision to send Patton on to another hospital for surgery, where doctors worked unsuccessfully to extract the fragment lodged in his side, finally deciding the metal could be left where it was.

After the operation Patton was sent to a hospital ward for post-surgical recovery before returning to the 11th. Patton awoke to a room with beds lined up in rows along the walls. Glancing about he noticed a young soldier in the next bed. The soldier was a double amputee, terribly injured in battle and extremely depressed. On the third night of his stay in the hospital Patton awoke to a soft moaning sound coming from the next bunk. Carefully holding his side, Patton stepped out of bed to see if he could be of help. In the faint light he saw a pool of blood on the floor and blood-soaked sheets where the young man lay near death. In his depression the soldier had severely slashed his wrists, dying just moments after Patton's shocking discovery. For Patton this scene was a graphic reminder of the many tragedies of the Vietnam War.

Early on December 1, 1968, following an Air Force fighter strike, the 11th launched a scouting mission over the north central portion of the area called the "Catcher's Mitt." Patton's troops detected movement and also spotted a few dead VC. Flying overhead, Patton, now back in action, made a decision to insert ARP elements, which immediately drew heavy fire. Under the ground command of Lieutenant C. W. Doubleday, the troops countered quickly, inflicting numerous casualties near a series of bunkers, some measuring thirty or forty feet in length and looking from the air like pipes sunk vertically into the ground. The VC had no real firing ports but would emerge from the end of the bunkers and shoot at the low-flying helicopters circling the area. The method commonly used to defeat such bunker positions called for soldiers to crawl up on top of the ventilation pipes and drop in either smoke or concussion grenades.

By afternoon it was determined that additional firepower would be needed, because evidence indicated the entire area was a base camp for a sizeable enemy force, perhaps even the headquarters complex for the elusive Dong Ngai Regiment. The battle continued throughout the afternoon, but by nightfall enemy contact appeared to slacken, and near 11:00 P.M. the enemy virtually ceased contact. To be certain, however, troops of the 11th undertook a resupply effort, and at dawn Air Force jets conducted a bombing run into the area. Later, after the air strike, scout ships were put into the air to assess bomb damage; infantry also went out and swept the area to count enemy dead. It was clear that Blackhorse troops had killed scores of enemy soldiers who had chosen to remain in the bunkers and fight it out. The air strike, meanwhile, had undoubtedly killed many more. The enemy decision to stay and fight proved to be a major mistake, since numerous important documents were recovered. Among the captured material were maps and plans for operations set to commence the following week. Because of heavy losses and the seizing of key information, the enemy had to alter its plans, thus allowing Blackhorse to gain some tactical advantage.

The toughest fight of Patton's career occurred in a huge forest of rubber trees called the Michelin plantation. The name came from the French-owned company which produces tires and rubber goods of all types for sale worldwide. Because of the dense nature of the terrain it was an excellent operating base for large contingents of North Vietnamese regulars and VC as well.

The beginning of the operation, called Atlas Wedge, which took place during the period of March 17–24, 1969, was the result of II Field Force intelligence that indicated the 7th NVA Division was moving southward from the Loc Ninh area passing through the Michelin rubber plantation towards Saigon.

Total enemy strength was thought to be in excess of five thousand troops, plus significant amounts of material. The regiment was alerted on March 15 that it might be called upon to help block the incursion. Because his regiment had never operated in the Michelin, Patton requested and received permission to carry out early aerial reconnaissance operations. On March 17 elements of the aero-scout platoon and key commanders took off in compliance with that mission.

By 9:00 A.M. on the 17th it was clear to the Blackhorse staff that the area was occupied by a large enemy force, which was making no attempt at concealment. Patton was radioed and apprised of the situation, whereupon he quickly called headquarters to obtain clearance to fire, including B-52 strikes in the area. Because it was a matter requiring a "decision by stars," meaning a general had to approve the request, Patton was forced to wait nearly ninety minutes before the request was granted. The reason for this delay was unquestionably the ever-present political side of the war. The Michelin rubber plantation, one of the largest in the world, was under French control; they did not want their trees damaged.

After approval was obtained the battle began; it lasted throughout the day, during which time nine air strikes were directed at the enemy. Two 11th Cavalry gunships, later reinforced by 1st Division helicopters, also made repeated attacks on enemy positions. During the night of the 17–18th Patton moved the 1st and 3rd Squadrons to a position from where on the afternoon of

March 18 they rolled into the eastern portion of the Michelin. Elements of both squadrons were immediately involved in heavy fighting, inflicting numerous casualties.

Fighting continued on the 18th, resulting in an additional 123 NVA killed and scores wounded. By March 19 both squadrons, reinforced by 1st Division infantry, continued to push northwest, killing at least fifty-one more NVA. During the evening of March 19 and the morning of the following day three more B-52 strikes were requested by the 11th ACR. Following the bombings Patton sent in damage assessment teams and discovered several large enemy base camps. Again, heavy fighting ensued, with body counts showing eighty-nine enemy killed. During the battle Patton also lost one of his key commanders, when Lieutenant Colonel McEnery was wounded and evacuated; McEnery would spend nine days in the hospital and later receive the DSC for his bravery in the action in which he was wounded.

The Michelin was to be the scene of several running battles, and on March 22, aero-scouts were sent aloft to develop additional B-52 strike areas. Flying towards the northeast, they discovered the enemy evacuating wounded soldiers; Troop C under Captain Lemos Fulmer, not then in heavy contact, was diverted and moved into the area. The NVA tenaciously tried to hold its ground, but results were again disastrous for the enemy, and their losses continued to mount. On March 24 the NVA finally broke off contact, and the Atlas Wedge operation came to a close. Atlas Wedge was by far the most significant test for the 11th and for Patton as a commander. The operation not only required the 11th to operate in unfamiliar terrain but kept it in continuous contact with the enemy over a stretch of several days. Atlas Wedge resulted in several hundred NVA killed, many wounded, and scores captured.

Patton learned a number of lessons during the battle. First, it required that he stress mobility and flexibility in operations, and take account of the complicated logistical demands. It also, upon reflection, occurred to Patton that despite his military education and previous experience his planning might have been better. But as he said later, a commander never ceases to learn how to wage war. As the battle progressed, Patton was also reminded of how important it is for a commander to have the ability to forgo sleep for an uncommon number of hours or days. Looking back at the Atlas Wedge operation, Patton feels it was good for armor, for the 11th ACR, and for the Vietnam War. Nonetheless, even years later, because of the loss of life during the battles in the plantation, Patton still refuses to look at a Michelin advertisement.

One more irony of war remains a memory for Patton, who recalls that during the confusion early in the Atlas Wedge operation, as he was desperately waiting for the battle plan to be approved, he was told by one general officer, "Colonel, I'm not sure exactly what your mission is, but don't screw it up!" Patton had to laugh, since the remark in some ways captured the essence of the Vietnam struggle.

In time of war, many a soldier has pondered which side God supports, and down through the ages military chaplains have been summoned to help commanders. General George S. Patton, Jr., called on a chaplain during the famous Battle of the Bulge to write and deliver a prayer for clear weather; George Patton, in turn, while in Vietnam asked Bob Hawn, chaplain, to write a "Blackhorse Prayer." It was delivered on Sunday, January 26, 1969, and included the verse: "Our heavenly Father, we of the 11th Cavalry are professional military men with the mission of destroying the enemy. At times it may seem that we stray from your ways, but we are striving to bring peace and freedom to this country and the world."

Patton often quoted the prayer and was surprised and pleased some months after leaving Vietnam to get a package from Chaplain Hawn, who sent him a set of brigadier general stars and a short note. It said, "I hope I'm not being presumptuous, I just know your ability and what the future holds in store for you. May these 'Blessed Stars' help in your future to remind you of your responsibilities to those you lead, to the Nation and to your service to God." He concluded with, "You are deeply and sorely missed in every aspect here in the Blackhorse Regiment."

For every successful operation in war, there are others filled with frailties and mistakes that cost lives. In late December 1968, Patton was called upon to inspect a fire base, called "Jack," which was being abandoned by elements of the 1st Division. When moving out of an operational area, troops were ordered to make sure nothing was left behind that "Charlie" could use. Patton decided to go to the fire base and make sure things were proceeding correctly. As his helicopter landed in a large field, Patton told the pilot to shut down the engine and with two others headed out on a walking tour of the area. Armed only with pistols and light weapons, they started checking the base. As Patton walked he looked back and saw the door gunners were out of the helicopter sunning themselves. Concentrating on scanning the deserted area for usable debris, the group was shocked to hear a burst of fire from a position about a hundred yards away. Sergeant Major Mulcahey went down with the first blast, and Patton dropped to the ground and crawled back to a nearby hole. Pinned down by the gunfire and without a radio, Patton tried to hand-signal the chopper, but the crew members were flat on the ground and could not get into the helicopter without being hit. Trapped without a radio or a machine gun and knowing Mulcahey lay wounded in the field, Patton realized he had made a serious error.

The helicopter crew members at length worked their way back into the chopper and cranked it up. Seconds later the helicopter hopped the two hundred yards to Patton as the door gunners blasted away at the enemy position. In the cloud of dust created by the chopper,

Patton climbed in and had the pilot move another fifty yards to the spot where Mulcahey lay shot in both legs. Under fire, the right door gunner, Corporal Tom Vogt, was able to get the sergeant major into the helicopter, which then flew on to Lai Khe, where medical treatment was provided. For saving Mulcahey's life Tom Vogt was awarded the Silver Star.

Because of the incident at the fire base, Patton modified procedures, and from that day forward choppers always had their rotors turning for a quick exit. Personnel were also instructed to carry a radio when leaving the immediate area and under such circumstances door gunners were ordered to remain ready at their guns.

Another mistake of sorts occurred in early January 1969, when Patton decided to check on some of his A Troop, which was working in the An Loc area. As Patton arrived by air he saw a convoy of American vehicles moving at high speed through what appeared to be an ambush. The drivers were practically standing on the running boards for a quick exit in case the trucks were hit. Patton circled the area at about five hundred feet looking for a place to land. The pilot found a spot on the east side of Highway 13 and put the chopper down by a group of ACAVs (armored cavalry assault vehicles) in order to ensure some security.

After landing, Patton hustled up Highway 13 on foot to the spot where A Troop personnel were now gathering. Patton quickly called together a group of officers and noncoms to get a status report on the ambush. The battle, near Quan Loi in Binh Long Province, had started as 1st Lieutenant Harold A. Fritz of Troop A, 1st Squadron, was leading his tank column on Highway 13. As the seven vehicles moved cautiously along the road a withering enemy crossfire attack caught the column. Fritz was hit and wounded but, heroically, he jumped to the top of his burning vehicle and directed the setting of a defensive position. He then ran from vehicle to vehicle helping the wounded and fighting the advancing enemy. Finally, Fritz, with a pistol and bayonet, led a counterattack which sent the enemy fleeing.

As Patton, Major Dozier, the regimental S-3, and the others were discussing the ambush, which would later result in Fritz being awarded the Medal of Honor, an RPG round whistled in and exploded nearby. The startled group hit the ground. Patton looked around and spotted Dozier bleeding profusely from a fragment that had pierced his arm. Miraculously, the force and shrapnel of the RPG had missed everyone else, including Patton. Dozier was quickly moved to a helicopter for evacuation, but here was another lesson, which Patton relearned and then put to use in commanding his regiment: No matter what, in a war zone, be it seemingly peaceful or secure, avoid standing in a group.

Patton's meritorious actions in command of the 11th earned him a variety of medals. In fact, in less than six weeks of intense action in the fall of 1968, Patton was twice awarded the Distinguished Service Cross, plus the Silver Star, all for extreme bravery. Patton also received the Purple Heart for wounds received in battle; the Air Medal for a series of twenty-five aerial missions in command and support of combat operations; and the Legion of Merit (First Oak Leaf Cluster) for "meritorious service while serving in a succession of assignments during the period January 1968 to April 1969." In addition, he received two awards for bravery from the South Vietnamese government, the first a Gallantry Cross with Bronze Star and the second a Gallantry Cross with Silver Star. Concerning the medals given him by the South Vietnamese, Patton later said, "I refused to wear the decorations, in view of the tragedy of Vietnam and the way in which U.S. forces left in disgraceful haste."

On the battlefield, Patton, after many months in the fight and seeking to fulfill his military heritage, admits to becoming *"pretty warlike."* His diary notations would seem to confirm this. In an entry dated September 4, 1968, he writes, *"I earned my pay this day."* Next to the entry is a follow-up note dated December 22, in which Patton writes, *"Apparently someone else thought so too. I just got the DSC* [Distinguished Service Cross]. *Well, Daddy, I'm trying!"* Then, in October 1968, Patton wrote, *"My inclination and total upbringing is to ATTACK. I have a lot of physical and moral courage. I'm getting to be a legend here and I must not overdo my part."*

It is clear Patton enjoyed the challenge of war, the smell of battle, and pride of command; he was not anxious to leave Vietnam. Ruth Ellen wrote a letter to her brother in January 1969 in which she dispensed some advice and reminded him of family history. In it she said it was perfectly understandable that he was not eager to come home, because "it means the end of something that has meant very much to you. You have been doing what you have been trained to do all of your life, and what you wanted to do; a race horse loves to race, a fighting cock loves to fight, a soldier of your calibre loves to soldier, and when the tour is over you know you will go back to the humdrum that you hate, and you, subconsciously or consciously, dread it." Ruth went on to caution, "Don't talk so bloody-minded to people as you do to me. I understand—I heard Daddy lament the passing of his fighting days after WW I. But if others—and everyone is jealous of your reputation and your decorations and your accomplishments—hear you talking with such blood lust, they will start a whispering campaign, as they did about Daddy, and for many of the same reasons you will be badly hurt and heart broken, as he was."

Joanne at this time was also concerned about comments in the press concerning George and expressed her feelings during a short respite they enjoyed together in Hawaii. In a letter to Ruth, she said, "George looks

marvelous. I have never seen him so lean and fit looking, albeit weary, but he is wound up pretty tight. I
tried to persuade him that the image of the professional
killer could use some tempering for public consump-
tion."

On the home front, Joanne and Ruth Ellen, along
with other family members, provided strong support
for Patton, and he frequently called upon them to visit
or phone the families of soldiers either killed or
wounded in battle. The family felt this was an important aspect, and extension, of Patton's command. These
visits were arranged without word to the media; it was
purely a personal, Patton family statement.

Patton, in spite of some of the publicity regarding his
feelings about being a professional military man, also
showed a very personal, and, in family tradition, a
tender side as well. In a diary notation in 1968 he
writes longingly of his wife. *"She is a real pro,"* he
writes, and then notes how intelligent and beautiful she
is. He concludes with, *"Joanne is such a great wife and
mother to us all."* Fellow officers also realized how important Joanne was to the Patton team, one saying,
"She was a wonderful influence on him," and another
commenting that she "tempered his comments" and
was the "perfect military wife."

Patton, like his father, also enjoyed writing poetry
and continued to do so on occasion throughout his
Army career. Near the end of his tour as commander of
the 11th ACR he wrote a poem about Helicopter 552,
which he called "Little Sorrel V," the last in a series of
his command aircraft; the original Little Sorrel had
been a mare ridden by the famed Confederate general
Thomas J. "Stonewall" Jackson. About the last Little
Sorrel, Patton wrote:

*You have done your part, through blistering heat and
Monsoon storms; through battle smoke, o'er jungle and
Burning fields. You've borne me faithfully.*

As did your namesake, in an earlier war, bear yet
   another
Leader far more apt than I before those sacred ranks of
Grey through Bull Run, Sharpsburg and then to final
Destiny at Chancellorsville—beneath the Virginia sky.

And as that supple mare jogged with her stern rider
Through those heroic years, a heritage was born which
   you
Would carry on. She, tho moving not so fast as you and
Tied to earth, helped him to act to mystify the foe with
Bold maneuver conjured up in mind.

Your gift was battle sense, a view of ground below that
   we
Might feel the points to place our power—to fight, to
   kill,
To chase, to fail and sometimes lose; but yet to start
   again
With confidence that we would overcome.

Your name, symbolically, has helped to forge command
Projecting it to sweating men below who face death
   daily
By my command and will. It recalls him who named you
First and who, on long hard days, seemed to sit by me
   as I
Rode above the land I've fought three years to hold—
   from
Tyranny.

Goodbye, old friend.

Though scarred by searing steel you, like your namesake,

Never failed the rider. What more can a cavalryman ask
   of
His own steed? Faithful, reliable, responsive, quick to
   turn

And dangerous to the foe.

I leave you now. Command me not to go!

—G.S. Patton
Col, Armor, Cmdg.
11th U.S. Cavalry

George S. Patton departed Vietnam on orders to the United States Army Primary Helicopter Center at Fort Wolters, Texas. His original orders, to the Army Armor School at Fort Knox, Kentucky, were changed because the Army leadership had decided that since the helicopter had shown itself to be so decisive on the battlefields of Vietnam, helicopter orientation and training should be provided to selected senior officers who would be continuing on active duty. It turned out that Patton was at the top of the list. After much thought and conversation with his family, General Abrams, and Major General Bob Williams, the senior Army aviator in Southeast Asia, Patton accepted this assignment in lieu of the scheduled Armor School position as Director of the Weapons Department.

Before leaving, Patton took the time to say individual goodbyes to his soldiers, visiting every regimental unit, including the contingent at Xuan Loc base camp. Emotional at times, especially when remembering the eighty-six troopers who died while under his command, Patton told his men that he admired their courage and perseverance. He also emphasized the accomplishments of the 11th ACR. In fact, his beloved regiment during the years of fighting in Vietnam had suffered fewer than 650 killed in action, and less than 5,500 wounded. Its members' bravery resulted in scores of medals, including three Medals of Honor, two of which were awarded posthumously.

John McEnery recalls that Patton's change of command was also an emotional experience. "General Abrams was there and he pinned a DSC on Patton," says McEnery. Following the ceremony, in which he said goodbye to his commanders and staff, Patton, not wishing to take anything away from the new Blackhorse commander, Colonel Jimmy Leach, departed by helicopter for Long Binh. His war was over, and, as McEnery recalled, "Patton flew off like someone going into the sunset."

Patton, having served in battle for the last time, departed Vietnam with mixed emotions. Pleased with the duties he had performed, intensely proud of his Blackhorse troopers, but eager to return to home and family, he sensed a feeling of foreboding and doubt. This *"sensing"* included a high degree of uneasiness concerning the future of Vietnam and the war. His thoughts and prayers reached out to such personalities as Creighton Abrams, Orwin Talbott, Jim Dozier, Meritte Ireland, Jim Leach, and all the other friends and close associates who *"continued dedicated service in that tortured land."* He believed that the people of the United States had finally lost their interest in a successful conclusion to the war, if they had had any to start with. Patton's concerns were deep, but he says, *"In retrospect, I did my best."*

In later years, *"after much reflection and a good deal of personal soul searching,"* Patton listed five principles that he says he learned the hard way during his thirty-three months in Vietnam. He wrote, *"These principles constitute my particular offering to those who deal with 'counterinsurgency' warfare. I consider them vital to any hope for success on this type of battlefield."*

Patton's Five Principles for Counterinsurgency Warfare

I

The nine classic principles of war as explained and demonstrated by Clausewitz definitely apply in this type of conflict. One principle should be added and that would be the principle of cultural understanding or familiarization.

II

Operations should be guided by good intelligence "now," as opposed to refined intelligence, for example, two hours from now.

III

Fully understand the form of warfare in a Vietnam type of conflict—call it counterinsurgency or whatever term is being used to characterize the so-called meeting engagement. Go within the training base and develop doctrine at all levels which supports this form of combat.

IV

When contact with an enemy unit is either present or expected, the commander must always hold a unit close in hand and in reserve to commit upon hostile contact. This reinforcement capability is absolutely critical in guerrilla warfare.

V

A commander may talk all day and most of the night on the subject of preventative maintenance in the field. However, it simply is not well done on the battlefield as there are far too many distractions, interruptions and poor facilities. As a result of my experience, I believe the best procedure is periodic withdrawal of armored units to a safe rear area where higher-echelon maintenance personnel can provide valid assistance. Although those who oppose that procedure would contest it all the way, I found that armored vehicle availability, especially tanks, increased in the long term.

12

LAURELS FOR THE SOLDIER

Sir, John Hays is riding in every vehicle in this column.
— B Troop 1st Sergeant

Observing events and American involvement in Vietnam and Southeast Asia through the years, Patton and many contemporaries saw a continual watering-down of objectives as administrations changed from Kennedy to Johnson and on to Richard Nixon. It simply became less and less clear what the White House, and indeed the Congress, was asking the military to accomplish. The leaders in the White House were, in large part, being driven by public opinion in the United States and, according to those on the scene, did not realize the effect on the military. However, Patton says, *"The deep level of dissent at home never permeated the theater while I was in Vietnam and therefore I could not see how important and vital it was until I came home in April 1969. But it hit me right between the eyes the night the 'Freedom Bird' arrived at Travis Air Force Base near San Francisco."*

After landing Patton stopped by the Air Force ticket office to purchase a commercial plane ticket to Washington, D.C., his home at the time. As he stood at the counter, filling out forms, one of his senior NCOs, who had been on the same aircraft, came in to report a disturbance in the outside parking lot. *"On this particular flight,"* recalls Patton, *"were three coffins, containing the remains of three Army soldiers."* As Patton walked out the door into the parking area, he saw that the coffins were the target of *"a group of hippies who were throwing garbage on them."* Patton's first reaction was to wade into *"this terribly tragic affair"* and do what he could to disperse the crowd. As he started to move an NCO pleaded, "No, Colonel. Please go back inside! We will handle this one." *"And they did!"* says Patton. *"The last I saw of those who had desecrated our dead comrades was a blue USAF pickup truck moving out with no less than six sets of legs hanging over the tailgate. I have no idea what their final disposition was, but I knew immediately that things had drastically changed on the homefront.*

"In the field, however, we felt we had a job to do and it took up all of our time. That was not the case with the enemy, who zeroed in on the protests in America and used them in the field," says Patton. This was made very clear one afternoon when Patton's unit ambushed an enemy contingent. One of the people killed was a North Vietnamese soldier whose principal duty, it appeared, was to incite his fellow soldiers to fight harder. When the Blackhorse troopers went through the dead man's rucksack they were shocked to find pictures and articles, in Vietnamese, about Jane Fonda and other well known dissenters of the war. The material, when translated, was found to demonstrate to North Vietnamese soldiers that famous Americans were in support of the North, and additionally that a majority of Americans were critical of U.S. operations and were in the streets protesting. Besides Fonda, there were news clips about Dr. Benjamin Spock and former Attorney General Ramsey Clark. The troops also found cassette tapes containing Senator J. William Fulbright's derogatory statements concerning the Vietnam conflict. The North

Vietnamese had dubbed in Vietnamese translations after his recorded comments. Patton later had the tapes copied and sent to the Senator, who never acknowledged receipt.

O'Meara remembers recovering a great deal of enemy propaganda. "Most of it contained anti-American themes," says O'Meara. "The material was written for reading by their own soldiers, and would usually say the American commitment was shallow. Interestingly, the propaganda would never mention they were communists. In fact, they would say they were non-communists. Obviously that was a facade."

Many incidents exemplify the American soldiers Patton served with in Vietnam, who he feels were extremely dedicated. He stated time and again that these were the best soldiers he had ever seen in combat, far excelling those he served with in Korea. Patton says they were superb, considering they were given difficult missions where the rules of engagement were not only complicated but also ever-changing. *"As an example,"* Patton remarks, *"what does one tell Sergeant Jones whose orders are to patrol and secure a local village? Can he shoot? Must he wait to be shot at? What are his specific instructions for engaging possibly hostile forces?"*

Despite the problems faced by American soldiers, they fought on bravely and with commitment. One story in particular demonstrates the loyalty of American soldiers to the cause. It involved a soldier named Stetson, a member of the air cavalry troop. He had been slightly wounded in the arm and was pulled into a nearby ditch to await a "dustoff" (a helicopter designated for medical evacuation). Because a medevac chopper could not be flown in soon enough to remove him, a decision was made to have a regular scout ship take him to the hospital. Moving into position, the chopper experienced partial engine failure over the ditch and settled. The tail rotor slammed into Stetson, instantly severing one arm.

Patton went to the hospital soon after to check on the injured trooper. He learned that although the soldier would live, despite losing his right arm, he was still in critical condition. After checking Stetson's situation Patton left, planning to return for a visit in the next few days. Patton always scheduled hospital visits at least once every ten days; however, a couple of days after the helicopter injury Patton received word of major problems at the hospital involving Stetson. Very busy at the time of the call, Patton passed a message back saying he would be there as soon as possible. "No," came the reply, "this is a serious problem with Stetson, please come immediately." Patton arrived at Stetson's bedside to find a depressed and angry soldier. He asked what he could do to help.

Stetson looked up and said in a sorrowful voice, "Sir, I'm being evacuated to Japan tomorrow and these sons of bitches won't let me sew an 11th Cavalry patch on my bathrobe!"

Patton started to choke with emotion and said, "Is that what you wanted to see me about?"

"Yes, sir," said Stetson. "I'm proud of my country and my service. I did a damn good job for you. I want to wear this patch on my way out."

Patton, his eyes welling with tears, grabbed the bathrobe and the patch and headed for the hospital commander's office. The next day he went down to see Stetson's departure, and as the wounded soldier passed by, lying on the stretcher, he winked at Patton and saluted his commander with his left arm. His Blackhorse patch was clearly visible on the bathrobe.

Another story concerning the type of American soldier Patton knew involved a fellow named Robert Roeder. Roeder was severely wounded by a claymore mine, an antipersonnel weapon that spewed small pieces of deadly metal. Patton went to the hospital as the soldier was being wheeled into surgery. He was under sedation at the time. The hospital commander was standing nearby, and Patton whispered, "Doc, how does it look?"

He slowly shook his head, "I don't think he's going to make it."

Patton looked down at the soldier on the stretcher and one of Roeder's eyes slowly opened, fixed a steely glare on the surgeon, and said, "Fuck you, Doc, I'll make it!" And he did.

Then there was the day Patton went to check on a troop in the An Loc area who were in support of the 1st Infantry Division. After landing he heard gunfire about a quarter-mile ahead and started up the road to see if he could locate and check on his people. Moving cautiously, Patton identified a lone soldier also heading towards the battle. It was not entirely unusual, except the soldier was hobbling along on crutches. Patton ran ahead a few feet and noted that the soldier, bearing an M-16, had a cast on his leg. Still closer, Patton recognized the Blackhorse patch. He stopped the soldier and shouted, "Just who the hell are you and what are you doing here in this condition!"

The trooper gave his name and his unit, and then said, "Sir, you got me."

Patton, perplexed, deduced that the soldier was AWOL (absent without leave) from the hospital. "Sergeant, what's your excuse for being AWOL?"

"Sir," he replied, "I was hit a couple of days ago in this area and I'm worried about the men I left behind. See, sir, I have some new men and I decided to come on up and check on 'em. You know, I'm responsible for getting them home." Inspired by the soldier's dedication Patton had the AWOL charges dropped.

Patton while in Vietnam also experienced the brilliant ability of medical personnel on the battlefield. *"The medics were simply the best and this was exemplified for me in late July 1968, in an area close to the Michelin rubber plantation,"* says Patton. As Patton landed in his helicopter to check on a column of troops he had spotted from the air, he noted a mine-clearing team busy on the road. While hustling toward the front of the pack he looked to his right and saw a soldier walking cautiously a few feet off the trail. A moment later there was a tremendous explosion. Thrown to the ground and momentarily dazed, Patton thought a mortar round had hit with deadly accuracy. Looking down and seeing he was splattered with blood, numbly wondering if he had been hit, he suddenly realized there was a hole in the jungle where the soldier had been walking a minute before. Patton, still fighting to gather his wits, could see no sign of him, nothing except decimated foliage.

In a matter of seconds, people realized the explosion had been caused by a land mine and began searching for signs of life. In the trees above the spot where the soldier had been walking the troops made a gruesome discovery: hanging from the twisted branches was a shredded flak jacket; a few feet to the left were a wallet and a helmet. Within moments voices cried, "Medic! Medic!" Nearly fifty feet away someone had spotted the soldier. Patton moved through a mine-cleared area to reach him, but he was unprepared for what he saw. The soldier was lying on the ground, his clothing blown away. He was missing both legs and bleeding profusely from his wounds. The shock was terrific, and in all of Patton's experience he had never seen anything like it. The soldier was barely breathing as the medic ran up, dropped to his knees, and started administering artificial respiration.

The lifesaving efforts continued for several minutes before troops could locate a stretcher and begin moving him to Patton's helicopter for evacuation. The medic had nothing available to place over the mutilated soldier and precious little time anyway, and as they were racing back through the column Patton noted the faces of the tank crews. Mortified at the sight, they were stunned into silence—everyone, that is, except the medic, who maintained complete control trying to save the man's life. The soldier died before they could reach the chopper, but the medic was fearless throughout, and Patton awarded him the Bronze Star.

The battlefields of Vietnam were filled with many heroic acts of bravery, and officers in combat like Dozier witnessed many examples. "The American army in Vietnam learned our training was very good," says Dozier. "When they learned how well they were trained, they blossomed in combat. The American soldier was first-class. In a year I saw only one incident which approached cowardice." Andy O'Meara concurs, "The U.S. soldier was really superb; they were enthusiastic and optimistic. We had exceptional morale."

Despite the high level of dedication there were some incidents that brought disgrace to the military. There is no denying, by military officers and others, that several events did irreparable harm to the war effort. The most famous incident was the My Lai massacre, about which Patton says, *"The stupidity and senseless brutality of that sordid happening was, in my mind, partially caused by the deployment program of Robert McNamara. We were simply getting to the bottom of the barrel in the regular Army because the president had decided against mobilization of Army Reserve and National Guard units, a major decision which, following the Vietnam period, took at least twenty years to cure."*

My Lai was located in an I Corps province called Quang Ngai. The murder of nearly 150 unarmed civilians occurred on March 16, 1968, when a platoon leader, William Calley, Jr., and his twenty-five men rounded up people and slaughtered them indiscriminately. The events of that day included not only murders but rapes and other atrocities. The incidents for the most part went unreported by either Calley's immediate superior or even by the division commander, Major General Samuel Koster. When the My Lai events finally came to light some thirteen months after the killings, Lieutenant Calley, along with others up and down the chain of command, faced a variety of charges. Calley was eventually convicted on murder charges and sentenced to life imprisonment. The others who were charged were found not guilty. Additionally, twelve officers faced court-martials for dereliction of duty. Koster, as punishment, was demoted to brigadier general, and his chief of staff was censured.

While in Vietnam as G-3 Patton had the opportunity to review General Koster's after-action "Senior Officer Debriefing Report." In Patton's opinion the report contained nothing particularly revealing. Patton is convinced Koster either was uninformed about the incident, as division commander at the time of the report, or was unwilling to mention it. As Patton says, *"In either case he was responsible and accepted the punishment without question."*

In the case of Lieutenant Calley, Patton elaborates, *"Here was an individual slipping through the cracks due to our need for junior officers. It was simply a case of not receiving enough raw material to choose from and thus having to take, in a few cases, second-best. We were so stretched that somehow this unsatisfactory officer got through the quality control strainer of what an officer is and is not, and so a situation got tragically out of hand. My own theory is that we were indeed lucky not to have had more Calleys. The worst case scenario is that possibly we did and don't know about them, their actions lost in the fog of war."*

An army in the field has trouble keeping everything under control, and clearly Calley was one example. Though they went nearly unreported, the military also had isolated discipline problems which resulted in death threats and, at times, "fragging." The term originates from the act of tossing a fragmentation grenade at a fellow soldier. Although no one was fragged in Patton's command, shortly after he departed Vietnam a major Patton had known at West Point was murdered this way; a grenade was rolled under his bed while he slept and exploded. His widow was never told how he actually died, only that he was killed in action, which, as Patton says, was in a sense a true statement. Many times fraggings stemmed from someone trying to enforce discipline or in retaliation for the decisions made by a particular individual on the battlefield. Some claim drugs also contributed, and Patton readily agrees. He goes further to say he is convinced that drug abuse contributed to the My Lai massacre.

Vietnam was a most interesting country to Patton, and over his three tours of duty he noted changes in the landscape and a people so affected by war. In the span of those six years he also noted a great deal of difference between the ARVN soldier vintage 1962 and those who fought in 1968. Along the way Patton met and became friends with many South Vietnamese Army officers, most of whom he later lost contact with after the North overran the South. In the early years, Patton met Duong Van Minh, known as "Big Minh" by the Americans. He also became acquainted with Nguyen Van Thieu, who before becoming president had commanded the 5th Division (ARVN). Later, when Thieu was president of South Vietnam, Patton briefed him a number of times on various actions in his sector. He found Thieu to be *"fairly dedicated"* and *"generally"* interested in the war effort. Of the many other South Vietnamese officers Patton came to know, he says, *"a majority impressed me with their desire to win, whatever win means in a war such as that. That question, 'What does win mean?' was a major item of discussion in the Pentagon from 1965–1970."*

Patton's assessments were formed mainly in his final tour, since in the early years he found the South Vietnamese officers were not particularly aggressive and in many cases were known to tamper with the payroll. *"I*

*believe the simple soldier wasn't as bad as many mem-
bers of the ARVN officer corps,"* says Patton. *"The
basic ARVN soldier that many of us came to know
seemed to require two things: to be paid regularly and
have the chance to care for his family. If he had those
two commodities, together with reasonably effective
leadership, he would do well."* However, it was very
clear to Patton over the years that the South Vietnamese
soldiers lacked the motivation of their enemy. Patton
recalls warning contemporaries as early as 1962 that
the United States had a long way to go with the ARVN
soldier. Most agree with Patton's assessment, including
Andy O'Meara, who says, "The South Vietnamese soldier was only as good as his leader, and those with
good missions tended to do well. The others didn't.
One must remember that during the American buildup
the ARVN was relegated to guard duty and things like
that. Units with such missions tended to stagnate."

However, in one area at least O'Meara feels the
ARVN had a clear edge over the Americans. "When it
came to village searches," says O'Meara, "we would
use the South Vietnamese soldiers whenever possible.
That was because Americans didn't really know how to
search a "hooch" (G.I. slang for a residence). We didn't
know how they stored their rice and where good hiding
places were likely to be. The Vietnamese soldiers knew
these things instinctively."

In a similar vein, Patton recalls a village search
where a Korean officer was assisting and was told by
the intelligence people that there were no VC around.
The Korean went into one particular house and saw a
woman cooking rice. There were three members of the
family, but she was cooking rice for at least nine people. *"He didn't say anything in the house but after we
walked out he warned us to watch the house closely,"*
marvels Patton. *"That night we killed several VC going
in to eat."*

Back in 1962, Patton remembers asking a number of
people on all sides of the scene how aligned the military

was with the ruling leadership. The answers were mixed, and even though it was 1962, the uncertainty of the relationship between the military and political branches of government bothered Patton considerably. *"In the early days of U.S. involvement, the leadership of the country had clear power, though the officer corps may not have been 100 percent loyal,"* he says.

The lack of trust between the military and the civilian leadership also affected the civilian population, who were distrusted by both groups. Patton remembers a good example from his first tour. *"There was a large parade held in Saigon,"* says Patton, *"with trucks and tanks all moving smartly down the road. Yet, all along the route there was an eerie silence since every window and door was closed and the streets were totally deserted. I inquired and learned that potential spectators had been precluded from watching the ceremony, which apparently had been staged for a few selected observers."* According to many military sources, things changed perceptibly, and the ARVN, if not the government, was clearly better by 1968 when Patton returned. A great deal of credit for the transformation is given to the United States military, which had committed top talent to the advisory chain. These advisory groups, largely unsung, did a yeoman's job of helping to develop a significant fighting force.

On the other side of the coin, Patton found the enemy and especially the Viet Cong to be tough fighters and excellent soldiers. Patton says, *"If you didn't know who you were up against in the first thirty minutes of contact, you weren't doing your job, since the VC were always much tougher and would hang on at terrible cost."* In addition to motivation, the VC had age and experience. The North Vietnamese Army, on the other hand, were not averse to putting children into the field. *"We were beginning to eat them up along about 1968 and 1969 and the very young soldiers being shipped down from the North were getting younger by the day,"* Patton remembers. *"I looked at kids fifteen and sixteen years old, dead in the field, and wondered if they even knew what the war was all about."*

The experienced enemy soldier, whether VC or NVA, however, was an interesting study, and one incident in particular gave Patton insight as to the hardened adversary he was fighting. In December 1968, during a Blackhorse operation, troops located a jungle-based enemy camp. Suddenly a North Vietnamese Army captain popped out of a hole, slightly wounded and hands up. He was taken prisoner, and Major Andy O'Meara called for an interpreter from his S-2 intelligence section. Upon arriving on the scene he began a series of questions, and within twenty minutes he realized they had captured a "live wire." Since the capture of commissioned officer personnel was a rare occurrence, Patton was notified and flew in quickly to assess the situation.

The NVA captain could speak French, and so Patton was able to converse with him, first asking the prisoner if he had been treated properly after capture.

"Yes, your soldiers have been gracious," the captain replied.

Patton asked if he would like a cigarette and a soda. He again said yes.

"Please relax," Patton continued, "I'd like to talk with you for a moment or two, and then we'll evacuate you just as soon as we can so that you can get medical care. How long have you been in-country?"

"I've been here eight years," the captain replied.

Patton asked where his family lived and how long it had been since he last heard from them.

"They live outside of Hanoi," came the reply, "and I haven't seen them in a very long time. I got a letter about a year ago brought down to me by a friend." He then reminded Patton that under the Geneva Convention he was precluded from asking about his family. With his eyes filling with tears, in a soft voice he said, "You shouldn't ask me such questions because it makes me very sad."

Patton moved off the subject and back to the immediate issue at hand, which was that the commander had a number of men dug into tunnel complexes in the base camp area. Patton asked him to go aboard a chopper equipped with a loudspeaker and order his men to surrender. The prisoner quickly refused, and Patton said to him, "If you don't go up in the chopper with me and ask them to surrender you have personally signed their death warrants, because I will be forced to obliterate this position." The NVA captain again declined, and Patton's frustration was evident.

He glowered at the man and said, "Goddamn it, who is winning this war?"

"You are," was the reply.

"Then in that case," Patton shouted, "why don't we save the lives of your soldiers and let us take them out and feed and medicate them?"

"Sir," he said, "you didn't ask who would win this war."

"Well, who is going to win this war?" Patton snorted.

"We will," the prisoner said forcefully, "because you will tire of it before we do."

The captain's comments proved prophetic and pointed out a weakness in an America not mentally geared for a long-term war of this particular brand. Minutes later, after a final refusal, the captain was put on a chopper. Salutes were exchanged, and he was evacuated. Within a short span of time Patton's troops overran the area with tanks and dropped charges in the tunnels. The base camp was destroyed before the prisoner reached his next interrogation.

The Viet Cong were not only good fighters in the field but also an intimidating force in the villages as well. Vietnamese peasants feared for their lives where it concerned the VC. Patton once had an old man brought to him and questioned him about infiltration in his village. Through an interpreter the elderly villager told Patton candidly, "I know about infiltrators and I know they come in here frequently, but I cannot say anything to you because you cannot guarantee my safety. If I tell you what I know, someday you will leave and I'll be a dead man." That sentiment was tough to overcome, and in most cases Patton and others were never able to get villagers to be fully cooperative. *"Generally,"* Patton says, *"we were incapable of permanently securing anything and as soon as we moved to another sector the vacuum was replenished with VC."*

In an attempt to subvert enemy ranks and gain valuable information, the U.S. employed the Chieu Hoi program to grant amnesty for Viet Cong soldiers willing to join the South Vietnamese side. In Patton's area one soldier had been a member of the Viet Cong for nineteen years and was a VC officer at the time he chose to switch sides. It was a rather significant occurrence, because he provided a great deal of information combined with a healthy historical perspective. In February 1969 that former VC officer wrote Patton a letter in which he thanked Patton for bringing him in to work with the 11th ACR and said, "I have followed the trail of the Viet Cong for nineteen long years. During this time they often distorted the truth, emphasizing that the United States was an aggressor in South Vietnam. Further arguing, the U.S. would murder innocent civilians and burn homes. To the soldier they shouted, if captured, he would be beaten until all information had been extracted, then killed." He went on to write, "After only a short time, their lies, hate and arguments vanished like bubbles from a stream." He concluded, "I very much admire you. Your talents as an officer and humanness as a man cause many men to open up their eyes and lay down their arms. Sir, when I first rallied I was warmed by your informal conversation, and honored that you would take my hand in friendship."

John McEnery, who commanded the 3rd Squadron, 11th ACR, remembers one incident involving a captured prisoner that once again pointed out the irony of war in Vietnam. "I had a captured VC for nearly two weeks, and violated orders in doing so since I was supposed to turn him over to a higher level within twenty-four to forty-eight hours," explains McEnery. "Every echelon was screaming and finally Patton came and took him from me under protest. We had so much confidence in this guy who was leading us to VC material caches and hiding places that we issued him an M-16 rifle. The day they came to take him he rode off in the helicopter alongside Patton, and there was this VC waving to my men like an old friend saying goodbye. It was absurd."

That same prisoner also made an interesting comment concerning the depth of VC indoctrination of their own fighting forces. "He was shocked upon his capture to learn that fires at some of our larger bases were merely dump fires to burn the garbage," says McEnery. "He had been told in the tunnels that the fires were the result of actions by VC contingents."

Valuable information was often gleaned from captured enemy soldiers, and according to Andy O'Meara, "After Tet '68, those we captured would generally tell you anything you wanted to know until they went to the POW camp, at which point their peers made sure they kept silent."

Aside from amnesty programs, the U.S. attempted to treat prisoners with respect and dignity, and was adamant about it. In fact, Patton's command post during his stay with the 11th was close to a prisoner of war camp, and he was asked by higher headquarters to keep an eye on it. Generally, Patton would send a staff officer to the camp to make sure all was going well. Every so often he would check it personally, and during one such visit asked the camp commander, as he always did, whether there was anything he could do for him.

"Yes," the commander replied, "the Vietnamese love to play volleyball and their net is frayed. Would it be possible to get them a new one?"

"You mean to tell me that's the extent of your problems?" Patton asked incredulously.

He nodded, "Yes, sir, that's it."

Patton arranged for a net to be delivered within twenty-four hours. Some time later, when Patton heard about what had been done to U.S. POWs in Hanoi, he was appalled. *"Here we had done everything we could to provide humane treatment, and they by no means thought the same way in the North,"* fumes Patton. *"Like many other examples during the Vietnam era, it clearly showed the difference in our cultures and approach to war."*

While the human element in war is perhaps the most decisive factor, technology can sometimes make the crucial difference. In Vietnam, the great equalizer was the B-52. The devastating power of the bomber, flying at high altitude, was a sight few witnesses will soon forget. One would hear a low drone from a great distance and then feel the earth shake as the heavy ordnance exploded on or near the target. Patton often employed these "Arc Light" strikes, as they were known, in the course of his time with the 11th. O'Meara also says, "We learned from captured prisoners how devastating our B-52 strikes were. We relied on the strikes but never knew how many we had killed. Yet, walking through bomb craters sometimes twenty-five feet deep and fifty or sixty feet across, with the ground covered in muck and trees blown away, you could smell death. It was from the prisoners we learned they had suffered losses sometimes amounting to companies of soldiers, huge losses which greatly understated our submitted body counts."

Patton's sector, combining farmland, jungles, and rivers, allowed the 11th to run a variety of operations. One of the basic principles of war, though not necessarily a classic one, is to follow firepower with maneuver. The B-52s provided that firepower when special needs were made known and approved. B-52 raids had to be planned well in advance, and Patton could not make even slight targeting modifications after seven hours before "bombs away." That sometimes meant Patton's forces could not maximize their effort. General Abrams worked with some success to provide the ground commander more input to coordinate late changes to the strike zone, which, if one placed it on a battle map, would resemble a box. The box at times might be a half mile long by two miles wide. Certain rules were applied to the bombing runs, including a restriction against other aircraft flying into an established bombing zone or putting anything into the air thirty minutes before strike time. These safety measures were implemented because concussions from the bomb blasts presented a danger to aircraft, especially helicopters, whose rotors could easily be damaged.

Because of the advance planning necessary for the B-52 runs, the Blackhorse staff would attempt to confuse the enemy as to what constituted the bombing box. After a few runs the enemy would catch on to the prebombing procedure and would scamper to clear the zone. Blackhorse staff therefore went to greater lengths to send mixed signals about intended target areas.

Immediately following a bombing run and the all-clear signal, Patton would order choppers into the air; he would actually have the rotor blades turning over during the bombing so that he could deploy the scout ships promptly. The scouts would look for human activity and assess the damage. When they determined where the most activity was occurring, Patton would deploy ground forces to mop up enemy soldiers, who were still groggy from the heavy bombing. Even with such intelligence, Patton never could trap an entire force within one of the boxes; some always escaped. Patton's troops were typically waiting three to four miles from the actual bombing area. After the strikes, in addition to looking for signs of life, they would attempt to root out the enemy by dropping either tear gas or incendiary grenades, which kept the fires going. Patton says, *"It sounds horrible and it was, but our job was to compress movement and destroy the enemy. Sherman was right. War is hell."* One technique which was frequently used involved putting tear gas upwind from the strike to drive the enemy in a certain direction. However, the enemy often proved elusive, and, as one of Patton's people told him one day, "These guys are like a bunch of ants; you turn over their hill and they scatter in every direction."

In war, the toughest thing one has to do is accept injury and the loss of life, and Patton lost many friends in Vietnam. Battle wounds and death were always at hand, and the circumstances were never pleasant. Patton, as a commander of men in battle, learned to accept the injuries and loss of comrades and still function.

After a bombing run one day, Andy O'Meara volunteered to go out for the bomb damage assessment (BDA). Patton was in the air doing something else and got a radio message from him: "I have noted Viet Cong leaving the area in numbers of twenty or thirty and they seem to have been affected by the bomb damage, but there are still some moving. I recommend that you put something in there immediately." (This was all done in voice code.) Patton replied, "What is your location?" O'Meara told him where he was and requested Patton also follow him to the hospital pad at the 93rd Evac. "The problem is that my pilot has been shot through the throat and is passing out at the controls," said O'Meara, "and I'm no helicopter pilot." He went on to say he was also wounded, having been shot through the leg. Patton says the message was very matter of fact, not a hint of panic, and yet they were twenty minutes from the pad. Patton called ahead to prepare the medics and followed O'Meara's helicopter as it landed. At the pad they called the CP, got the Blackhorse surgeon, and requested the blood types of O'Meara and the pilot. The pilot meanwhile had lost a lot of blood, and O'Meara was by now in bad shape.

Because O'Meara was a major and Patton a colonel, the hospital commander showed up. He looked at O'Meara and said the leg had to come off. Patton interjected that he didn't think so. The hospital commander immediately became angry, challenging Patton's opinion of O'Meara's condition. "Who are you to tell me?" he cried. Unmoved by the outburst, Patton replied that he wanted a second opinion immediately. The doctor finally backed off and asked a medic if there was another orthopedic physician in the area who could provide a second opinion. The medic said he thought such a person was located at MACV in Saigon but that he was too far away. "No, he's not," Patton said. "Get him. I've got a helicopter right outside and I'll send it down there now." The helicopter returned with the doctor, who then examined O'Meara and said, "I can save that leg." After it was over O'Meara had a long recovery and today walks with a slight limp, but as Patton says, *He has two legs and was able to go on with his career, retiring years later as a full colonel.*

Death as a daily companion in Vietnam had an intense effect on some soldiers. As part of Patton's mission he was required to contribute a troop of cavalry once a month to help in the defense of Saigon. The commander, Major General Fillmore Mearns, was in charge of assigning the contingent after it reached Saigon. Mearns was an old soldier and a West Point graduate. One day he went out of his way to ask Patton who was going to be assigned to him as the troop commander. After Patton gave him the captain's name, the general looked away and said, "I hope he'll be all right. I'm tired of burying my classmates' sons." It was one of the most telling comments Patton heard during his time in Southeast Asia.

One of the more poignant episodes in Patton's career brought home directly the issue of life and death on the battlefield. B Troop was commanded by Captain John Hays, a regular Army officer and a U.S. Military Academy graduate (1965). In early November 1968 it had come to Patton's attention that the troop had been nearly ineffective for more than two weeks. In fact, the troop had completely ignored and failed to make contact with a sizeable enemy force that passed by while the troop was in a night ambush position. Not a shot was fired by either side, and the enemy company had continued its uninhibited movement, most likely toward the Saigon area. Armed with this information, Patton called the squadron commander, requesting his opinion on the fighting efficiency and readiness of B Troop. The commander responded that he had been watching this organization closely and was about to relieve Captain Hays.

Patton approved his recommendation and agreed that the relief should take place when the troop returned to the 1st squadron fire base. A few days later he was informed that Hays had requested an appointment. Hays entered the tent and after an exchange of amenities informed Patton that he was "used up," had no more interest or drive left for command. He asked to be relieved of his B (or "Bravo") Troop responsibilities. He agreed with all concerned that his troop was generally ineffective and that he was responsible. Patton informed Hays that he had already approved his relief but felt Hays should stay in command until he was able to improve the situation and then depart. In that more positive way the troop could be, once again, marked as an effective fighting force. It would only be fair to the new commanding officer.

Hays in response to Patton said, "No, sir. I want out now. Let someone else do the dirty work of bringing B Troop up to speed." Patton told him that if that was his final position, he had no recourse but to let him go; however, he insisted that Hays think his decision over for an hour or two and then return for a final action. He agreed and left to consider his decision, returning within the hour. "Sir, I was wrong," Hays reported. "I am a West Pointer and I will stay on and get Bravo up to speed. I cannot leave. My West Point training will simply not permit me to leave this troop in its currently unsatisfactory condition."

Over the next few days Patton held B Troop in a rear area, allowing Hays and his troops time to correct the long list of deficiencies and shortcomings. Two weeks later the troop was declared ready and was ordered once again into a very heavy engagement, in which a brigade of the 1st Infantry Division was fighting. As Patton stood on the side of Highway 13, Bravo passed by. One could tell at a glance that a transformation had taken place. As the last vehicle passed by, Captain John Hays pulled over and dismounted. "Colonel Patton, this troop is ready! We are at top condition and on the way. I am glad you talked me into hanging on." As Hays departed he saluted and shouted, "Sir, we are going to battle and I will meet you on Fiddlers Green!" His prediction was accurate. Three days later Hays was killed in action leading his troop in a firefight.

After days of further action on the battlefield, B Troop was once again placed in a training and rehabilitation situation lasting several days. Following the "rehab" period, Bravo was reassigned to the 1st Division, which was still locked in heavy contact with NVA forces near Loch Ninh. Once again, Patton stood on Highway 13 waving B Troop on, this time under a new commander. As the last vehicle passed by, the 1st Sergeant dismounted and reported to Patton that Bravo was combat-ready and moving. Patton exclaimed, with tears in his eyes, that he wished John Hays could see how great that troop looked. The answer from the 1st Sergeant was one he will always remember: "Sir, John

Hays is riding in every vehicle in this column." And Patton believes he was.

No incident in the Vietnam War affected Patton like the John Hays exchange. *"I will carry the remembrance of Bravo Troop moving to combat always,"* says Patton. *"The watchword was 'Duty' which could not be set aside. Hays epitomized the type of American soldier I knew and admired in Vietnam."*

Death in Vietnam had little respect for rank, as evidenced by the number of high-ranking military officers killed during the war. General Keith Ware, Commanding General, 1st Infantry Division, who died in a helicopter crash, is but one example. On the day Ware died, Patton was attending an intelligence briefing at Division Headquarters. Patton normally went to the briefings three or four times a week, since they were helpful in setting objectives. The meetings usually started around 6:30 or 7:00 A.M. and included only division and brigade-level commanders and senior staff members, those cleared for a certain level of intelligence information.

During the briefing that day a staff officer interrupted to inform Ware about heavy fighting in an area to the north, but within the division area of operation. Ware immediately said he was leaving, and another officer under Ware began to move as well. Ware turned to him and said, "No, you're not going, because you're leaving on R&R [rest and recreation] today."

The officer replied, "General, I can postpone my trip. Let me go with you."

Ware looked at him and snapped, "God damn it, this is an order: you're not going!"

Ware left the meeting, and four hours later he was dead. Military experts never fully ascertained the circumstances surrounding the crash of his command aircraft; however, Patton's theory is that the VC shot the chopper's tail rotor off. During the hours before Ware's death Patton's units became involved in heavy fighting north of the Dong Nai River near the village of Than Yuen, and Patton called headquarters for an additional rifle company to come under his control as a small but available reserve. Patton was told by radio, "Sir, I can't tell you anything but there are no troops being moved anywhere until we receive further orders." Patton knew something was up but did not find out that it was Ware's death that had stopped tactical movement until later that day, Friday, 13 September 1968.

Death and wounds received in battle not only knocked at the division-commander level but also affected the command of the 11th ACR through the years. Jack MacFarlane, who took command of the regiment in December 1967, was seriously wounded and had to relinquish command to another close friend of Patton's, Colonel Leonard D. Holder. Holder and Patton had served together in the Korean War and at the Armor School. Only a few months after assuming command Holder would die in the crash of a chopper. "Tex," as people affectionately called him, was a likeable person and his death reverberated through the command. It also reminded Patton, when he took command of the 11th, of the very real dangers he would face on a daily basis.

The battlefield, despite constant death, does have its comic relief as well. Patton tells the story about one particular day which started rather quietly. As was often the case, fighting picked up and soon a heavy battle was raging along Highway 13, north of Lai Khe. *"I landed behind a line of vehicles stretched across the road,"* says Patton. *"We were receiving fire from the woods and pouring some in. Gunships were working from behind on the other side of the woods. Gunfire and the smell of war was everywhere and as I looked the area over I saw an APC to my front about seventy-five yards from where I landed. I decided to move up to it for a better view of the battle. As I got to within a few yards of the vehicle a sergeant in the turret spotted me and yelled, 'Colonel, it's too dangerous for you up here! There's all kinds of fire and you shouldn't come any closer.' I told him to open the back of the APC anyway because I wanted a look. He shouted back again, 'It's too dangerous; besides, you can get a better view if you stand off to the side of the track.' I yelled, 'Open it, now!' Well, he came down and opened the doors to let me inside. As I climbed in, I realized that on the bench seats lining each side of the vehicle were two door gunners getting it on with a couple of Vietnamese women they had picked up along the road. I said, 'Get them out of here!' I busted the sergeant a grade but he took it rather matter of factly, and deep down I couldn't help but appreciate the endless irony of war."*

An army is composed of a variety of soldier personalities, but it is generally the mavericks or renegades one remembers. This was true for Patton and a young man nicknamed "Pancho." Patton met Pancho after heavy fighting in the northeastern corner of the Catcher's Mitt. During the battle Patton had been given a 1st Division infantry battalion. The battalion, codenamed "Dracula," had been in the field about three days, and Patton went in to see them after the enemy had taken heavy losses and withdrawn.

When Patton arrived one of the officers said he had someone for Patton to meet. They walked down a twisting path until they came to a soldier sitting on a log cradling an M-16. The soldier was very small and sported long sideburns and a big black mustache. Introductions were made, and the officer began to tell Patton about the remarkable soldier in front of them and how he had killed four VC with four shots.

Patton asked Pancho if he would show him those he had killed and explain how he managed to pull off such a feat. "Señor Colonel," said Pancho, "the enemy is just over there under the tree." So the group walked over and lying underneath a large tree were four of the enemy, and they had all been shot through the head.

"Pancho, that's really good shooting," Patton exclaimed.

"Yes, Señor Colonel, very good shooting. Pancho shoot very good," he replied.

As the story began to unfold, Patton found out that the soldier was a loner who worked best by himself. It seemed he disliked groups. Generally, this is not a very good trait for an everyday soldier, but Pancho was not just an everyday soldier. Pancho went on to explain that he used single shots to kill instead of automatic fire because he didn't like to waste ammunition. "But," said Pancho, "the main thing for me is to shoot them through the head so they don't move around, they just fall soft. When they move around it makes me nervous." Impressed with the man's fighting ability, Patton tried to recruit him on the spot for the Blackhorse, but he wasn't successful. Pancho's own commanders were very aware of his value.

Patton later looked into Pancho's background and found he had a prison record, had troubles with drugs within his own battalion, and obviously was not a disciplined soldier. Yet, he was one combat veteran every commander would love to have. Patton recalls that the last time he saw Pancho he asked him if he intended to stay in the Army. "No, Señor Colonel," he said. "I go back to Laredo, Texas, to work as an artist's assistant and do a little smuggling on the side. I'll be okay."

13

A SOLDIER'S GENERAL

No officer I ever met, either above or below me in rank, could touch General Creighton W. Abrams. He was the best soldier I have ever known, including all the members of my family.

—George S. Patton

Long before the American public got to know General Creighton W. Abrams as Commander, U.S. Forces, Military Assistance Command Vietnam (MACV), he was already a legend in the United States Army. Tough, irreverent, often gruff, yet flamboyant, Abrams commanded respect. The penultimate "tanker's tanker," and a general who would eventually command a half million soldiers during the war in Vietnam, Abrams was known to his legions and friends simply as "Abe." Reviewing his stellar career, many military historians now rank Abrams among the very best fighting generals in the annals of the U.S. Army.

Abrams first tasted success and acclaim under General George S. Patton, Jr., in World War II, when as commander of the 37th Tank Battalion, 4th Armored Division, he spearheaded the relief of Bastogne during the famous Battle of the Bulge. Born on September 15,

1914, in Springfield, Massachusetts, Abrams was the oldest of three children born to Creighton and Nellie Abrams.

The Abrams family, while poor materially, were rich in the lessons they taught their children, and young Creighton was a beneficiary. During his high school years he would become the president of his class and editor of the school newspaper, and be recognized by his classmates as the boy most likely to succeed. Nearing the end of high school Abrams was offered a scholarship to Brown University, but owing to the family's financial constraints he decided to seek an appointment to West Point.

Abrams entered the Military Academy in July 1932 as a member of the Class of 1936. Among the 382 who entered, 276 would graduate, including William Westmoreland, Bruce Palmer, Jr., and a host of other officers who went on to have distinguished military careers. Following graduation in June 1936, Abrams began a career that would culminate in his appointment as Chief of Staff, United States Army.

In early 1949, George Patton, an infantry first lieutenant recently transferred from the 1st Squadron, 2nd Cavalry, located in Augsburg, West Germany, and further assigned to the 7767 European Command Tank Training Center at Vilseck, would seek a transfer to the 63rd Heavy Tank Battalion. Permission being granted, Patton thus joined the only tank battalion in Germany at that time and went to work under the command of Lieutenant Colonel C. W. Abrams. The transfer commenced a long association between Abrams and Patton. During his career Patton would serve with Abrams in Korea, Europe, and Vietnam, and work with him in the Pentagon as well.

"From my Dad and others, I had heard a lot about Abrams in my younger days," says Patton. *"Of course the Abrams story was rich with great exploits including his having chewed up several command tanks during*

*his dash across Europe, starting with a tank he nick-
named 'Thunderbolt,' and concluding the war in the
turret of Thunderbolt VII. The story of Abrams and the
37th Tank Battalion was the stuff of legends."*

The 37th Battalion of the famous 4th Armored Division was a favorite of General George S. Patton, Jr.,
and was truly suited to the aggressive style of Abrams.
The famous and often chronicled story of Abrams and
his battalion had its beginnings in July 1942. At the age
of twenty-seven and the rank of captain, he took command of the 3rd Battalion of the 37th Armored Regiment, a part of the 4th Armored Division, activated at
Pine Camp, New York, in 1941. The battalion's war
began in earnest when it landed on Utah Beach in Normandy on D + 35, that is, thirty-five days after the first
assault. From there the battalion began ringing up victory after victory, crossing the Seine in August 1944
and the Saar River in early December. Lewis Sorley, in
his definitive book about Abrams, *Thunderbolt*, recounts a story told by the journalist Jimmy Cannon,
that Patton was discussing Abrams with a gathering of
newsmen. Patton is supposed to have said, "If you are
going to write about him, you better do it right away.
He's so good, he isn't going to live long."

Later, during the Battle of the Bulge, Abrams was
fighting in the Saar when he learned that the 101st Airborne Division was surrounded and trapped in the village of Bastogne. Under orders from Division, Abrams
fought tenaciously, steadily leading the relief force to
rescue the besieged and beleaguered soldiers, holding
on by a thread, just one day after Christmas, 1944. The
brilliant military maneuver caught the attention of the
media, which trumpeted his exploits throughout Europe and America.

In 1949 George Patton first commented on Abrams
in his daily diary. He wrote, *"Abrams is quite a guy, he
can be described in one sentence: he means business. He
is very forceful, rough, kind, generous, understanding,
thinks of his men, has great personal attraction and the*

ability to inspire. I am possessed of the feeling that he wants men around him who respect him but who are not afraid of him in the end." On a more personal level, Patton observed that Abrams enjoyed cigars, with one usually punched in the side of his mouth, and drank "*a fair amount.*" To the end, Abrams, at five feet, nine inches and heavyset, would remain the embodiment of a true warrior in Patton's eyes.

After Patton had moved from Vilseck to Grafenwöhr, the major training area for the U.S. Army in West Germany, to become executive officer of C Company, 63rd Heavy Tank Battalion, Patton quickly learned how Abrams worked. "*In those first weeks after Abrams took command he did nothing but observe,*" says Patton. "*Then one morning he called a meeting of the company commanders and his battalion staff. When we assembled Abe announced we would take a short walk. We started in the HQ motor park and terminated in the C Company motor park. I'll never forget it. He had fifty or so officers on the tour and he said, 'Each time I raise my swagger stick the problem I point to will be corrected in twenty-four hours. And I don't care what the problems are. If you need more time to fix the situation call Major Lance Booth, the Executive Officer, and give us a precise time when it will be corrected. But be damn sure you are right on that, because if you are not I am going to fire you.' So we walked and observed tools rusting in the sun, spare tires and pieces of machinery, dirty glasses and dishes, and broken furniture. Conditions were incredible. But more incredible was how the place changed overnight following the walk-through. It was crystal clear to all concerned that Abe meant business!*"

Shortly thereafter, Abrams received orders to relocate the battalion at Sullivan Barracks in Mannheim, leaving the training facilities in Grafenwöhr, which everyone agreed were the best in Germany. Sullivan Barracks, however, proved to be a well designed military kaserne, with a horseshoe layout for Headquarters

Company and A, B and C companies, plus the ordnance group and an MP contingent. Abrams, as post commander, continued to whip the 63rd into shape, concentrating on the important issues, including maintaining readiness for battle. Abrams believed in helping to facilitate good battalion-wide intercommunication, so he instituted a weekly coffee call where every commissioned and warrant officer would assemble, have coffee, and speak with the battalion commander and staff. *"This contributed greatly to unit cohesion,"* remarks Patton.

At one of these meetings Abrams expressed disappointment that though the battalion had a new chapel on base, not many people were attending services. Throughout his career, even during the time he was Army Chief of Staff, and except in time of war, Abrams always spent Sunday with his family and encouraged others to do the same. Church services were important to Abrams, and he wanted the attendance problem improved. As the C Company commander, Patton was partly responsible to fulfill Abe's request. One day Abrams told his personnel that he was going to buck up the services but he did not say how. *"On the appointed day and hour we assembled and a respectable group of soldiers all went in,"* chuckles Patton. *"As the service started the famous missionary hymn, 'Onward Christian Soldiers,' sounded and here came Abe carrying a large cross down the center aisle, leading the choir in song. He was singing at the top of his voice although slightly off key."*

During Patton's time with the 63rd under Abrams, an incident occurred that left an indelible impression on the young officer. A maneuver was being carried out near Kitzingen, involving infantry elements advancing on a town. In meetings before the maneuvers began, Abrams cautioned tank units about moving through and destroying what the troops called "the first row of beets." Patton, in looking back, remembers that units were seldom permitted to deploy in mass across the wheat, corn, and soybean fields of West Germany. *"We worked hard to make sure our tanks did not do indiscriminate crop damage and there was a great deal of command emphasis on that particular subject."*

During the maneuver, Patton, whose company had been in a short, simulated firefight, was experiencing delays caused by the umpires, who were making determinations of gains or losses by particular units. Patton, his unit stopped once more, received a call from Abrams, whose call sign was "Arson King." Abrams said he understood Patton had been administratively halted and wanted him to move his tanks off the roadway rapidly to allow B Company, commanded by Sidney S. "Hap" Haszard, to pass through and continue the attack. Patton was then to report in as a division reserve.

Patton started carrying out his orders from Abrams, but in a somewhat cautious fashion so as to avoid damaging the crops on the side of the road. *"I was carefully deploying my tanks when in a cloud of dust came Abrams,"* says Patton. *"He stopped his jeep in front of me and stormed up. It was clear he was burning mad. 'Patton, you are too goddamn slow moving your tanks off the road!' Then he balled up his fist and slugged me in the face. I went down to the ground. I recall that the only people who saw the incident were Corporal Albert Cash, who was my driver, and Abrams's driver, a soldier named Harris. After getting up and dusting myself off I can tell you I got those tanks off the road with a new sense of urgency. Abe disappeared just as quickly."*

That night C Company entered an assembly area behind the reserve regiment and Patton received word that he was to report at once to Battalion HQ. *"I figured this was it. Georgie, you're going back to some obscure infantry platoon somewhere out of sight and mind and start over."* Patton walked into a small wall-tent where Abrams was sitting on a folding chair, behind him a small folding table. On the table a candle was flickering, providing a surreal setting, and Patton noted a single piece of paper lying on the table.

Saluting he said, "Lieutenant Patton reporting, sir."

Abrams fixed a look on Patton and said, "George, what I did today was wrong. Rather than explain what I'm going to do I want you to read this memo."

Abrams leaned forward and handed the paper to Patton. Patton's jaw went slack. The memo contained the facts needed for a court-martial of Creighton W. Abrams. Under a section of the Uniform Code of Military Justice known as Article 96, a form was made out for Patton's signature and charged Abrams with conduct unbecoming an officer, with one charge and two specifications concerning the incident.

"Sign it," Abrams said to Patton.

"I was shivering from the top of my head to the soles of my feet," recalls Patton. *"Abe waited for a moment and said again, 'Sign it.' 'Sir, I was wrong out there in not moving fast enough and you were wrong in hitting me, but I was the source of the problem,' I blurted out. Then I simply tore up the charge sheets and threw them into the waste can. There was silence and tension for a few moments before I saw a trace of a smile come over his face. Then he reached under his table and pulled out a bottle of Scotch. We had a drink and from that day forward to the end of his life, the incident was never again discussed."*

In 1950, after Abrams had given Patton command of C Company, Patton would learn of yet another side of Abrams when one of Patton's soldiers was tragically crushed between two tanks. The troops had been unloading material at night in response to a general alert when the soldier was killed. Patton went to Abe and told him he accepted full responsibility for the accident. Patton was especially upset because the unit had been attempting to beat another company's unloading time.

Attempting to shave time was normal, and competitions in loading and unloading went on constantly. In this case, however, Patton felt he had failed to make sure the company was acting in a safe manner. He went on to tell Abe that he was ready to be relieved on account of the accident. Abrams looked at Patton and said no, that unloading and loading times were critical to the defense of Europe. *"It was just another example of his measured and thoughtful response to a problem,"* remarks Patton. *"His eternal gaze was always on his mission which, in this case, was very simply success in war."*

In 1951, Abrams and Patton would go in separate directions to take on new assignments. The separation would last for three years, until they would work together again in Korea. *"Throughout those years we would see one another sporadically,"* says Patton, *"and when we could find time we would get together to fish for bass and trout, and eventually he almost became like an older brother to me. I especially enjoyed our fishing and hunting trips because he was a very personable, an enjoyable companion. I can't begin to outline the amount of time we spent together. He was a lot of fun to be with in or out of uniform."*

Patton believes his two years of service under Creighton Abrams with the 63rd Heavy Tank Battalion not only influenced his entire military career but set the pace for his selection for flag rank in 1969. Patton adopted many of Abrams's techniques. Others must have also followed suit, since that 1949–1951 period in the 63rd produced four general officers. Throughout his career Abrams produced leaders, and good ones. As one of the selected officers said one day, "We learned how to do it right."

In July 1953, about the time active hostilities were concluding in Korea, Abrams accepted an offer to work for an old friend, Lieutenant General Bruce Clarke. Abrams and Clarke had served together in World War II in the 4th Armored Division, and Abe was one of his protégés. He would be Clarke's chief of staff in I Corps; eventually he served as chief of staff of three successive corps before leaving Korea. *"At the time I was there,"* says Patton, *"Clarke directed the formation of the I Corps Reconnaissance Battalion. Concurrently I was given orders to turn over my A Company, 140th Tank Battalion, then located west of the Punchbowl, and join that battalion as S-3."* George Patton remembers that Clarke both admired and respected Abrams, and that Clarke was quoted in a *Time* magazine article in 1961 as saying of Abrams, "No one is more deliberate in planning for war. No one is more violent in execution."

Watching Abrams in Korea, especially during a time of uncertain peace, was very instructive for Patton. *"The mission of the provisional recon battalion was to support I Corps HQ in the evacuation of former POWs,"* says Patton. *"Some POWs refused, for one reason or another, to return to mainland China but selected Taiwan* [Formosa] *as the only alternative. There were thousands of these men who had fought against UN Forces during the Korean War. Some even went to the extent of a tattoo on their back informing the world that they had fought under Mao but were now throwing in with Chiang Kai-shek."* During the evacuation of former POWs the provisional reconnaissance battalion reported to Abrams. It was complicated, highly political, but necessary, and Patton learned new skills from Abrams in the process.

After Korea, Abrams returned to the United States and was assigned as Chief of Staff of Fort Knox and the Armored Center and School. Patton, too, carried on, next working for Abrams in 1959, when he transferred to G-3, USAREUR.

Early on, it was clear that Patton and Abrams enjoyed their time together, often finding humor even in the context of business. Patton recalls accompanying Abrams and a major general on an inspection of a mess hall. *"Along comes the general to look for dust and see how clean the tops of catsup bottles were. Meanwhile,*

Abrams and I are tagging along. The general got to a corner of the snack bar and reached under the stove and with his white gloves pulled out a gob of foul grease. He showed it to the snack bar sergeant and said, 'Your snack bar is in atrocious shape!' The sergeant beamed and said, 'Yes, sir, and we intend to keep it that way!' Abe and I looked at each other and could barely keep from laughing. I mean it was tough and we all moved away to keep from bursting. I knew if I looked at Abe we would lose it. A few minutes later we walked out into the street and the general turned to Abrams and said, 'What does that guy mean, he intends to keep it that way?' 'I think he has a language problem, but I'll straighten it out,' Abrams said."

Toward the end of 1961, Creighton Abrams turned over the 3rd Armored Division, with which he had received national recognition, and was assigned to the USAREUR DCSOPS in Heidelberg. As was the case throughout his career, however, Patton would go only a short period of time before hooking up with Abrams once again. They frequently saw each other when Abrams was in the Pentagon as Army Vice Chief of Staff and Patton was *"pushing paper."* Patton marveled at how Abrams could adapt to any assignment. *"Time or location never diminished his intensity, even in the Pentagon."*

A story Patton tells about Abrams and the Pentagon is illustrative of his intensity and love for the Army. At the time Secretary of Defense McNamara and his staff had ordered the services to review every organization carefully to be certain that soldiers and units being deployed to Vietnam were truly required. Most of the office of the Assistant Chief of Staff for Force Development (ACSFOR) was heavily involved in the review. In view of McNamara's established urgency on this matter, ACSFOR representatives continually looked for times when it would be possible to brief Abrams or his boss, General Harold K. Johnson.

During one of these meetings, as Abrams was listening to a presentation by the ACSFOR himself, Lieutenant General Collins, a dedicated infantryman, General Collins informed Abrams that one way to reduce deployments and overall expenses would be to remove the tank from the tank company commander and let that individual use his jeep instead. *"I was sitting there on pins and needles because I knew what was going to happen just as sure as God made apples,"* says Patton. *"Abe pulled out a long cigar and lit it slowly. The room fell silent as he took a couple of puffs, finally looked directly at Collins and said in a very low voice, and you could barely hear him, 'Art, the day you take the tank away from the company commander is the day I will take the parachute from the parachutist! Next briefing!' With that one comment, one lieutenant general, five colonels and two lieutenant colonels got up and left the room immediately."*

After General William Westmoreland returned to the United States in the summer of 1968 to become Chief of Staff, U.S. Army, following General Johnson, who was retiring, Abrams took over as commander of MACV. Southeast Asia brought out the best in Abrams, although the limitations of the conflict would be a heavy cross to shoulder. In one of the lasting quotes of the war, reported in a *New York Times* Sunday magazine article, came an anonymous quote from a high-ranking official who said, "Abrams is one of the most impressive men I've ever met. You know, it's too bad. Abrams is very good. He deserves a better war." Lewis Sorley in his biography reports then–Secretary of Defense Melvin Laird as saying Abrams was not well liked by President Richard Nixon; however, the late president, in a letter to this author in 1991, said, "General Abrams was an outstanding commander in Vietnam. He found service in that war very difficult."

Despite the difficulties of fighting in a protracted, politically entangled war, Abrams carried on, and Patton remembers he left no stone unturned in the quest for excellence. *"I can recall one time when I was getting ready to go to a 1st Division briefing, while I was commander of the 11th,"* Patton recalls. *"Dozier came running out to tell me that he had received a message from 'Moonshine,' which was Abrams's call sign at that time in Vietnam, that he wanted to land at our location. The helicopter settled and Abe stepped to the ground. He was wearing a steel helmet pulled well down over his eyes, which we always knew spelled trouble ahead. I reported to him and we started walking towards my CP. I began to brief him and offered that we could go out and talk with the soldiers. He growled, 'I only want to talk with you.'*

" 'You got any whiskey?' Abrams asked as we went into my CP. 'I've just come from Qui Nhon and the depot there and it was terrible,' he said. 'I got to rummaging around and what do you think I found? I found a crate with two thousand jock straps. So I said to the depot commander, "Show me where these jock straps are listed in your computer runs." And he was standing there and after a considerable period of time, he reports he can't find them.' Then Abe said to me, 'You know what I did? I assigned one more goddamn worthless staff officer to the USARV G-4 section.' He started to smirk and shake his head, then waving his arms in the air he yelled, 'And about those jocks, they were all medium. God damn it, we aren't over here for a PT [physical training] session with the enemy!' "

Having served under Abrams on four separate occasions, Patton knew that after months of command responsibility the war was consuming Abrams mentally and physically. Under tremendous pressure, Abrams was running the war from a windowless office in the MACV headquarters, nicknamed "Pentagon East," next to the Tan Son Nhut Airport, about three miles from downtown Saigon. For relaxation, when time permitted during his seven-day-a-week schedule, he enjoyed listening to music and had an impressive collection of albums, mostly classical, but with a wide variety of other kinds as well.

Abrams, even under great strain, would, when needed, always respond with the fire and enthusiasm Patton had known and loved for so long. Yet at the same time Patton knew Abrams missed his family greatly. Julie Abrams, his wife, and their three younger children were living in Bangkok, but he rarely found time to visit them, because he simply refused time off. Patton also felt the military brass in Washington were running Abrams to the point of exhaustion, yet he carried on. Patton says, *"Abe was a great supporter of what we were attempting to accomplish in the war and gave it his all."*

The fighting spirit of Creighton Abrams was illustrated one day when he came to Patton's area. Patton had arranged for Abrams to present the Distinguished Service Cross to an A Troop corporal who had shown extreme bravery in a fight. Just about the time the ceremony was to convene an aide ran into the CP and said, "Colonel Patton, there is a hell of a battle going on at Chanh Luu."

Patton looked at Abe and said, "General, we can postpone this. Would you like to go up and take a look?"

Abrams grinned and said, "Hell! Screw the ceremony, let's go to the fight!"

The enthusiasm of General Abrams was, in fact, felt throughout the Blackhorse. "An utterly fantastic leader," John McEnery called him.

Jim Dozier recalls Abrams and Patton's relationship as very close, and with very amusing moments at times. "I remember one day when Abrams came in and soon he and Patton were in the field observing a fight. Abrams quickly noticed one of the mortars had no sights. He looked at the first sergeant and said, "Don't you think it's a little dangerous to be shooting those mortars without sights?"

"Don't worry about it, sir," answered the sergeant, "those people we're supporting are only the ARVN."

Patton, thinking about the leadership style of Abrams, says, *"As a commander he was quite adept in making sure he praised you when you had done a job well."* Patton recalls leaving a briefing room with him in December 1968. *"He looked weary that day,"* says Patton, *"and had a number of important issues rolling around in his head. Yet he still took a moment to tell me that I was one of the most respected commanders in the theater. He said that opinion had been echoed by my various bosses. Coming from him it ranked as one of the finest compliments anyone had ever given me."* That compliment ranks a close second to what Patton considers his finest military accolade, one that came to him from Abrams in the form of an inscription on a photograph. The photo shows Abrams and Patton standing together at a helicopter pad, and Abrams had written: "To George S. Patton, with respect and admiration for a proven combat leader of unequaled professional excellence."

Abrams could, at times, be very emotional, which was really brought home to Patton one afternoon when the commander landed at the Blackhorse Command Post shortly after Patton had received word that a particular sergeant of his had been killed in action. Patton had known this NCO for many years and thought very highly of him. Abrams came in and saw the tears streaming down Patton's face and asked what was wrong. Patton gave him the background, explaining the long association. Abrams listened, and with tears in his own eyes he said in a hushed tone, "Don't ever get too fond of them." Patton says he never forgot the advice. *"Abrams meant that emotions can't be your guide. You have a mission to accomplish and you can't let your heart rule your head. One must turn his attention to those who are alive and still seeking guidance. When*

Abrams told me not to get too fond of my men he meant only to remind me of my responsibilities, because he then softened even more, placed his arm around my shoulder and said, 'Believe me, I know what you're going through.'"

At Abrams's change of command ceremony, before leaving Vietnam, a party was held, mostly with first sergeants, master sergeants, and sergeant majors, some officers, but mainly just the troops. Over and over, people went to Abrams telling him how he had positively affected their careers or otherwise had taught them a valuable lesson along the way. Finally, after several minutes of this, Abe came over to Patton and said, "You have to get me out of here because I'm ready to burst into tears." *"The idea of these soldiers coming up to him one after another to thank him, during the middle of a war, was too much for him to handle,"* remarks Patton.

The kindness of Abrams was also visited upon Patton many times in their years of friendship, but never more so than in 1974. Patton had been assigned in European Command as J-7 (security assistance) and was becoming increasingly lame as a result of a broken hip suffered in Europe in September 1970. In Washington, D.C., meanwhile, Abrams had been named Vice Chief of Staff under Harold Johnson, jumping thirty-three three-star generals and twelve four-star generals on the seniority list to be named to the post. In 1972 Abrams reached the pinnacle of Army command, when he was selected and appointed to the Army's top job, Chief of Staff.

One day in 1974 Patton was asked to report to General Jock Sutherland's office. *"Sutherland was Chief of Staff to General Eade, US EUCOM Commander in Europe. He said to me, 'I have good news for you. Abrams has selected you as Commanding General of the 1st Armored Division.' I immediately started to get the shakes,"* remembers Patton.

Mustering all the courage Patton could find within

his system, he told Sutherland that he was not physically able to command a division because of his hip and requested leave to meet with Abrams personally. Patton arrived shortly thereafter at the Pentagon and was ushered in to see Abrams to explain his situation and the physical problems that left Patton feeling that he would be unable adequately to command the division. Abrams said, "That takes guts, because you may never be offered another division." Patton responded he was fully aware of that, but it was not fair to the soldiers in the division to have a commander not fully fit to command. By that time Patton even had trouble climbing into a jeep or helicopter, could barely walk, and was in pain all the time. Patton asked Abrams for permission to get checked out through the Walter Reed Medical Center and then be allowed to see a civilian physician he had heard about, Dr. William H. Harris, a teacher at Massachusetts General Hospital, and reportedly a pioneer in reconstructive hip surgery.

Patton wanted to leave immediately for Walter Reed after the meeting, to get the process started. Abrams concurred, and in a move that spoke to their long friendship, told Patton to take his sedan and driver and start right away. *"That was in 1974, and while I was feeling bad, I knew that Abe didn't look good. Sadly, it was the last time I ever saw him,"* says Patton. While Patton was still in Massachusetts General recovering from his hip replacement surgery, General Abrams entered Walter Reed, diagnosed with cancer. He fought to the end, even attending an important meeting at the White House with President Gerald Ford, four days after the resignation of Richard Nixon and just three weeks before succumbing to the disease in September 1974. By the time Abrams passed away, Patton, using a cane, was returned to duty at Fort Devens, assigned as deputy commander to Major General Morgan Roseborough. He was informed that Abrams had passed away and was asked to be a pallbearer at the funeral. *"A singular honor,"* says Patton.

The funeral for Abrams, the first Chief of Staff in United States Army history to die in office, was held at Fort Myer and was attended by a host of dignitaries, including nine former Chiefs of Staff. In fact, Patton was the most junior pallbearer in a phalanx of military and civilian dignitaries, including Ellsworth Bunker, Harold K. Johnson, Bruce Clarke, Fred Weyand, Walter "Dutch" Kerwin, and Bruce Palmer. *"It was a sad day,"* says Patton. *"The whole Abrams family was there, his lovely wife Julie, a Vassar graduate from a family of five daughters, and his sons Creighton, a major general, John, who is now a lieutenant general, and Bruce, who is also coming along very well in the Army. Abe's three daughters were there, each an outstanding human being. What a testimony to a marvelous man who understood and loved what he was doing."*

Having served under numerous commanders, Patton feels Abrams taught him more about war, life, and the Army than anyone else. *"I'll never forget the lessons he passed along to me,"* says Patton. *"His formula for leadership was based on honesty, integrity, commitment, knowledge, and love of the soldier and the love of soldiering. Because he was a busy man he wasted little time on the things he didn't feel were very important. He had a tremendous influence on me. In fact, I probably used more of Abrams's techniques and examples than I used from my dad's experience. But perhaps Abrams picked up much of it from my father, although they were entirely different personalities. Abrams could be flamboyant, but I think more humble than my dad. My father was kind of patrician. For example Abe never really looked good in a uniform—he was kind of scruffy and a little overweight. He was neat but he didn't dress with a flair like my father did. That was not his way. But I so clearly remember one piece of advice he gave me on this score. He said, 'Always remember to be yourself; people who are not themselves are nobody at all.' Abrams was himself, and smart enough to understand what he was all about."*

In perhaps the highest compliment one soldier can pay another, Patton says, *"If Abrams gave me a mission with the chance of staying alive at 1 in 10, I'd ask, when are we moving out? I never felt that way about an officer before or since and I worked for some good ones. No officer I ever met, either above or below me in rank, could touch General Creighton W. Abrams. He was the best soldier I have ever known, including all the members of my family."* Patton was especially pleased in 1980 when the highly praised M1 main battle tank rolled off the assembly line designated the "Abrams." *"That was the least his Army could do for him,"* Patton remarks. *"May he rest in eternal peace."*

14

TURBULENT WORLD

George Patton, the Army needs someone like you right now. You can't quit.

—Joanne Patton

In April 1969, as Patton was making a decision concerning whether to go to flight school, he spoke with Major General Robert Williams, then head of Army aviation in Vietnam. He told Williams that the only way he could accept a change of orders from the Weapons Department at the U.S. Army Armor School, Fort Knox, Kentucky, in favor of flight school was to experience the entire nine-month program. *"I do not agree with the policy that a senior officer can take a get-rich-quick course lasting only three or four months and know all that he needs to know. He simply becomes dangerous."* After accepting a spot in flight school and taking a short leave, Patton moved his family to Fort Wolters, Texas, for primary helicopter training. Completing that phase, he would then go to Fort Rucker, Alabama, for instrument qualification training, a course which lasted about three months.

The first instructional phase was ground school, followed by flying the actual aircraft. The students were supervised by solid—and, Patton adds, *"patient"*—instructor pilots, who taught the students to fly. Of course Patton had flown hundreds of hours in his various Vietnam assignments, but only as a passenger. Now, as a pilot in the right seat, he experienced the challenge for himself. *"Believe it or not,"* says Patton, *"I sat many nights with two plumber's helpers, one for the 'cyclic' stuck to the floor, while the second one, the 'collective,' was attached to the wall behind me. This arrangement, suggested by Billy Choate, my long-suffering instructor pilot, was a very helpful idea."* At the school it was generally felt that the first and most vital challenge to rotary qualification was learning to hover. It was a difficult maneuver to teach; the student pilot had to learn the feel for it by gently placing his hands over those of the instructor during the hover. After much practice the skill finally came. When a student hovered successfully, and then executed a 360-degree turn at the hover, at three feet of altitude, he was on the road to qualification.

Patton was forty-six years of age when he learned to fly a helicopter and soloed in thirteen hours. *"I always felt pretty good about the experience,"* says Patton. *"The average time in our class was ten or eleven hours, but most of our guys were half my age. The graduating exercise,"* recalls Patton, *"was a solo cross-country flight to Fort Sill, Oklahoma, about an hour and a half away by air."* During his solo Patton was flying along when he received a radio call from the monitor aircraft that was checking on student performance. They believed that Patton had strayed slightly off course. Patton called back with a chuckle, saying, "Colonels don't get lost in this school, they get temporarily disoriented." Patton descended quickly to a six-foot hover, read the road signs on the ground, went back up to about 1,200 feet, and corrected his course for Fort Sill, landing there without incident.

The basic school at Fort Wolters lasted nearly six months, and just before Patton was scheduled to move to Fort Rucker in September 1969, for instrument training, he was informed that he had been selected for promotion to brigadier general. *"I was elated,"* says Patton. *"I had worked hard and could enjoy achieving yet another benchmark in my Army career. Moreover, I wanted additional responsibility!"*

Now a promotable colonel, Patton still needed to undergo instrument training in the helicopter to complete his flying program. *"While we did not qualify totally for instrument flying,"* says Patton, *"what we received was a tactical instrument ticket which allowed us to fly under U.S. Army aviation flight rules in Vietnam. Because I took this training post-Vietnam, I never really used all the skills we were taught. However, I did learn much about Army helicopter employment and maintenance."* Later, when he was stationed in Europe, Patton continued to fly and did so until he was grounded by a U.S. Army policy that general officers not specifically assigned to an aviation unit would not be authorized to fly as pilots.

When Patton was about to graduate from Fort Rucker with a set of Army aviation wings, he contacted General James K. Polk, Commander in Chief, United States Army Europe, and asked to join his command. Polk offered Patton an assignment as Assistant Division Commander for Support, 4th Armored Division, in Nuremberg. *"I was one of three generals in the 4th Armored Division. This was my first tour as a general officer and I failed to realize what I was getting into. The position was very disagreeable because of the condition of the Army at that time. As a matter of fact, this was the most troublesome assignment in my thirty-four years of service."*

Patton arrived in Germany in early 1970 and was faced with a host of problems. Soldiers from Vietnam who had five and six months to go to complete their military service obligation had come to Germany already unhappy with having to play out their time away from the United States. *"During my 1970–1971 tour in*

*Europe elements of the division received twenty-seven
bomb threats, whereas I had about nineteen threats on
my life,"* says Patton. *"The unrest was palpable, com-
pounded by terribly rundown facilities."* For example,
Patton was responsible for building maintenance and
supply, yet had practically no maintenance dollars. He
recalls visiting an Erlangen-based mechanized infantry
battalion one morning and learning that the barracks
containing nearly six hundred men had one working
urinal in the entire building. The soldier occupants of
that particular barracks were urinating from the win-
dows, and the odor was terrible. Improving the buildings significantly was difficult to justify officially,
because the view prevailed that the United States would
soon pull out of NATO, which, as events transpired,
did not occur. Patton says such thinking created a so-
called *"bow-wave"* syndrome: *"Let it go for just one
more year and we will then get after the problem, when
things really become critical. This concept obviously
did not work out to the benefit of the soldier,"* Patton
says. In another example, several barracks assigned to
Division Artillery, 4th Armored Division, had no heating system. As an alternative, a primitive Herman-Nel-
son heater was used to warm the barracks.

Patton also was a first-hand witness to the height-
ened racial tensions then being visited upon American
society. One morning Patton received information
through "privileged intelligence channels" that there
was trouble brewing in Bamberg, where a brigade of
the 4th Armored Division was located. *"The CID
[Criminal Investigation Division] report indicated black
soldiers were planning to march on the Rod and Gun
Club in the Bamberg Kaserne, break in, steal the guns
and raid the post,"* Patton remembers. Since intelligence
sources were generally reliable, Patton flew to Bamberg
and met with the brigade commander and his staff. Patton felt the need for more military police to offset the
threat, so he then talked to the corps commander, who
happened to be in Bamberg at that same time. Knowing

there was a Corps MP company in Stuttgart, he asked to have that unit, or at least a portion of it, deployed on alert in the Nuremberg area. The corps commander responded, "That sounds like a good idea. I'll return to Stuttgart and support it." Patton had several additional meetings with intelligence personnel, chaplains, and various staff levels and formulated antiriot plans. They even considered putting two battalions on practice alert in order to defuse the situation. As he and his staff were working on the plans, Patton was summoned to a telephone to receive the corp commander's bad news. "My staff and I have looked the situation over and we can't spare the MPs. Just do the best you can with what you have," the commander reported. *"My heart sank. I felt very much alone,"* says Patton.

As a disappointed Patton walked back to rejoin the security meeting, he noticed a copy of *Stars and Stripes* in the S-1's office (Personnal and Administration at the brigade, regiment level, or below). An article about a performance by the comedienne Martha Raye in Grafenwöhr the next day caught his eye. *"This famous actress was well known to the troops, having done so much entertaining in Vietnam,"* remembers Patton. Knowing the Grafenwöhr commander very well, Patton called him on the "old boy circuit" and outlined his problem. "If I stage a surprise show by Martha Raye it may well break the tension here," explained Patton. He replied, "I understand completely; consider it arranged." Patton sent a chopper for Raye and following her arrival briefed her on the problem. She said, "Don't worry, I'll put on a show that will knock their eyes out." *"And it was a great show,"* Patton recalls, *"and it eased the situation and our crisis vaporized."*

The challenges plaguing Patton, and indeed the European command according to some observers, reflected a general lack of understanding by senior officers concerning the tensions that were permeating both U.S. society and the Army. Problems with drugs, alcohol, racial discontent, and previous Vietnam service were new to the senior levels, and they were struggling to deal with them. Patton remembers having meetings with intelligence personnel three or four times a week. *"I later learned that one general was physically attacked during a riot and was eventually relieved for letting the situation get out of hand,"* says Patton. *"And he should have been! One cannot allow himself to be degraded when one is in uniform, especially a general officer."*

The problems in Europe, according to the same observers, were exacerbated by the USAREUR manpower level, which had been drawn down in order to support Southeast Asia requirements. Duty assignments that called for majors and captains in brigade and battalion staffs were being filled with lieutenants. These officers, although eager to do whatever was required, were *"simply devoid of the experience to handle the problems which existed in this theater,"* agrees Patton. He credits General James Polk, Commander in Chief, U.S. Army Europe, with holding the theater together. *"Had he not been at the USAREUR helm during those difficult times, with the Army at its lowest ebb since the final days of World War II, we could have been literally blown away. His experience and his sense of trust for his subordinates were largely responsible for our survival,"* says Patton.

During this time Patton also dealt with prison riots, and even murder in the barracks. *"One time a black senior NCO was forcibly filled with drugs and thrown out a third story window to his death, as just one example. This was a senior noncommissioned officer trying to do his job. His refusal to provide black militants with his support cost him his life,"* claims Patton.

In an attempt to deal with the problems within VII Corps, Polk set up a time on Saturday mornings when the offices of all general officers would be open for visits from anyone, from 8:30 A.M. to 11:00 A.M. The purpose of this "open door policy" was to reduce tension within the community, encouraging enlisted personnel to address any subject with their commander. The problems and solutions, if appropriate and supportable, would then be transformed into action at higher headquarters. *"One day,"* Patton remembers, *"a soldier came in and said, 'I represent a group of black soldiers and we have a major problem.' He said, 'You know there are whorehouses in Nuremberg.' I indicated my awareness of that fact. He went on to say, 'The whores downtown are not equal opportunity employers. They won't take us in. The brothers request that you meet with the madams and see if you can get it straightened out.' I looked at him and said, 'Fella, I've been in the Army twenty-seven years and this is the first time I ever received a request like that. I will not do anything about it. Get out!' I sat there wondering what the Army was coming to and he started toward the door, then turned around. 'General,' he asked, 'don't you have a little blonde daughter that walks to school every morning by herself?' I glared at him and said, 'What's that to you?' 'Nothing,' he muttered, then he threw me a sloppy hand salute and walked out.*

"Needless to say, I had that soldier shipped back to the United States under an official 'quick check,' a privileged communication between myself and General Polk with information copies to division and the VII Corps commander. That was the single time I used that special privilege of communication in my career. The soldier was gone within two days."

Meanwhile, bomb threats in the city of Nuremberg were becoming such a problem that special arrangements even had to be made for the REFORGER (Return of Forces to Germany) dinner held for senior officers participating in the annual exercises. REFORGER was designed to deploy CONUS troops to Germany in predetermined positions in order to demonstrate the effectiveness of this contingency in the event of a Soviet threat. At least one division and sometimes two were brought from the States for the event. Arriving with their individual weapons, but no heavy equipment, the troops would obtain supplies stored in Europe, join a corps, and proceed to maneuver against an opposing force. They would do this for a week or more, usually in cold weather months to avoid excessive crop damage in the countryside. They would then return their equipment and redeploy to their CONUS location.

One afternoon Patton received word that General Polk's train was halted in Nuremberg and the general wanted to see him. Polk asked for a status report and Patton detailed the latest news concerning bomb threats, racial tension, and a number of other concerns regarding VII Corps and its assigned units in the Nuremberg community. Polk confirmed with Patton that he was hosting the REFORGER dinner to be held in the Bavarian American Hotel in downtown Nuremberg. Among the attendees would be the Secretary of Defense, the Supreme Allied Commander in Europe (SACEUR), and other senior dignitaries and staff. *"The lowest-ranking military person attending the dinner would be a lieutenant general,"* says Patton.

"Polk then asked me, 'Specifically, how many bomb threats have you had in this area in the past six months?' I answered fifteen. We then discussed the dinner, and I mentioned that there was a very real possibility of a bomb threat that evening. Polk replied, 'If there are bomb threats on the night of the REFORGER dinner you will join the ranks of the unemployed. Your job is to stop all that and get it under control.' My aide was the only person with me, so I wheeled around sarcastically and said, 'Staff, Attention!' 'Patton, what do you mean by that?' Polk shot back. I said, 'This fellow is my staff, sir. The CID, CIC [Counterintelligence Corps], *MPs, and other agencies whose mission is to deal with such problems do not work for me, and I have no control over them. They work for headquarters in Munich and elsewhere in the FRG* [Federal Republic of Germany].*'*

"'I'll take care of that,' Polk concluded, and while

on his train he dispatched a message saying Brigadier General Patton was in charge of security for the REFORGER dinner and all necessary agencies are to report to him and comply with his orders."

After General Polk's message was relayed to various agencies, Patton began putting together a coordinated plan for added protection, security, and intelligence collection. Even with the effective intelligence nets placed throughout the city, anyone could enter a phone booth, any place in the city that night, and call the hotel claiming they had planted a bomb. In further preparation for the dinner Patton added on-site security personnel and spread the dignitaries throughout the city so that not too many were billeted at any one hotel. Special transportation and escort services were also arranged to support VIP movement.

On the day of the dinner, Patton established a control and information CP in the hotel and conducted a building search from top to bottom. A map was placed in each room to provide guests directions to an alternate location if the hotel had to be evacuated quickly. As the evening began, Patton sat in a jeep in a pouring rainstorm watching the dignitaries and their wives arrive. Some greeted Patton, including General Andrew Jackson Goodpaster, SACEUR, whom Patton had known for many years. He could plainly see that Patton was faced with a long evening. Patton sweated out the hours until the conclusion of the evening's activities. After the dinner the last person to exit was General Goodpaster, who stopped by Patton's jeep and said, "Well, we got through it, George. Everything went well, the food and wine were excellent and we had no bomb threats. Glad everything worked out."

Not long after all the guests had left the dinner for their hotels, Patton was called by his MP master sergeant, who was on the second floor of the hotel in his control headquarters. He asked Patton to join his men for a beer to celebrate a successful evening. Patton went up to the hotel room, now overflowing with security people, and congratulated them on a good job. As he was chatting with members of the detail, the lobby desk clerk phoned and stated that he had just received a call warning that there was a bomb in the hotel. *"I looked at my NCO,"* says Patton, *"and asked, 'Well, what do you think we ought to do?' He replied, 'Have another beer.' I was tired; we had protected the dinner guests and that was it. I took an awful chance on that decision, since some of the generals were staying in the hotel. If anything had happened I would have gone for the long course at Fort Leavenworth* [i.e., to prison]," Patton chuckles, *"but everything worked out fine. It was a long night and one in which I must admit—I earned my pay."*

During his time in Europe Patton was asked to write his thoughts concerning the subject of the racial tensions facing the 4th Armored Division, VII Corps and all U.S. troops in Europe. In a memo addressed to General Polk, Patton highlighted his solutions to the problem:

- First, in any dealings with racial areas or problems, the by-word must be complete impartiality, always and everytime. One must be colorblind.
- Hard meaningful work, tough and demanding training and enforceable disciplinary programs are basic requirements. The equipment and funds to support this type of training must be made available.
- I am compelled to again emphasize the continued development of a meaningful, feasible and manageable intelligence program which, through the incident center, produces intelligence for the commander that he can use.
- Finally, I would mention the PIO [public information officer] aspects of the racial problem. We are in need of additional emphasis wherein public information personnel cover such events as Service Opportunity Seminars within a given unit; AER grants to

destitute black soldiers; and photographs of enlisted men, NCOs and officers of all ranks, who make meaningful contributions to the unit mission.

He concluded with a quote from Thoreau which seemed applicable: "There is no ill which may not be dissipated like the dark if you let in a stronger light upon it. If the light we use is but a paltry and narrow tape, most objects will cast a shadow wider than themselves."

As Patton's bleak European assignment wore on, with troubles piling upon troubles, he became so disgusted with the situation that he went home one night and started to prepare his resignation from the Army. *"That is the only time I ever did that,"* says Patton. *"But Joanne came into the room and asked me what I was writing and I told her. She reached over my shoulder, took the paper and tore it up. She said, 'George Patton, the Army needs someone like you right now. You can't quit.' It was a great compliment, which I am not sure I deserved."*

To add to Patton's problems, in late 1970 he had incurred the hip injury that would eventually put his military career in serious jeopardy. As a part of Patton's official duties he was the Nuremberg community commander, in charge of dependent affairs, schools, athletic programs and, as he says, *"acting as sort of a mayor."* In September Patton was scheduled to attend a district meeting of the Boy Scouts of America in Berchtesgaden. He could not leave until late that afternoon, arriving in Berchtesgaden after 9:30 P.M.

At the desk he was informed that he would have to go to a parking lot a quarter of a mile from the hotel. Leaving Joanne in the lobby, Patton found the non-illuminated designated area and started walking back to the hotel. As he prepared to cross over toward the hotel's entrance he realized, too late, that he had been

walking on a large stone wall and not a road. Stepping
out into thin air, Patton fell eight feet to the road. When
he hit the ground Patton heard something crack and
realized he was seriously injured.

A few minutes later a bus came by filled with American women from a religious retreat. The passengers
spotted Patton in the road and took him to the hotel.
Being moved by those well intentioned people was unfortunate, as it caused further bone displacement in
what turned out to be a fractured right hip.

*"As luck would have it, the ranking USAREUR sur-
geon was in attendance at the hotel conference and ordered an ambulance to evacuate me to an Army
hospital in Munich. I underwent surgery there and was
released to return to Nuremberg after a week or so. I
was on crutches for a while, then a cane, and was able
to regain fair mobility for a period of time."* Several
months later Patton had to undergo additional surgery
to remove the pins in his hip. Patton's orthopedic ad-
ventures had just begun.

During the winter of 1971, Patton learned that the
Assistant Commandant's position at the Armor School
at Fort Knox, Kentucky, would be vacated. Ever since
being commissioned, twenty-five years previously, he
had hoped for that assignment. Fed up with the situation in Europe, and feeling deeply that there was little
more he could personally do, Patton contacted General
"Dutch" Kerwin, who was now the Deputy Chief of
Staff for Personnel, and the transfer was accomplished.
Patton, as a former member of the staff and faculty at
the Armor School, was intimately familiar with Fort
Knox and the Central Kentucky environment; soon the
Patton family was on its way back to the United States.

When Patton reported to his new boss, Major General William R. Desobry, he was given three guidelines
concerning their working relationship. First, General
Desobry would teach four hours of leadership to each
career course. Second, he would have the final decision

on the assignments of War College graduates to the Armor Center. Finally, Patton was to stay out of local politics in the Radcliff-Elizabethtown, Kentucky, area. Everything else with regard to the relationship between the Armor School and headquarters of the Armor Center was Patton's responsibility. *"It was brief and to the point,"* says Patton, *"and I considered it unique and very acceptable. Bill Desobry was one of the finest bosses I had in my entire career of service."*

At the time of his arrival, fighting was still going on in Vietnam. Yet when Patton took over the school, he was appalled to find that there was not a single unit of instruction on Vietnam or Southeast Asia. Most of the instruction was for armor over the rolling plains of Europe, "tank country." He took care of that oversight quickly. *"The Armor School was still back in World War Two, not withstanding the fact that most of our students were either coming from or departing to Southeast Asia."*

The primary mission at Knox was to work with lieutenants, assisting them in becoming technical experts on armored equipment. The curricula included several courses in various training disciplines for different levels of officers. Training was also provided to other areas and people, such as radio operators, tank mechanics, and vehicle maintenance personnel.

Patton, always creative, was continually plagued by a shortage of commissioned instructors. One day he decided to raid the hospitals in search of some *"walking wounded"* to allow his staff to be filled to its authorized level. Several of these officers were about to be discharged for physical disability, and Patton turned them into instructors. Those who were not able to teach for one reason or another were placed in administrative duties in support of the school. Patton feels his major accomplishment during his tenure was bringing the Armor School into a modernized posture. *"Of great importance—we were able to organize an air cavalry*

*course of instruction which included the enlisted scout
observer."*

Summarizing his Fort Knox assignment, which lasted
over two years, Patton reflects that it was perhaps his
most enjoyable peacetime experience in his thirty-four
years of service. His department directors, all War College graduates, were among the best he had ever served
with. He felt the Army had been good to him in this
assignment, perhaps paying off for the Nuremberg experience, which had been less than satisfactory.

Another satisfying aspect of the assignment to Fort
Knox was helping bring the Patton Museum up to standard and seeing it moved to a permanent site. It was
relocated in a new building that overlooks heavy traffic
on Highway 31W, the route running right through the
Armor Center. *"We were fortunate to receive a large
donation from the State of Kentucky and gifts from
other sources,"* explains Patton, *"since we were prohibited from receiving congressional appropriations for
this purpose."* To assist in bringing the museum up to
speed, a number of businessmen in Louisville and Eliza-
bethtown organized a fund-raising dinner; the guest of
honor was George C. Scott. *"This was just about two
years after the movie* Patton *was released,"* Patton explains. *"I had never met Scott, and after a luncheon we
toured the entire Armor School. The museum really
took off at that time and I was honored to be involved
with its progress."*

In 1973 Patton was transferred from Fort Knox,
once again to Europe. He was informed that he was
going to Stuttgart, Germany, as the J-7 for European
Command. Patton remembers at the time he was teaching an advanced class of senior officers. The room was
full of generals and colonels; Patton announced his departure and then asked if someone could tell him what
a J-7 was or did. There was an uneasy silence. No one
knew. Patton learned later that J-7 was a security assistance person who exercised Joint Staff supervision over
the MAAGs in Europe, the Middle East, and several

countries in Africa. His assignment was to be Director of Security Assistance with Headquarters U.S. European Command, under General George Eade, USAF.

After arriving in Europe, Patton had Joint Staff jurisdiction for twenty-one Military Assistance Advisory Groups, located in France, Germany, Spain, Portugal, Belgium, Holland, Norway, Denmark, Jordan, Saudi Arabia, Kuwait, Tunisia, Morocco, Mali, and Ethiopia. *"We had to deal with budgets, programs and attaché people who monitored the security assistance programs in those nations,"* says Patton.

When the Israeli-Syria War started on Yom Kippur in 1973, Patton was in Spain visiting the MAAG. As Patton says, the alert status for the United States *"went from casual to not quite so casual,"* and he called his boss, Lieutenant General Jock Sutherland, in Stuttgart to ask him if he was going to be recalled. Sutherland said no, but requested that Patton watch the progress of the war very closely. After hostilities ceased, Patton traveled to Jordan. He knew Jordan had resisted joining the war on the Arab side for a period and had then given in to political pressure and had sent one armor brigade to the Golan Heights area, where it was decisively defeated by the Israelis. The irony for Patton was that after the war, Jordan had asked the United States for both new and replacement tanks. The request was approved in Washington. Patton later had a frank talk with a Jordanian major general, saying he could not understand how Jordan could have entered the war contrary to the wishes of the United States, been "whipped," and then had the nerve to ask for more and better tanks. His answer was, "We fought very slowly."

While Patton was in Jordan, he visited a truck rebuilding plant. Using limited funds the Jordanians were restoring a great many salvaged American vehicles, rebuilding them from the bottom up. There was an American civilian technical representative available to the Jordanians to answer any technical questions about the equipment. Patton asked him what he did specifically.

He replied, "I do very little, General. They don't want me in the factory because they want their people to scratch for their knowledge and I am not to be a crutch." Patton found the Jordanians to be efficient from a military point of view. On one occasion he visited an airfield in northeastern Jordan. Fighters were deployed along the airstrip and Patton asked how long it would take them to get in the air; he was told eight minutes. Patton replied, "Let's see it." They were airborne, Patton remembers, in seven minutes, fifteen seconds.

Patton was invited to have breakfast with the brother of King Hussein, Prince Hassan, a meeting that proved to be very educational and pleasant. "*I was one of the first U.S. officials to visit there after the war and consequently I was heavily guarded and well escorted. The Jordanian Army staged a review for me which was one of the most faultless exhibitions of military drill that I've ever seen,*" marvels Patton. The Jordanians held a luncheon in Patton's honor, and one of the dishes was a large bowl of mutton in a cream sauce. The bowl was about three feet across, and in the middle, looking straight up, was the unshorn head of a sheep. The host reached and scooped out one eye, saying it was traditional for the guest of honor to have one. Patton said, "What would you like me to do with it?" "Pop it down, old boy," came the reply. Patton swallowed the golf ball–size eye to hearty applause and could feel it all the way down. "*Later, when it was convenient to do so I went outside to do some deep breathing and almost threw up,*" says Patton.

While in Jordan on that particular trip, Patton had an interesting incident. The group went to the Allenby Bridge, a crossing point between Jordan and Israel. Patton had heard all about the problems of peace and mutual cooperation, and as he says, "*all the buzz words from the State Department*" about these two countries. Arriving at the bridge, Patton saw Israeli guards on the west side and Jordanians on the east. Each crew had a mounted tripod machine gun facing the other at a distance of fifty feet. The crews were not with the guns. They were out shooting dice in the middle of the bridge. Once again Patton was left musing about the ironies of war and peace.

Patton found Saudi Arabia an entirely different story. He talked at length with retired U.S. service people who were maintaining the aircraft. Patton asked why the U.S. was providing so much support; a technician replied, "The Saudi pilots don't even kick a tire, they expect us to do everything." *"The Saudis obviously had huge quantities of money, and I simply drooled when I toured their air defense school and saw the available instructional equipment,"* says Patton. *"Everything was state of the art, the best money could buy. For instance, they had installed microphones at each seat in the lecture theater thus enabling students to ask questions or comment without leaving their place."*

During this period, the head of the MAAG in Denmark, an Air Force colonel, came to Patton with a major problem. The fighter aircraft in the Northern Tier countries of NATO, including Denmark, Norway, the Netherlands, and Belgium, were getting old, and there was heavy pressure on those nations to purchase French aircraft. The pressure came from political, economic, and military interests. The Chief MAAG said he was getting nowhere with the Air Force in having the U.S. make a competitive offer. He had tried everything and asked if Patton could help. Patton explored the problem through channels and found out that he too hit a dead end. *"I decided then to contact my friend General Alexander Haig in the White House,"* recalls Patton. *"Within three weeks the tables were turned and U.S. aircraft were purchased by Denmark. For me the incident illustrated Haig's influence and dedication to America, but also demonstrated how solid, long-lasting relationships in the military produced results."*

Patton, as J-7, also had a very rare opportunity to

meet and confer with the Ethiopian emperor, Haile Selassie. *"We had a scheduled visit to Ethiopia to do an
annual inspection to assess their problems, strengths
and needs,"* says Patton. *"I knew through message traffic that Haile Selassie had run into a problem with the
U.S. Congress concerning his grant aid package. Accordingly we were prepared to discuss the situation
when we travelled to Ethiopia for a two-week visit."*
During the stay, Patton's team got word through the
ambassador concerning what day he was to call on the
Emperor. He looked forward to the visit, since Selassie
was such a well-known international figure. Patton met
with the ambassador, and they went over the problems
and challenges as they both saw them and came to common agreement about an agenda for the meeting.

Patton remembers driving to the palace, parking,
and walking around to the back side, which also served
as the VIP entrance. *"As we approached the palace, we
encountered a lion in the driveway. Now, Haile Selassie
was known as the Lion of Judah and this lion was obviously his personal property,"* he says. *"The lion was
secured with a chain, just a few feet from the door. As
we walked gingerly towards the entrance, hugging the
wall away from the lion, he let out a huge roar. I'll tell
you this got our attention!"*

At the door the group was met by a slight gentleman
in a blue suit, who said, "The Emperor will see you."
Patton went into a room, sat down, and was given tea.
Fifteen minutes later another, more ornately dressed,
gentleman came and said, "The Emperor will see you";
off the group went into yet another room, and again
were given tea. Still another man came in, and again
they were moved, to yet another room. By this time, an
hour and a half had gone by, and Patton was certain
they had run out of time and tea.

"Finally the great moment came," says Patton. *"Another gentleman in a swallowtail coat with spats, a
wing collar and many medals and ribbons entered and
said, 'The Emperor is ready to see you now.' We*

*walked into a huge room, perhaps seventy-five to a
hundred feet square. On the right was a fireplace, about
fifteen feet in width. Even though this was September
we were cool, at seven thousand feet in elevation, so
there was a roaring fire going. As I looked around the
room I noticed all the couches were covered with zebra,
leopard and various animal skins. Several chihuahuas
were also in the room, as well. In the far corner of the
room to the left was a huge desk and behind this desk
stood a little tiny man, alone, with a small dog under
each arm. We bowed and the ambassador took two
steps forward and said, 'Your Imperial Majesty, I present Major General George S. Patton, Director of Security Assistance, U.S. European Command.' The
Emperor moved out from behind his desk, stood about
twenty feet away, bowed slightly and said, 'Yes, General Patton.' Those were the only English words he
spoke. The rest of the conversation was held through an
interpreter."* The ambassador later told Patton that
Haile Selassie had a very good understanding of English
but that the interpreter was there to give him time to
think before having to respond.

The Emperor conveyed to Patton that he was unhappy with President Richard Nixon. He had asked for
a certain amount of money and believed that Nixon
had agreed. Patton, who had already done considerable
research on the issue, explained to Selassie that the difficulty was in the United States Congress, which had
slashed the appropriation. It took Patton a few minutes
to explain the circumstances, and when Selassie realized
it was not President Nixon's fault he asked Patton to
send the president his warm personal regards. The rest
of the time, Patton chatted with Selassie about the Emperor's World War II experiences. He showed Patton
and the ambassador around his office and pointed out a
collection of photographs of the leaders of the twentieth century. The list of international VIPs was absolutely incredible, recalls Patton. *"He had photographs*

of himself with Woodrow Wilson, Chiang Kai-shek, Eisenhower, Stalin and Churchill. All were autographed to this famous little man who had held Ethiopia together for so many years." After the briefing a servant came in with a tray of raw meat and coffee. *"It was tough to make it look like I was enjoying raw meat,"* says Patton, *"but I figured I just had to eat it. When you are with people in their country they expect you to eat their food. If you don't they are rightly insulted."*

After visiting the Emperor, Patton's escorts took the J-7 group to visit tank units near Jijiga in the Atlas Mountains. *"East of Jijiga is Somalia and between the two is an absolute flat and arid piece of ground known as the Ogaden,"* says Patton. *"We visited a tank company there. When we arrived the whole outfit was lined up for me to inspect. They looked first-class. I had a chance to meet one tank driver, who through an interpreter said he had been a driver for eight years. I turned to the tank commander and inquired as to whether this fellow was promotable. The commander said, 'No, sir. He needs more experience.'"* Patton laughed to himself, that a tank driver after eight years in the same job still needed more experience, but at the same time he could not help but admire the extremely well trained troops. Patton, aware that they had been having difficulties with Somalia, asked how long it would take the unit to move out when ordered. The answer was ten minutes; Patton asked the troop commander to get them under way. *"I never saw anything like it in my life,"* says an admiring Patton. *"Within ten minutes, they had the tanks lined up on the road, engines running and every man with his field equipment in place. I was impressed."*

Patton, who traveled a great deal in the J-7 assignment, also went to Israel on an orientation tour with the army, escorted by General Moussa Peled, commanding general of the Israeli Armored Corps. *"In the U.S. Army a corps commander would be responsible for his corps only. Another general would be responsible for the training base. In the Israeli Army, as I understood it, one commander did both jobs,"* explains Patton. *"The Israeli military has always been a first-class fighting force which is motivated, disciplined, and innovative, but on the outside scruffy,"* Patton says. *"Israeli soldiers are not noted for their appearance; however, underneath there is a high degree of professionalism. They are motivated because they have something to fight and die for. During my visit I observed a* [simulated] *night attack conducted under radio listening silence. It was a very well done military operation. In the attack, in which live ammunition was being used against paper targets, the task organization of the battalion changed twice under listening silence, without communication, other than flares."*

Patton found the Israeli reserve and call-up systems also remarkable. *"When they execute a call-up of reserves, people leave banks, offices, drug stores, and hospitals in order to drive tanks, shoot howitzers, fly aircraft and fill the ranks,"* says Patton. During one visit Patton, staying in Caesarea, had to attend a departure meeting and briefing at the embassy in Tel Aviv. He was riding along in the taxi and enjoying the countryside when the driver suddenly heard on his citizen's band radio that his unit had been ordered to activate. The driver brought the cab to a stop about two miles from the embassy. He turned to Patton and said in English, "My unit has been called up. I'm first sergeant of an artillery battery and you must get out of my cab, sir."

Patton, loaded down with three suitcases, said, "Can you get me another cab?"

"I'll try," he replied, but within seconds had unloaded Patton's suitcases, placed them on the side of the road, did a 180-degree turn in the road, and raced off in the other direction.

While Patton's travel schedule and workload were daunting, his injured hip was also progressively deteriorating. Warned at the time he broke his hip in September 1970 that he would eventually need a hip replacement, Patton had asked, "How will I know when?" The doctors in Munich said, "You will know." And he did. In 1973 the Pattons drove to Paris for the Christmas holidays. It was a seven-hour drive, and when they arrived at the hotel Patton was in so much pain he could barely get out of the car. *"I couldn't walk two hundred yards without stopping,"* he says. *"At that point I was living on aspirin and in constant pain."* In the midst of this came the offer from Abrams to command the First Armored Division, a dream that would have to be put on hold, perhaps forever.

15

HELL ON WHEELS

*I'd follow that man to hell and fight the devil himself
'cause I'm damn sure he'd lead me back.*
—2nd Armored Division tanker, of Patton

Patton underwent successful hip surgery in June 1974
and by fall was looking around for something to do,
with the proviso that he stay near his doctor. After calling a friend in the Pentagon, Patton was assigned as
Special Assistant to the Commanding General of Army
Readiness Region I, Major General Morgan Roseborough. The duty station was Fort Devens, Massachusetts, near Boston.

In the winter of 1974, little more than a year after
being promoted to major general, Patton received a letter from General Frederick Weyand, Chief of Staff,
United States Army, with devastating news. The Army
had decided to retire Patton because of his hip. *"I was
in shock,"* says Patton. *"When I was at Fort Knox, I
had people working for me with one leg, one arm or
one eye."*

For Patton, the day he was notified of his forced and
imminent retirement was one of the saddest of his life.
He felt the Army medical people were offended because

he had requested that Dr. Harris in Boston perform his hip surgery rather than the personnel at Walter Reed Hospital. He was particularly upset because he loved the Army and knew he could continue making significant contributions.

Patton discussed the problem, first with the Fort Devens Army surgeon, Bert Goldberg, who provided a copy of the regulation that apparently mandated retirement after hip replacement, and then with Joanne. Together they decided to seek advice from Dr. Harris, who was astounded when he heard the Army's opinion, that Patton had a disease of the hip and could not possibly continue his service. Harris reviewed the findings and considered them "a personal insult." Hip surgery had progressed much further than was recognized by the Army Surgeon General's Office, and the state of the art had outdated the regulation that condemned the operation. At the time Harris was considered the top hip surgeon in the United States. He told Patton, "You have 85 percent use of that hip and remain very active. There is no reason why you cannot serve as a general officer. You couldn't serve as a private, but you are not a private." Harris called in his secretary and dictated a letter to the Army Chief of Staff, General Weyand. He wrote that he was the surgeon who had performed the operation on Patton, and that whereas the Army had stated that Patton had a disease of the hip, the disease had been excised and he was fit for duty as a general officer. Placing his dictated letter in final form, he mailed it to the Chief of Staff that evening.

A month later Patton was at work at Fort Devens when a soldier came running into his office. "General, the Chief of Staff Army is on the phone." Patton picked up the phone. "George, this is Fred. That doctor of yours certainly writes a good letter. The judgement of the surgeon general's office has been reversed, and I'm not sure what I'm going to do with you old friend, but I'm going to retain you on active duty." Breathing a sigh of relief, Patton replied, "Sir, I'm perfectly qualified and able to command, and I'll do whatever you want me to do provided I can stay in the service."

Patton remembers the month between the retirement letter and the call from General Weyand as a very tough time. *"I wasn't ready to leave the Army and called several friends about the situation. They went into action."* One in particular, Lieutenant General Orwin C. Talbot, Patton's former division commander in Vietnam and influential in Patton's receiving his first star, flew from Fort Monroe to Washington to meet with the Chief of Staff about returning him to active duty. General Bruce Clark, the hero of St. Vith and a protégé of Patton's father, although long retired, also communicated with the Chief of Staff on Patton's behalf. Patton respected and admired General Weyand for overruling the Army medical staff and keeping him on active duty. *"Dr. Harris's letter, coupled with Weyand's decision, provided five more years of service for me. I appreciated every day of it."*

Shortly after arriving at Fort Devens, the commanding general, Major General Roseborough, retired from active duty, and Patton assumed his spot as CG of Army Readiness Region I, covering reserve and National Guard activities in the six New England states and the state of New York. While Patton had little experience with either the Guard or reserves, his exposure to them during this period stood him in good stead when later, at Fort Hood, he became involved with training responsibilities for the Texas National Guard.

For Patton, time at Fort Devens was a long holding pattern, yet he did his job with the usual vigor, even though the confusion and turmoil of the last days in Vietnam were visited upon him, especially in 1974. In April the mayor of Cambridge, Massachusetts, asked if Patton could provide troops for the reenactment of George Washington's commissioning ceremony. Patton looked around and told the mayor that the best that he could send to represent the Army were a couple of detachments of the 10th Special Forces Group, stationed at Fort Devens. The mayor said no, the Special Forces, the Green Berets, represented everything people were protesting in these anti-Vietnam days, and he did not want to have the day marred by protests. He then asked Patton if he could have the medics or engineers who were at Fort Devens. Patton refused. The mayor relented, and on the day of the celebration a large crowd was assembled with many people dressed in continental uniforms. A group of businessmen had reenacted the ride from Philadelphia to Cambridge, including a person playing George Washington. Patton's detachment was led by a sergeant major dressed in fatigues and a contingent of Green Berets, some with jungle machetes. Patton also brought along a color guard and a band.

Just as the actors were to present "Washington" with his commission, a young man with ribbons in his long hair broke loose from the crowd and ran up to the sergeant major, who was standing at attention. He stuck a flower in his face and started shouting, "Baby killer." The sergeant major turned to Patton and said, "General Patton, what should I do?"

Patton replied, "Use your own judgement."

The sergeant major turned to the protester and hollered, "Get lost, motherfucker, before I waste your motherfucking ass!"

Patton laughs, *"I will say that guy disappeared immediately and the mayor, wide-eyed, stuttered, 'It sounds to me like he means business.' It was an incident which so epitomized the tenor of the era."*

While Patton was dealing with a variety of problems in Region I, the Vietnam War was in its final and most inglorious phase. The last American troops had departed Vietnam in May 1973, yet the war continued despite a truce. In fact, over fifty thousand Vietnamese were killed in battle in the twelve months following the signing of the truce. The taking of Phuoc Long province near the Cambodian border in January 1975 set the stage for the final communist offensive, which began in March with major attacks in the Central Highlands.

South Vietnamese President Thieu soon ordered the evacuation of the highlands, and South Vietnamese Army forces began to break up. Saigon was occupied on April 30, 1975. Most of the top anticommunist leaders left with the last departing American civilians, and the war was over.

Patton watched the television reports of the final collapse in utter dismay. *"I was terribly ashamed that our great country would leave that little nation in such shambles,"* says Patton. *"I observed the helicopters being pushed off carriers into the sea and the Vietnamese attempting to break into the embassy and other U.S. buildings. I was heartbroken. To me, and certainly to many of my contemporaries, the final days and hours of the Republic of Vietnam were disgraceful and marked the low point of the military as we knew it. Given the situation at the time, it was inevitable that South Vietnam would collapse totally and surrender to the enemy."*

In the summer of 1975 Patton attended the Fort Myer, Virginia, retirement ceremony of a long-time friend, Brigadier General Joseph McCarthy. The formation was held in the riding hall where Patton as a boy had taken riding lessons from his father and other distinguished horse cavalrymen. In the middle of the McCarthy ceremony, a soldier whispered to Patton that the Chief of Staff, General Weyand, was on the phone and wished to speak to him. Patton located a phone in a janitor's closet.

"George, this is Fred. How would you like to take over 'Hell on Wheels' at Fort Hood in August?"

Patton stammered, "Yes, sir," finished the call, and then broke down and cried. In a matter of months Patton had gone from being told that he would be retired to becoming the first officer in the history of the United States Army to command the same division as his father.

While awaiting his assignment to take over the 2nd Armored Division, Patton travelled from Fort Devens to see other divisions. He visited the 101st Airborne at Fort Campbell, Kentucky, as well as Fort Knox, Fort Sill, Oklahoma, and Fort Benning, Georgia, soliciting advice on division command.

When Patton arrived at Fort Hood, Texas, he realized he was a part of military history. He remembers his first day vividly: *"I went to the chapel by myself and prayed on my knees asking the Lord to let me do a good job and to be a credit to the Army and my family. I could really sense my dad's presence in that chapel with me. My reaction to his presence was simply intense pride."*

The 2nd Armored Division—commanded from November 1940 through January 1942 by George S. Patton, Jr.—now witnessed his son commanding from August 1975 through October 1977. Originally activated in July 1940 at Fort Benning, "Hell on Wheels," as its motto proclaimed, was ordered ready for combat not long after activation. Training became the responsibility of brigade, and later division, commander Colonel George S. Patton, Jr.

Following the division's training at Fort Benning, Hell on Wheels took to the field in a series of maneuvers about which the senior Patton issued General Order Number 67, which read: "You have completed six months of active duty field training under severe conditions. Through the Tennessee, Louisiana, and Carolina maneuvers, you have acquitted yourselves individually and by units as soldiers. You were commended by the highest and most experienced officers in the Army for your appearance, your discipline, your soldierly deportment, and your combat efficiency. By every test short of war you are veterans. I charge you to protect your record." The 2nd Armored Division did indeed protect, and enhance, its record, as the division fought in North

Africa, Sicily, and through four months of heavy combat from October 1944 through January 1945 including continuous action during the Battle of the Bulge.

On the day in 1975 that Patton took over, all division units except those in Germany were turned out for the change of command review. Afterwards, the retiring commander asked Patton how he enjoyed the ceremony. Patton answered that it was fine except for the fact that the band had not played the "2nd Armored Division March," composed by his mother, Beatrice, in 1941; passing in review, the band had played the theme from the movie *Patton*. *"I was upset, feeling that it was wrong to interject my dad into my ceremony,"* says Patton. *"I asked the outgoing commander why they omitted the '2nd Armored Division March' and he said it had been played so much that everyone was tired of it and thought it would bore me."* The next morning Patton summoned the bandmaster and told him that from then on the "2nd Armored Division March" would be played just before the "Army Song" at any ceremony. The bandmaster replied that he had never heard the march but that he would immediately send to Washington for the music. *"Basically,"* says Patton, *"in all candor, I had been told a bald-face lie by the previous commander."*

In addition to playing the *Patton* theme at the change of command ceremony, Fort Hood had put on an elaborate display, including signs welcoming George Patton to "Patton's Own." James Davis, assistant public affairs officer at Fort Hood at the time, recalls, "We had brochures published, murals painted, and many displays. The day after he took command Patton issued a direct order to everyone that any reference to the Pattons would be stricken from the division, to include the signs, brochures and paintings, unless they were of direct historical reference. For about three days there was a concentrated effort of whitewashing and scrubbing."

Davis also remembers that every major news agency and television network wanted to attend the change of command. "Although Patton valued his privacy," says Davis, "we explained that we could not prevent the news people from coming. He did meet with the media for about five minutes after the change of command address, where he gave a fantastic speech which concluded with, 'Good luck, God speed and I will see you in the field.'"

In assuming command Patton followed a personal guideline he had used his entire career. It was similar to the orders routinely followed in the old Royal Navy: *"Unless posted in an emergency, the oncoming officer of the deck will not change the setting of the sails until he has been on deck for thirty minutes,"* says Patton. *"My interpretation of that is, don't take over a unit and make a lot of changes until you have been there for a while."* Patton would quickly find that such a directive would be hard to follow in this particular case.

Before taking over the division, Patton had reviewed the division readiness reporting system, which relayed to higher headquarters, including the Department of the Army, the division's capability to conduct combat operations. The report was immaculate. Then, just a day before taking command, Patton was called in by General Robert Shoemaker, his immediate boss and classmate. He informed Patton that he did not believe that Hell on Wheels was as ready as currently reported. Since Patton had received similar information from other sources, with Shoemaker's concurrence Patton took a close look at the validity of the current readiness reporting system and found it badly inflated. *"I asked Shoemaker why he had not explored this problem prior to my arrival,"* recalls Patton. *"He simply stated that he was leaving this problem to me, since he knew I could handle it."* In Patton's opinion the real cause was a desire not to stir up controversy which could have negatively impacted Shoemaker's career.

After Patton's discussion with Shoemaker and following his experience with the change of command music at his ceremony, warning lights began to flash in

Patton's head that there were some serious problems in Hell on Wheels. He procured a readiness report from a mechanized battalion that indicated conditions were excellent; Patton methodically checked out the unit and then asked the commander directly if the actual readiness condition was excellent. He said, "No, sir." Patton ordered him to rewrite it immediately to reflect the proper figures.

Readiness reporting, even in the mid- to late seventies, was clearly believed to be the bedrock of the U.S. Army readiness system. Patton was displeased to discover that some reports were not totally accurate. *"A commander cannot knowingly violate a readiness report. They must display the true readiness picture of the unit. Honesty is essential,"* exclaims Patton. Readiness for Patton was the top priority. At the time he took over the 2nd there was a standing order saying that when a tank battalion moved to the field, all the tanks would go. Yet shortly after Patton took over, he observed a tank battalion on the march to training. All fifty-four tanks in the battalion were in the column, but five had their guns in travel lock (in travel lock tank turrets face the rear with the gun barrel secured by a clamp). One had only a driver and no crew. Patton talked to the battalion commander and asked about the guns in travel lock. He was told, "Sir, the turrets don't rotate."

Patton then asked about the tank with only a driver. "We are short of crewmen," he replied.

Patton was irritated and inquired as to what policy he was operating under. "That of the previous commander," was the answer. In violation of Patton's Royal Navy rule, he effected a change on that day. He ordered the commander to send the inoperable tanks back to the motor park and put them on deadline for repair. *"I saw the trace of a smile on his face and I know a great load had been lifted from his shoulders,"* says Patton. *"From that time on, as far as I know, the division never submitted a dishonest readiness report, although the readiness reporting, readiness rating decreased markedly. I received inquiries from higher command levels about the decrease and I had to tell them, without mentioning names, that major discrepancies in earlier reports had been located and corrective actions were under way."*

Patton, in his usual style, soon began stamping his imprimatur on Hell on Wheels. In August 1975 Patton issued his description of the successful armored commander. *"An armored commander has got to be a quick thinker. He must be bold and prepared to take a chance,"* Patton wrote. *"He must know the difference between a gamble and a risk. Lastly, notwithstanding the oceans of ink and mountains of volumes written on leadership throughout history, the one guiding precept that he must have is simply this: He must be reliable."*

During Patton's tour as commanding general of Hell on Wheels, his major responsibility was to deploy troops successfully to Europe under a program known as Brigade 75. The deployments involved one tank battalion, two mechanized infantry battalions (one of them provided by the 1st Cavalry Division), one direct support artillery battalion, and one armored cavalry troop, all at Readiness Condition One. It was a monumental task. Under the required criteria, personnel had to be at nearly full strength. As time went on, however, it became clear that the division could not support either the numbers or the rank distributions of the semiannual requirements, due to insufficient numbers. For Patton and the division this caused a high degree of turbulence. Deployment involved sending soldiers to Europe for six months at a time; Patton had to contend with a variety of problems at home, most especially with families, including divorce and general marital unrest. To provide assistance, a "family dependent unit" was established offering a range of services designed to minimize the difficulties caused by the long deployments.

With four brigades assigned to Hell on Wheels and one (the 3rd Brigade) permanently stationed in Europe, at Grafenwöhr, Patton had the largest division in the U.S. Army, numbering over eighteen thousand troops. Therefore, equipment transfers and general logistical concerns under Brigade 75 were particularly bothersome; it was a great relief to everyone when the Brigade 75 deployments and redeployments were terminated, not long after Patton departed Fort Hood. *"The biggest headache,"* explains Patton, *"was that under Brigade 75 the battalions going to Europe picked up the equipment of a battalion returning to CONUS, while the departing battalion in Europe would return to Fort Hood and take over the equipment of the group recently deployed. Keeping track of equipment was a nightmare. Even so, the elements of the division did a magnificent job."* Interestingly, Patton had no command-related responsibilities while the brigade was in Western Europe, although he worked closely with the people on the scene. *"One of my closest friends was commander of USAREUR and I could cut through a lot of red tape with him and improve efficiency,"* says Patton.

Fort Hood was a highlight of Patton's career. *"Every good soldier hopes to command a division. It is the ultimate,"* he says. Patton's view was that higher assignments became too political. *"When you are a division commander you are still around and with soldiers,"* he concludes. Nearly every day Patton visited a different mess hall, making himself available to the troops. Sometimes he would go in the morning, but often at suppertime as well. Unannounced, he would also drop in at the NCO club on post. This policy of being very mobile made some of his commanders nervous, since they never knew when or where he might show up. *"I made up my mind when I took that command, that I would visit at least two battalion-size units daily. I did that religiously unless I was absent from the post. I told my people that they could expect to see me in out-of-the-way places and they did."*

The Hell on Wheels assignment renewed many memories for Patton. *"I had two battalions of the 66th Armored Regiment, whose insignia was designed by my father during World War I. The battalions fought with the 2nd Armored during World War II, and I can remember as a teenager seeing them in training at Fort Benning, Georgia. While Hitler's legions were overrunning France, Poland and the Low Countries, our totally unready force was maneuvering with trucks that had 'TANK' chalked on the sides. I observed 2nd Armored soldiers training in the field with two-by-fours instead of rifles. They had to dress in blue jeans and civilian shirts since the availability of fatigues and individual equipment was nil!"* Patton believes the United States had not followed George Washington's motto, "In time of peace, prepare for war"; within a short, two-year period, units of the 2nd Armored would be locking horns with Rommel's panzer army. Hell on Wheels of 1975–1977 had come a long way from those hectic days of preparation for battle—a long, long way, to be sure.

Under a staggered schedule, field training for all division units was a seven-day affair. *"I worked every day but I loved it,"* Patton says. Units responded with enthusiasm to Patton's obvious respect and care for the soldier. The mutual admiration between Patton and the troops was highlighted in an article that appeared on Sunday, July 20, 1980, in the nearby *Killeen Daily Herald.* It said in part, "During the Joint Readiness exercise Gallant Crew, conducted at Fort Hood in 1977, when Patton was commanding the 2nd Armored Division, a group of young tankers—wet, dirty and tired—had just been visited by their general. After Patton was out of earshot, one soldier said to his buddies: 'I'd follow that man to hell and fight the devil himself 'cause I'm damn sure he'd lead me back.' His fellow tankers agreed."

Patton found that motivating peacetime soldiers was a constant challenge. His experience over the years was that nearly every soldier wanted to be in a good unit, so that it was usually competition that motivated people. Patton therefore found ways to inject competition in nearly every task imaginable. *"A commander in peacetime must keep his troops at the ready,"* instructs Patton. *"Doing our job well was so important. NATO Europe, during my entire time with Hell on Wheels, was fully expected to be the flashpoint for the next war."*

During Patton's command of the 2nd Armored Division at Fort Hood, future president George Bush, who was director of the CIA at the time, paid a visit. Bush had requested a division operational and deployment briefing, along with an orientation on division-level intelligence equipment. Patton's troops from the newly formed Combat Electronic Warfare Intelligence (CEWI) battalion placed on the parade ground every piece of intelligence equipment available at division level, for Bush's perusal. Patton led the briefing and explained the division's wartime mission, including details on embarkation plans and time-phasing at various ports. During the walking tour, Bush stopped at a vehicle loaded with electronic equipment designed to intercept hostile communications and report battlefield information to the commander. Following some small talk with the noncom in charge, Bush said, "I understand your division and this equipment have a Europe-reinforcing mission. Would you tell me about it?"

The soldier gave Bush an overview; however, knowing that the mission involved intercepting communications in Europe, Bush asked the soldier what languages he spoke.

The soldier replied to Bush, "Sir, I speak Cambodian."

Bush turned to Patton and barked, "Cambodian? What the hell is going on here?"

"Sir," Patton said, "I have the requisitions out for

the proper language capability but we have not received them as yet."

Bush gruffly turned to his assistant and said, "Make a note of that."

Later he wrote Patton a letter in which he said, "I've explored your assignment problems and there is nothing I can do about it at this time. We will just have to wait for the language training area to catch up to requirements." Patton wrote back thanking him for his interest and said he was pleased that Bush realized the problem was not the fault of the 2nd Armored Division but much broader in scope.

Patton, while at Fort Hood, always conscious of history, invited the elderly General Ernest Harmon, the only man to have commanded the division twice—once in Africa and once in Europe during World War II—to attend the July 1977 2nd Armored Division reunion. *"We had a dinner, ceremony and a tour of the museum for General and Mrs. Harmon, but we were not permitted to have an official review for him since Army regulations prohibited this type of ceremony. So I arranged for what the Germans call a 'march past.' Harmon came to the division when it just so happened I had the entire 4th Brigade training in the field,"* smiles Patton.

General Harmon was in a World War II–type scout car hidden behind a large berm, where he could not be seen by his veterans in the stands. At the appointed time, Patton had "Old Gravel Voice" brought to the bleachers in the scout car. As he approached the announcer said, "Ladies and gentlemen, veterans of the 2nd Armored Division, the former Commanding General, Ernest N. Harmon." Patton and Harmon stopped in front of the reviewing stand, and with a little help the elderly soldier dismounted and was seated. Patton then signaled by radio to pass the brigade by. The brigade units were outstanding, and the applause was deafening. *"That 'pass by' was Harmon's last appearance,"* says Patton. *"He died a short time later."*

As Commanding General, 2nd Armored Division, Patton was often sought after by Texas newspapers and other media, including national publications, which frequently carried lengthy interviews related to division affairs and Patton in particular. In September 1975, not long after assuming command of the division, an article about Patton appeared in *People* magazine; the cover gave a glimpse of the article inside with the headline, "General Patton, chip off the famous block." The story contained seven photographs and recounted some of Patton's early years as an "Army brat" traveling with his parents. Patton said later of the article, *"I am not a chip off the block and regardless of random comments concerning my upbringing and character, I went out of my way to be myself always and every time. Certain characteristics that did pertain to my father were simply not my 'cup of tea' and I went out of my way to discount them."*

As for the media, then–assistant public affairs officer James Davis says, "The general preferred not to be around reporters, mainly because I don't think he had a great liking for the profession. Yet, there wasn't a week that went by that we didn't receive a request from some member of the media to talk to Patton. It went all the way from the *National Enquirer* to foreign media. We finally had to have a set of guidelines if they wanted to deal with him or request an interview."

Those who worked for Patton at Fort Hood remember various facets of his personality. On the humorous side, one story in particular is of the three little flags the general's chief of staff used to keep just outside Patton's office. Those coming to visit Patton could tell how the day was going by noting whether the red, green, or amber flag was in place; they had to evaluate the seriousness of their problem and how badly they needed to see Patton. While the flags were kept out of Patton's line of sight, most think he knew about them. One officer recalls, "He was generally a good natured guy and very approachable so the green flag was out most of the time."

Patton was also noted as a stickler for detail. He made certain that his plans and policies were acceptable and workable, since as far as he was concerned the division would use them every day. He never let his commanders forget that the mission was to prepare for war. One day the subject of a particular meeting was what would happen if the enemy got into the rear area and attacked the Divisional Tactical Operation Center.

Patton said, "If that occurred then our intelligence was bad and we were blindsided. I don't ever want to experience a situation where I know the enemy is going to overrun me."

"Sir, I can guarantee you if that happens I'll be there," the G-2 said.

Patton grunted, "I'm glad you will because I won't. I will be dead."

After twenty-six months at the helm, Patton's time in command of Hell on Wheels came to an end on October 16, 1977, when he turned the division over to a temporary commander, Brigadier General Walter F. Ulmer, on Sadowski Field at Fort Hood. Patton inspected his division at a walk. Then, speaking before three thousand soldiers standing in formation, Patton said, "To Hell on Wheels, by God I'm proud of you. For the last time I challenge you to honor courage, punish weakness, disgrace cowardice, and with that time-tested approach, develop the warrior soul." Newspapers covering the event reported Patton shed tears of sadness as he heard music played at the ceremony selected as a tribute to him. The music included the by now well-known "2nd Division March," "Ballad of the Green Beret," "Scotland the Brave," and "Enroute," a Red Army march played as a salute to the 3rd Brigade for its success in demonstrating to Soviet General E. F. Ivanovsky, during his inspection in Europe, that the brigade was ready and would be a worthy adversary if ever tested in battle.

During an earlier speech to the officers and senior NCOs, Patton also provided a glimpse of his military heritage, saying, "I admit that I am unique here because of my particular heritage. I put my tiny hand in the scalp wound of General Washburn, who received it in the Apache War, and lived to tell about it. I was bounced on General of the Army Pershing's knee. I groomed Eisenhower's horses. I was taught to shoot by the immortal Paddy Flint, the hero of the 39th Infantry of World War II. I saw Douglas MacArthur come into my house as a small boy. I walked General Marshall's hunting dog." Patton concluded the review of his life by saying, "I came to realize what the Army truly was and by God I loved it."

Those who served under Patton in the 2nd Armored Division learned, as others had in the past, that he possessed an inspiring persona. In August 1977, Lieutenant General Robert M. Shoemaker, commander of III Corps, including the 2nd Armored Division, also recognized Patton's ability. Writing in Patton's efficiency report, he said, "Patton is unique among our general officers in many ways. In appearance, manner and demeanor, he personifies the American warrior spirit and heritage. . . . His style of command is personal, emotional, and rooted firmly in methods which have been successful for him (or other successful leaders) in the past." Patton was not only a leader but a teacher as well, once writing in his 2nd Armored Division Commanding General's notes, *"Look for the guy that makes errors of commission not omission. Correct the error but do not destroy the soul."*

In November 1977 Patton became Deputy Commanding General, VII Corps, in Germany, under Lieutenant

General David Ott. *"I really didn't want to go back to Europe,"* said Patton, *"particularly to Stuttgart, where I had served three tours."* Patton had read the "tea leaves" and knew that if the Army had future plans for him they would have given him command of III Corps, since it was located at Fort Hood. Patton thought about retiring from the Army at that point but just could not bring himself to take the ultimate step and leave the life he loved.

Upon his arrival in Germany, Patton quickly went to work, *"doing things that the corps commander wanted me to do that he wasn't particularly interested in, but that were important."* Patton's job included working with the various Army facilities such as the Stuttgart Community, which had a large commissary and PX and was supporting many dependents. As the Community Commander in the region, Patton was responsible for all of the cafeteria services, Rod and Gun clubs, PXs, commissaries, and the schools at both the elementary and high school levels. Additionally, Patton was the rating officer for the 2nd Armored Cavalry Regiment, which was part of VII Corps on the border, and also had responsibility for the nineteen battalions in corps artillery. Along with his various day-to-day activities, when the corps commander was absent on business, which was fairly often, Patton assumed the role of acting corps commander.

Patton went about his duties in Germany, working on numerous tasks; one day he was informed that General Ott was retiring. Little did Patton know, but he would soon face yet another career-threatening event, one that would do irreparable harm to his Army career. Word had come down that Ott was going to be replaced as corps commander by General Julius Becton, a black officer whom Patton had known well at Fort Hood while he was CG 1st Cavalry Division and Patton was CG of the 2nd Armored Division. Having served with General Becton as a division commander, Patton could not see his way clear to serving under him as a corps commander. Patton is adamant today that his feeling had nothing to do with race. *"The bottom line is that he was a division commander on the same post and at the same time I was. He was slightly junior to me, and in my opinion, the division I commanded far out-performed his organization. I just could not report to him, so I applied to come home. I told him exactly what I was doing and he gave his approval."* Joanne told George at the time, "They are going to get you. They will claim racial discrimination." *"My situation indeed got to the Secretary of the Army, who was also black, and he construed it, as Joanne predicted, to be a racial problem,"* says Patton. The inference that he was unwilling to report to Becton because of his race hurt Patton very personally. The worst, however, was yet to come.

When Patton returned to the United States in 1979, he was assigned to DARCOM (Army Material Development and Readiness Command), as Director of Readiness. This assignment, instead of a highly desired corps command, which many of Patton's contemporaries believed he deserved, came despite an outstanding efficiency report noting that Patton, as deputy commanding general for a corps stationed in Germany, had been responsible for eighty thousand troops and eighty-five thousand dependents. In his rating of Patton Lieutenant General Ott had written, "This colorful officer has many professional attributes well known in the Army. I've singled out his character and moral courage because I believe it typifies his absolute dedication to both the Army and his country. I don't believe I have ever served with an officer who is less a 'yes man' than General Patton. Major General Patton exceeds any officer I have ever known in thirty-seven years of military service in his love for the Army. There is literally nothing that he will not do to make it better. The magic of his name, the distinctiveness of his appearance motivates soldiers on their first contact with him and he is able to use this motivation in a highly effective manner."

Nevertheless, Patton had been shunted aside. No corps command was in the offing, and the job he was taking was logistics-oriented. The staff was mostly civilian employees. Even to take the job, Patton had to put all his personal assets into a blind trust. *"I did so because it was said that some of the corporations in my portfolio did business with the Department of Defense and that supposedly constituted a conflict of interest,"* explains Patton. *"Afterwards I had been told by the Judge Advocate staff that I was clean and the blind trust was adequate. For reasons unexplained the Secretary of the Army* [Clifford L. Alexander, Jr.] *overrode that opinion and said what I owned was still a conflict of interest. I am convinced Secretary Alexander fixed it so I would have to retire."*

Patton was bitter about the situation. He had done what was asked to avoid a conflict of interest, yet was left hanging. *"Ironically, I was later told, again by someone in the Judge Advocate General's office, that they deliberately assigned me to DARCOM and further that I had been considered for other jobs which were disapproved. I firmly believe I was assigned to DARCOM in order to create a conflict of interest and accordingly ease me out of the service."*

Unaware of what may have been occurring behind the scenes, Patton took his situation to the Chief of Staff of the Army, General Edwin C. Meyer. *"He asked me what I might want to do, and although I actually halfway enjoyed my service with DARCOM, I mentioned I would like the position of Commandant at the Army War College."* In the end, however, Patton was offered only a training-related role in the Pentagon. Equally disturbing, he learned he would have to be subordinate to an officer who was his junior. That was more than Patton could take, and he applied for retirement that day.

Even though Patton's career was coming to a conclusion, he performed well at DARCOM, and in May 1979 Lieutenant General Eugene J. D'Ambrosio, Deputy Commanding General for Material Readiness, DARCOM, wrote in his appraisal, "Patton has performed superbly as Director of Readiness. . . . He should be selected to command an Army Corps." It simply was not to be.

Patton could not bring himself to retire from the DARCOM assignment, *where they give you a Distinguished Service Medal and everyone has cake and coffee.*" Patton instead requested that he be allowed to retire in the monthly retirement ceremony sponsored by the commanding general at Fort Knox. As fate would have it, Colonel Andy O'Meara's brigade would be the host unit for the retirement. Since O'Meara had fought under Patton in Vietnam, it seemed a fitting end. *"I just went out there with those noncoms and a couple of majors who had put in their twenty years and stood there with them. I really wanted to go to Fort Hood and retire with the 2nd Armored Division, but I figured it would tear me up too bad,"* says Patton.

The retirement ceremony at Fort Knox was deeply emotional for Patton. He was leaving his beloved Army and *"something I had devoted my life to."* As Patton stood at the retirement he reviewed in his mind what he had done and had not done, what he had done right and what he had done wrong, over his long and meritorious career. Afterwards, Joanne and George hosted a cocktail party just across from the parade ground. When Patton got to the club he welcomed everyone and thanked them for coming. *"My whole family was there along with many people I had served with and it was a wonderful and memorable day and at the same time tinged with so much sadness. My time in the Army was finally over."*

Although concluding his Army career, Patton still, on August 31, 1980, felt compelled to send a lengthy missive to General John R. Guthrie, then Commander of DARCOM, in which he made suggestions for improvements. He also needed to vent his feelings concerning how the Army was treating someone who had given his all. *"I have but one major regret,"* he wrote. *"Through this duty, I obviously improved upon my capacity to serve this nation. However, my capability for that service has been curtailed by the powers that stand above us. . . . This has had a significant dampening effect on both my warrior soul and the Patton family, since in the final analysis, the only true wealth we who serve the nation enjoy is our name. Nothing else matters."*

In a letter to General Meyer, also dated August 31, 1980, Patton wrote what he called *"both a tour end and a career termination effort."* In the lengthy critique of the Army, he ended by saying, *"I hope and pray that your newly forming team will be able to prepare the Army for the awesome tasks which may face it when the killing starts again."* Meyer responded in May of 1981, saying in part, "I have delayed answering your final active duty letter because I wanted to think more fully about some of the views you related. Over the intervening months, particularly at those times when my conscience has had to deal with issues especially critical to the future of the Army, I have valued its counsel. The observations come from a soldier whose contributions I have always admired, whose actions have displayed that characteristic so critically short in our ranks, the fingertip-feeling of the art of war which the Germans call *Fingerspitzengefuehl.*

"My overall reaction to your letter is one of great sense of loss. As you know I would much rather you'd have stayed on active duty to help me address some of the enormous issues you raised." Meyer concluded his letter by writing, "Notwithstanding, we're kindred souls in our mutual love and concern for this great Army. You know I will always be open to your advice." Patton later would wryly remark, *"He never got around to calling."*

So for George Patton the music played for the final time at Fort Knox; yet another Patton had rendered full service to his country. He prepared to return to the family home in Hamilton, Massachusetts, to face new challenges and begin reflecting upon his long and illustrious military career.

QUIET REFLECTION

If I were to say that I didn't miss the Army, I'd be lying. I didn't have any idea what it was that I would miss the most but it turns out to be the fellowship of the Army environment.

—George S. Patton

Major General George S. Patton, after thirty-four years of Army service, arrived home in 1980 and immediately set to work pursuing business and personal interests. In the years since leaving the service Patton has finally had a chance, perhaps for the first time in his life, to consider fully his unique legacy and the future of the Army which he so loves.

Looking back over his career, Patton says he watched history repeat itself. *"Nothing has changed in a thousand years,"* remarks Patton. *"Military decisions reverberate for years. It's like throwing a stone in a pond. The ripples take a while to reach their point of destination. Because of politics and other factors, it seems the military, not only in this country, but historically, have always fought the last war. In my lifetime I've watched this great nation start World War II with equipment from the World War I era, and witnessed that repeated in Korea, with equipment from World War II. But the military must respond to the political leadership. At times the message is fuzzy, and lacks direction. In many ways this was certainly the situation in Vietnam."*

When studies are done on Vietnam thirty or forty years from today, Patton believes, they will focus most intently on the decision of consecutive administrations not to mobilize the National Guard and Army reserve forces. *"One very important difference between Vietnam and Korea was mobilization of the reserve forces in the Korean War,"* explains Patton, *"which meant American society as a whole had something at stake. That didn't happen in Vietnam, and the consequences were tragic. When we finally mobilized National Guard units in Vietnam after Tet '68, we ended up destroying units to build units."* To illustrate the point, Patton tells the story of an incident at Fort Hood in 1975, when as the 2nd Armored Division commander he was on the tank range observing a sergeant tank commander maneuvering and firing his tank, and doing it very poorly.

Patton called the tank commander aside from his crew and asked him to comment on his performance. The sergeant replied, "Sir, I realize I fired very badly, but I just haven't been in tanks very much. All during Vietnam I served in a terminal service company." The mission of a terminal service company during the Vietnam War was to move cargo from ship to shore, and the reserve components of the Army had several such companies. Westmoreland, Patton recalls, at the time had put in for numerous terminal service companies to fill the ranks. *"However, instead of calling up the reserves, they pulled men, such as my sergeant, out of other units,"* explains Patton.

An order to call up the reserves in Vietnam was not issued until after Tet '68, although according to Patton it was recommended to the president several times. *"I know personally that the Chief of Staff Army, General Harold K. Johnson, went to the president twice on the question of mobilization,"* says Patton. *"But it didn't fly."* Meanwhile, the legacy of misassignments, such as that which Patton encountered at Fort Hood, blew holes in career patterns, especially for enlisted personnel. Tragically, officers were also misassigned and were held in positions outside their specialties.

Patton says that many problems of the era, including the lack of mobilization, misassignments, and the "Band-Aid approach" to complex problems, could have been at least partially avoided by drawing, as he describes it, a "goose egg" around North Vietnam, South Vietnam, and the offshore islands, perhaps calling it the Southeast Asian Theater. Patton then would have placed a four-star general with a joint staff in charge and let them guide the war in the theater. *"Sadly it sometimes takes a Vietnam to produce a victory such as we had in the Gulf War,"* observes Patton. *"Of course it should not be forgotten that the young officers who had served in company and battalion levels were the senior officers of the Persian Gulf experience. We clearly learned lessons in Vietnam which we later applied quite successfully."*

Patton, like many veterans, attempted to put Vietnam in perspective years ago. He is now noting changes in attitude about the war, seeing less bitterness on the part of veterans particularly. Even so, Patton believes questions still remain about why the United States was unsuccessful in Vietnam. *"You can cut it anyway you want, but we lost that war to an eighth-rate power, not on the battlefield, but politically,"* charges Patton. *"Somehow you always pay for something you do wrong, but things have changed and hopefully we learned from our mistakes."*

Today, despite success in the Gulf War, Patton believes the United States military faces many problems and decisions as it moves into the twenty-first century. One abiding concern for Patton is the use of the American military internationally, especially as it relates to the United Nations. This for Patton is particularly true given the number of world hot spots where the United States has provided, or been asked to provide, peacekeeping forces. The ever-simmering Bosnia-Herzegovina situation is but one example. Patton issues a warning concerning all future UN missions that involve American forces: *"It will always be difficult to put U.S. armed forces under a foreign commander, though we've done it before,"* says Patton. *"And I can see where you may have a UN commander who is a figurehead in a place like Somalia and then have a U.S. general officer who commands those troops and follows the UN commander's policy directions. But caution is required. In theory we worked with the Vietnamese Army, but we always maintained control."*

Patton believes before the American military ever operates under the UN umbrella, there should be a requirement that all forces in the coalition have a standardized training program, including radio procedure, map reading, map making, resupply, and the all important rules of engagement. In reviewing the list Patton says, *"I'm not sure we are there yet."*

More fundamentally, Patton has another concern about the use of American troops by the United Nations. *"At the end of the day we have to explain to a mother and father how their son or daughter died in battle, and dying in vain for some cause which isn't clear, under a commander who isn't an American, is the worst possible situation. We need to think about that seriously as a nation each time a call is put out for our involvement."*

On the other hand, once involved, Patton is adamant that Americans and the American military take into account what he calls *"cultural empathy."* As he did in Korea and Vietnam, Patton insists that one must understand the culture with which one is working, regardless of the kind of warfare. *"The British will tell you that from their operations in the last century in Afghanistan and India,"* claims Patton. *"One of their problems was that they neither understood nor sympathized with the basic motivation of the people with whom they worked. Understanding the religion, the food habits and the economy is vitally important."* Patton believes his success in his third tour in Vietnam was due to the fact that he had worked in the village defense program with the CIA during his first tour, where he learned much about Vietnamese culture and history.

"When my dad was set to deploy in Casablanca, in World War II, he read the translated Koran from cover to cover," says Patton, *"simply to gain an understanding of the people he would be working with. I think it's a mark in his favor that instead of worrying about whether a guy had two canteens or the proper equipment, which was somebody else's job, he sat down at night in his stateroom and read the Koran in order to understand the Muslim religion and way of life."*

On the subject of cultural empathy, Patton once said in an address to a group of Massachusetts business people, *"I can truly say that one of the many problems during that rather tragic period involving Vietnam was our almost total lack of understanding of the cultures, customs and languages or dialects of the Southeast Asian people."*

Patton's feeling about cultural empathy and the understanding of a particular country is coupled with his observations concerning the ever-increasing need for language skills, which he believes are of paramount importance. *"I was raised in a family where French was spoken and it is a good language to know but it is not nearly the dominant language it was. Why do we still teach French in our schools? We should be teaching Arabic, Spanish, Russian and perhaps Chinese."* Patton calls such languages the *"challenge languages"* of the post–World War II twenty-first century. He believes Arabic is perhaps the most important because of world events. *"If anything ever happens in a world war sense, it's going to be in the Middle East. That's my belief,"* argues Patton. *"Some say it could be elsewhere, but I believe the need for oil represents the greatest threat. But whether one is learning Arabic or another language, it is the process of accepting the fact that others may not think as you do that is so critically important."*

Today, Patton often reflects on the many changes visited upon his profession, some good, and some that he feels weakened the military. While publicly supporting the concept of a volunteer force during his Army career, Patton nevertheless harbored reservations. He often fretted about difficulties in filling divisions with professional volunteers. His real concerns were on a higher plane, on the philosophy of service to the nation, which he believed then, as he does today, to be a sacred obligation of its citizenry. Patton is convinced that a core of patriotic dedication and devotion to the nation still exists within the character of the country's youth. *"The sacred theme of the citizen's obligation to contribute some form of national service to his country in order to protect the society in which one lives is valid and deserves a prominent place in our appeal,"* he says. *"We tend to underestimate it or to consider it an anachronism. It is not."*

Exploring various elements of an all-volunteer force, Patton calls on history, saying, *"The concept of an all-voluntary force is not new. Other nations, at similar stages of progression, have tried it."* To support his thesis, he refers to Colonel Denison's classic, *A History of Cavalry*, written in 1913, wherein is discussed the transformation of the Roman army. *"What is important here is that as the army changed character, so did the nation it supported, for the worst. Denison described the problems facing Rome, including the diminution of discipline, pay increases, refusals to carry the heavy fighting armor, which had made the legions unconquerable, and this came at the beginning of the end. In fact, Denison wrote, 'Arms, equipment or tactics could do nothing to save a nation where the guiding principle was lost, where there was no longer patriotism, where the national life was dying out, and where the indulgence of selfish luxury was the ruling sentiment.'* "

At the core Patton believes that the future success of U.S. military forces will depend on the caliber of the individual soldier who enters the service. He is, however, like many professional soldiers, equally concerned that the resources necessary to pay for a truly quality active military will be lacking. Patton believes that for the national well-being, the military must reflect the cross-section of the country's *"able-bodied citizenry, whose age and health award them the privilege of bearing arms in their nation's defense. I cannot identify a historical case where hired soldiery was not symbolic of fading power."* He concludes by saying, *"I deeply believe that you cannot pay a man enough to make him willing to die. There must be something more."*

In addition to concerns about an all-volunteer force, Patton cites other challenges and threats to national security. During his career, for example, Patton saw first-hand the rapid rise of the nuclear threat and a variety of nuclear weapons put into military arsenals. *"Unfortunately, we had to spend billions and billions of dollars on nuclear weapons,"* says Patton. *"For years we were attempting to avoid nuclear blackmail and it was a time of high tension and even as we trained preparing for a nuclear exchange I couldn't help but think our greatest risk was coming from nuclear banditry and terrorism which may be the real threat to the free world."*

In fact, Patton's main problem with the issue of nuclear weapons was almost never with the recognized international military commands. *"I don't believe a weapon can be launched or shot inadvertently by a country with a legitimate command structure,"* explains Patton. *"Systems are in place which involve numerous steps with several headquarters confirming a decision."* Ironically, the complicated approval process actually concerned Patton. He felt the use of such a weapon after a complicated authorization process might not mean much, because the time involved would result in a target lost. *"Targets on a battlefield are fleeting. If you want to hit a tank battalion with an overhead four-kiloton blast, it could be thirty miles away by the time you get everybody saying, 'Roger.' There are so many controls, it's almost mind-boggling."* Patton's concerns therefore reside in the realization that rogue individuals, terrorist organizations, and various nations wish to possess nuclear weaponry.

Given his long-standing fears of the theft of nuclear weapons, Patton always appreciated security measures designed to thwart such a possibility. One time Patton was outside one of his own nuclear weapons storage facilities in an area that was also a first-class German partridge-hunting spot. He was in an open field, perhaps a couple of miles across, hunting with a group of German nationals. Patton, in time, shot a partridge, which fluttered inside the fence of the facility. At the gate was a soldier, with an M-16 at the ready and watching Patton's group very carefully.

Patton went up to the soldier on guard and said, "I'm General Patton. I've got my bird in there and I want to come in and get it."

"I'm sorry, sir," he responded, "you can't come in unless your visit is authorized."

Patton pulled out his identification card and showed it to the soldier through the fence. He nodded and said, "Yes, sir, but you still can't come in."

An exasperated Patton finally exclaimed, "Do you know I'm responsible for this site?"

"I know that, sir, but I still won't admit you."

"It was just that tight and he was absolutely following his orders," concludes Patton.

Patton believes the threat of nuclear terrorism will remain a very significant concern well into the future. *"Weapons can be made or stolen, especially with the thriving black market in the wake of the Eastern European collapse. It doesn't even have to come in the form of an explosion. Nuclear waste, as an example, can be spread so that responsible people wouldn't be able to access an area for many years. How we defend against that, I don't know."*

Since the beginning of his career—and, as Patton will admit, even from his childhood—he has studied leadership. His scholarship on the subject leads him to conclude, *"Leaders aren't born, they are made, and that's why I've always been fascinated with what motivates people."*

General George S. Patton, Jr., often said there are two types of generals or leaders, persuasive and obtrusive, and he added that some are a combination, although they are rare. George Patton agrees with his father. *"For example, Eisenhower—persuasive, Bradley—persuasive, MacArthur and Napoleon—both are a rare combination,"* he says. *"Frederick the Great—obtrusive, Lord Nelson—persuasive, Halsey—obtrusive, Nimitz—persuasive. Marshall—probably both, although Marshall was not a fighting soldier. I would say, like my father I was obtrusive because it fit me better, not because of my dad's style, it just always seemed the road which best fitted my personality."*

Depending on the circumstances, George Patton, at times, might use elements of both styles. *"For instance, if you run into a soldier who looks like he slept in his uniform, using the persuasive style you would perhaps say, 'Well, fella, you don't look so good today; you've let down the reputation of this platoon by your appearance and you really ought to be ashamed of yourself. You should go out and think about it.' That's persuasive. Obtrusive is, 'God damn it, you look like a piece of shit! Now clean up, goddamn it!' "*

Reviewing military leaders, especially from the American Civil War forward, Patton says that he very much enjoyed learning about Confederate General "Jeb" Stuart, who he believes was very close to a born leader, although another famous Confederate, General "Stonewall" Jackson, in his opinion was not. *"Jackson was more famous and more reliable than Stuart,"* explains Patton, *"but he was an introvert. He was nevertheless successful because he grew up in the area where he was fighting and knew every nook, cranny and trail. He knew the terrain but mainly he had a will to win. The Union general U. S. Grant, in my view, was a butcher, yet he had fine subordinates in Sherman and Sheridan, plus superior numbers of men and a better supply line."*

For World War I, Patton cites General Pershing as an aloof person, not at all close to his soldiers, but successful. A telling story concerning Pershing was floating around West Point when Patton attended the Academy. The vignette had actually come from one of the instructors who had been in the First World War. *"He said one of General Pershing's aides came to him one day and said, 'General Pershing, you've got to get closer to the troops, you've just got to mix a little more.' The general agreed and went out walking among the troops and came upon a soldier who was debugging himself. In an attempt to be friendly Pershing said stiffly, 'Well, son, I see you're picking them out.' The perplexed soldier turned to the famous general and could only utter, 'No, sir, I'm just taking them as they come.' Such stilted conversation didn't surprise me in the least,"* remarks Patton. *"Pershing, although a great soldier and commander, was just not the type of officer to mix informally with the soldiers."*

Thinking about leadership in World War II Patton observes, *"My dad's style was totally different from that of Omar Bradley, and was more on the MacArthur side. There were more similarities between my dad and MacArthur than between himself and Bradley or Ike. Interestingly, there were some similarities between my dad and British Field Marshal Montgomery. One of my favorite exchanges in the movie* Patton *is between Karl Malden, who played Bradley, and George C. Scott, who played my dad. Scott says something like, 'We're both prima donnas, but the thing about me is I admit it and I enjoy it and you don't.' My dad was certainly a prima donna."*

Looking at the similarities and differences of commanders during World War II, Patton believes MacArthur stands out as an altogether unusual personality. *"He carried a different level of prestige,"* says Patton. *"I don't think anybody would fool with him. MacArthur was MacArthur and everybody was subordinate to MacArthur,"* he says. *"For his part and with regard to leadership, MacArthur commanded a theater, and of course his responsibilities far transcended those of my dad. He was a superb leader and was probably the greatest general this country ever produced."*

The study of leadership was a continuing process for Patton and one that he took very seriously throughout his Army career. Each technique or nugget of leadership he learned along the way was later used, if it was applicable. At one point in Vietnam, he had a commander who was not doing well; he tried everything he could think of, but nothing seemed to work. Finally, one night when the commander performed well in battle, Patton went up to him, threw his arms around his neck, and said, "How the hell's my fighting son-of-a-bitch?" *"I took that from my dad,"* says Patton. *"The fellow just beamed. He was a super company commander from that day forward. I had found the combination to his safe and it worked."*

On June 6, 1944, D-Day for the invasion of France, Patton, Commanding General, Third Army, wrote his son a letter on the subject of leadership. In the missive he wrote,

All men are timid on entering a fight, whether it is the first fight or the last fight. . . . Cowards are those who let their timidity get the better of their

manhood. You will never do that because of your
bloodlines on both sides. . . . Your knees may
shake, but they will always carry you toward the
enemy.

To be a successful soldier you must know history.
Read it objectively—dates and even minute details of
tactics are useless. What you must know is how man
reacts. Weapons change, but man, who uses them,
changes not at all. To win battles you do not beat
weapons—you beat the soul of the enemy man.

Take calculated risks. That is quite different from
being rash. My personal belief is that if you have a
50% chance you should take it, because the superior
fighting qualities of American soldiers led by me will
surely give you the extra 1% necessary.

The most vital quality a soldier can possess is self
confidence, utter, complete, and bumptious. . . .

What success I have had results from the fact that
I have always been certain that my military reactions
were correct. Many people do not agree with me;
they are wrong. The unerring jury of history, written
long after both of us are dead, will prove me correct. . . .

Well, this has been quite a sermon; but don't get
the idea that it is my swan song, because it is not. I
have not finished my job yet.

Patton learned much about leadership from his father. *"As an example, I emulated my father's belief that
a commander should stay in the field,"* says Patton.
*"When I had a company, I was in the field all the
time."* Like his father, at night, Patton would do his
paperwork including correspondence, the processing of
decorations, letters of condolence, discharges, and
courts-martial. *"The techniques that I learned from my
dad, clarity of orders and letters of instruction, helped
considerably,"* says Patton. *"My Commanding General
Notes in particular were based on his way of doing
things."* Patton believes that most of the time, soldiers,

particularly those who get promoted, garner techniques from other soldiers for whom they have worked—because, as he explains, *"There is nothing new about soldiering. Man doesn't change, therefore the techniques of motivating him don't change too much."*

Patton realized time and again throughout his career how much one person can influence a unit. He had a commander at one point who had not done well, including missing deadlines and generally setting a bad example. Patton put a new officer in charge and told him what was wrong and said he was going to leave him alone but would be back in ten days to look the place over. *"When I came back the transformation was just unbelievable. The place was straightened out. One person can make a difference."*

An important aspect of leadership, Patton contends, is the appearance of fearlessness. *"You have to overcome fear, and like my father said, 'Anybody who says he's not scared is either a fool or a liar.' Later, as one advances in the military there is generally less contact with the enemy, so you're not scared for yourself, you're scared for your unit, you're scared that you'll screw something up for your unit and get a lot of people killed or hurt unnecessarily. Fear transfers from a lack of physical courage to a lack of moral courage, where you're afraid that you'll make the wrong decision."*

The fear factor has been the downfall of many leaders throughout the centuries, claims Patton. *"You just have to know in your heart you are doing the right thing. You have to have the ability, which I think I had, to put yourself in the soldier's shoes. Maybe I inherited it, maybe I developed a sense for knowing what the soldier needed. Someone once said the number-one requirement is self-confidence; alternatively, my number-one requirement is reliability, particularly in combat. Care of the soldier is also terribly important, along with knowing what's going on, and attending to details. As Abrams told me in 1949, when I took over my first company, 'Never forget to look in the dark corners of your organization.' "*

Over the years Patton had the opportunity to observe well-known military leaders, both on the battlefield and in staff jobs. But he also closely watched and often was troubled by the civilian leadership in the military structure, from the Secretary of Defense down through the organization. *"This is blunt,"* says Patton, *"but an example of what I'm referring to is Robert S. McNamara. I don't believe he ever really understood the nature of the Vietnamese conflict or the people trying to conduct the war on either the North Vietnamese or the South Vietnamese side. I don't think he was a people-oriented man. I think he tried and was dedicated, but for some reason, known but to God, he was incapable of really understanding the nature of sub-limited warfare. I might add that he had plenty of company in that regard."*

Patton also believes McNamara's basic lack of understanding about the military produced in him a procrastinator who failed to help provide a specific national strategy for conduct of the war in Vietnam. *"In fairness, though, it is tough to criticize a man who comes out of an automobile production company and is faced with a challenge such as that, which many others did not understand,"* says Patton. *"But I know his systems analysis approach didn't work. In my view, the Secretary of Defense must have some military experience in order to understand fully the performance of the branches of the service."*

Another problem Patton identified during his service was that too many higher-echelon civilian employees in the Pentagon were using their positions in the office of the Secretary of Defense as a stepping-stone in their career paths. Some he believes took political appointments only for future gain. One story in particular illustrates Patton's point. The Pattons went to a cocktail party one night for an Assistant Secretary of Defense who was departing governmental service. As he and Joanne walked in, the Secretary's wife was saying, "Now that my husband has done his stint at the Department of Defense we are going home to cash in on this for our business." Hearing the remark, Patton promptly put his hat back on and said, *"Thank you very much, but I'm not here to celebrate such a thing."*

Joanne's recollection of this event was somewhat different. She recalls that the wife said, "Now that he has done his thing in the Defense Department, we are returning to the real world and make some money!" Joanne remembers that the husband already had business cards printed that said, "former Assistant Secretary of Defense." *"Either way,"* says Patton, *"Joanne wasn't too happy about my manners, but I wasn't going to associate with a guy who can come into a job like that and literally destroy something over a one- or two-year period that we had taken years to build."*

Patton also recalls that, during his tour as assistant commandant of the Armor School at Fort Knox, the Secretary of the Army visited with the objective of examining a certain type of tank and to receive an orientation. Patton had everything lined up on the tank range for the distinguished visitor and had a noncom, Sergeant 1st Class "Spitshine" Smith, his weapons department VIP spokesman, perform the briefing. *"The Secretary and 'Spitshine' entered the turret and they fired a couple of rounds,"* Patton explains, *"and as they emerged the Secretary said, 'Spitshine,' you're the finest noncom I've talked to since becoming Secretary of the Army. Call me by my first name. Spitshine came to attention and said, 'Mr. Secretary, I can't do that.' The Secretary was speechless and came over to General Abrams and me with the question, 'How come he won't call me by my first name?' Abe said, 'Mr. Secretary, we'll explain later in the car.' We went ahead with the rest of the tour but it was a good example of failing to understand how things must work in an Army."*

During his time at the Pentagon, Patton also concluded that the division of civilian and military responsibilities in the Pentagon are almost hopelessly confusing. *"There was a civilian secretary of each service and a military chief of the service,"* he says. *"Some civilian secretaries exercised hands-on management and others left the services alone. The problem is that the civilian role is what the individual makes it."*

Patton does believe the civilian approach can work well if everyone pulls together. He cites the Persian Gulf War as a case in point. *"The president, [Secretary of Defense] Dick Cheney and others let [General] Norman Schwarzkopf pretty much alone, thanks to JCS Chairman Colin Powell. I believe Powell became a buffer between Schwarzkopf and the politicos and I further believe that President George Bush was super in that war because he let them do it. He stayed out, unlike LBJ, who would not stay out of Vietnam. I was particularly impressed by Schwarzkopf, who followed the Clausewitzian principle of Unity of Command. You have to have a single guy who is responsible. That was done in World War II with great success, but we've slipped a few times since.*

"Keeping Israel out of that war was also a masterpiece. [Secretary of State] James Baker and the State Department get much credit for that effort. It showed how the military and civilians can work in concert and perform brilliantly." Patton also was truly proud of the military during the Gulf War, because he felt it exorcised the demons of Vietnam and particularly because many officers who worked for him in Vietnam and in other assignments held command positions during the war in the desert and did well.

On a personal level, George Patton, given a family history and with a famous father, worked hard to find his own direction. In looking back over George's life, Ruth Ellen once recalled, "George worshiped his father." Yet for all the similarities, there were differences. She also said, "My father was a reader but he didn't like going to movies. He didn't like parties particularly, but when he did go, he had a good time and was often the last to leave. George, on the other hand, loves to go out, and loves to talk to people."

Ruth Ellen believed that it was never easy for her brother. "I'll never forget his graduation day in 1946. It was also a reunion day for my father's class of 1909. George was carrying his sword and it was banging on his white trousers so he gave it to me to hold. About that time an old guy came up and said, 'Well, George, you'll never be the man your father was, but congratulations.' I picked up the sword in both hands and hit that old man so hard across the backside he almost fell down. I was so angry. What a thing to say, yet he's had that all his life."

The late President Richard Nixon, in an interview with the author, addressed the difficulty. "While I did not have the privilege of knowing General Patton's son personally, I knew him through General Don Hughes, who was my military aide and who was one of his many friends and admirers. It is very difficult for the son of a bigger-than-life personality like Patton to live up to the legend of the father. Winston Churchill's son, Randolph, who would have been recognized as a brilliant writer in his right but who was always compared unfavorably with his father, is a cogent point. From what General Hughes and others have told me, Colonel [later Major General] Patton was an outstanding officer and would have made his father proud of his service in America's most difficult and divisive war."

Nixon also alluded to the difficulties of military service for those, like Patton, who served in Vietnam. Referring to George's father, Nixon remarked, "Patton would have been particularly outraged by some of those in the media who wrote more positively about the enemy than they did about our American forces. On the other hand, if Patton had served in Vietnam, he would have probably raised so much hell about this situation that the media might have given more balanced coverage to the war effort."

On the lighter side of things, Ruth Ellen recalled a story about her brother selling vegetables at a roadside stand after he had retired. "He had on one of those fisherman's caps and was dressed in his dirty old clothes. He was just one of the gang. A reserve officer and some soldiers stopped to buy vegetables for the mess. George complimented them on their appearance and chatted. The next day the general in command called George and said, 'Oh, have I got one for you. This lieutenant came back last night with some vegetables and said there's an old farmer in Hamilton that thinks he's General Patton.' Bless his heart, he told that on himself."

Ruth Ellen observed, "My brother has lots of friends, but not in Hamilton. George is very dependent on friends and he has them come to stay and gives them all a wonderful time. But I always had the feeling he thought he'd let Daddy down by not becoming Jesus Christ II. He keeps thinking that he was expected to do more. I said 'George, you can only do your best. There isn't any more that anybody can do.' It's awful to live under somebody's shadow. I'm positive that my father wouldn't have wanted it that way."

When George Patton retired in 1980 he did a little consulting in Washington, D.C., as he was getting ready to return to Massachusetts and devote himself to creating what is now known as Green Meadows Farm. *"After my dad died, my mother continued to live at Green Meadows, and when she died in 1953 my sister and I divided up the land. Ruth Ellen then bought a place called Brick Ends Farm with about sixty adjoining acres and each of us ended up with a little over 150 acres."* Patton says he would have preferred to live in Virginia or North Carolina, but felt compelled to come home. *"I had Green Meadows and I decided to try to do something with it,"* he says. *"I have put some of the*

acreage into the Greenbelt Association under a conser-
vation restriction, so while I still own the land, and can
use it as I want, I cannot build on the property."

Since 1981 Patton has actively been working his
land. The Green Meadows Farm produces fruit and
vegetables, which are sold at Patton's own produce
stand and at the local farmers' markets. *"We currently*
farm thirty-two acres, and while we do a little whole-
sale our goal is to become totally retail," says Patton.
Additionally, Patton's operation also markets nearly
three hundred cords of firewood a year. *"I'm deeply*
involved in this farm, which I've adopted as my second
career, and I'm going to see farming it through," remarks Patton.

The farm fields at Green Meadows still have a military connection, of sorts, and they whisper silent tribute
to Patton's fallen comrades. Signs with the names of
men lost in battle under Patton's command in Vietnam
are placed along paths through the food crops, naming
the individual fields for those departed troopers. One
sign in particular Patton erected in special memory of
the battle in the Michelin rubber plantation. It's a sign
which he passes daily, a grim reminder of Vietnam battles fought long ago.

George Patton has often speculated on whether, if
his father had survived, he would have eventually returned to Green Meadows. *"If he had, let's just say*
you'd never see him on this farm pruning blueberry
bushes. He might go out and check a couple and chew
some ass if they were not done right, but he would not
go out and prune like I must do to set an example as a
working farmer. I think he would have been riding fast
horses and doing other things. There was even some
talk of politics at the time." Ruth Ellen agreed, "He
would not have come back and planted things. He
wouldn't have liked that very much."

President Richard Nixon spoke about the subject of
Patton's possible postwar activities, including politics.
"Like other Americans, I followed his career with great

admiration during World War II. Before the days of
television, I knew him primarily through newspaper
and magazine accounts. I vividly recall reading about
the famous slapping incident and thought at the time
that the media was overreacting against one of America's most able and colorful military leaders. I recall,
too, that before I ran for Congress, I heard of the possibility that since he was a resident of San Marino, he
might become a candidate. If he had, my political career
would have ended before I got started!"

While Patton works with the farm, much of his time
is also spent handling Patton family business. *"I get a
fair amount of correspondence,"* he says. *"Veterans and
research people write asking for data, but I simply do
not have the time to answer requests for specific information which require research. Instead, I refer them to
either the Patton Museum or to West Point."*

At the Patton Museum, in addition to a library
where people can do research, there is also one room
dedicated to the Patton collection. *"Some might enjoy
the displays containing my dad's medals, bedroll and
personal items. His truck, in which he slept during
World War II, is also there. It was a relief to get all of
the material shipped to places where it could be properly displayed."*

People tend to focus on the movie *Patton* when
thinking of the World War II general, and George un-
derstands. Even if veterans or historians dispute the
portrayal of Patton, most still conclude the film is inspi-
rational. President Nixon, for instance, once told the
author, "I read the book [*Patton: Ordeal and Triumph*,
by Ladislas Farago] at Camp David before seeing the
movie. It was one of those rare occasions when the
movie faithfully captured the qualities of the man,
which were described in much greater detail in the
book. I, incidentally, would urge those who liked the
movie to read the book because it describes at greater
length Patton's life-long love affair with history and his
outstanding intellectual capacity."

George C. Scott would later reprise the role of Patton in 1985 in a three-hour drama produced as a Chrysler Showcase Presentation on the CBS Television Network. "The Last Days of Patton" also starred Eva Marie Saint, as Beatrice Patton. In researching her role as Patton's wife, the actress relied on the memories of Ruth Ellen. Saint recalled later, "I learned so much about Beatrice from Mrs. Totten. She was wonderful, and sent me a package of photos telling me she did so 'to make a character come alive through a talented actress.'"

Looking back at his life and military career, Patton mentions few regrets, but he knows the army life was tough on his family. *"The very fact that none of my children selected a military career may be indicative of the problem. We did move around a lot, particularly after returning from Vietnam. At times we moved during the school year and most of the kids were involved in secondary school at the time. I am the first one to agree it was hard on them."* While the military life offers negative aspects for children, on the positive side Patton maintains it taught the youngsters to make friends quickly. *"When they went to a post such as Fort Hood or Fort Knox there were other children their age who were going through the same thing and who had also learned how to make friends quickly. They didn't waste a lot of time in moving into their portion of society whether it was baseball, fishing, touch football, or the Scouts."*

Patton believes the benefits derived from the opportunities to travel and meet interesting people are also a significant aspect of a military upbringing. Benjamin, Patton's son, for example, has been to Israel and all through Tunisia. *"He saw the battlefields on which his grandfather fought in World War I and World War II. He stood on the spot where his grandfather was wounded in World War I along with Martin Blumenson, author of* The Patton Papers, *who made the trip with us,"* says George Patton. *"The children met Man-fred Rommel and had Christmas dinner with him, and along the way met other important people."* Patton says his interest in seeing that his children met well-known people goes back to his own childhood and being given the same privilege. He believes such links to history overrode some of the deficiencies to Army life, which included *"living in inadequate quarters, attending marginal schools and a lot of uprooting, the vagabond side of the military, as some people call it. Children need a degree of permanence in their upbringing as far as location is concerned. Army life does not lend itself to that."*

Life in the military, including frequent family separation, takes its toll. Along that line Patton recalls a particular incident at West Point that always stayed with him. *"A very senior general was coming to visit his cadet son and I was assigned to escort him. I learned that his son would be coming out of class around 3 P.M. and they were to meet at the east sallyport of Central Barracks. I had told the cadet that I'd be standing there with his dad. Just before the cadet showed up the general tapped me on the arm and said, with his eyes a little teary, 'Nudge me when you see him because it's been so long, I'm not sure I'll recognize him.' His own son! I'll never forget that and it's one of the prices one pays for military life."*

In reflecting on his many years of service, George Patton is very quick to add that his Army career, with its constant upheaval and challenges, was aided immeasurably by Joanne, who, he says, was the key reason things ran well around the Patton household. *"As an Army wife, her familiarity with the service because of her father's time in the Army, contributed to her ability to handle our life and make it a good experience for our five children, Margaret, George, Robert, Helen and Benjamin, each a unique and wonderful individual. During my time in the Army she was also instrumental in Army community service, to include a long list of associations and groups, all directed to producing a better Army and happier Army families."*

In addition to his many activities since retirement, Patton has been involved with West Point, serving on the Fund Committee, which takes him back to the Academy for meetings scheduled at least three or four times a year. The Committee is a not-for-profit organization which, under the Association of Graduates, provides money for activities not covered by government appropriations. The Fund Committee supports bus rides to sports meets, the choir, the glee club, and many other activities. *"We don't usually find a lot of money,"* says Patton, *"but one of our members did give $3.5 million to move the museum to a better location several years ago. We also have a scholarship fund, set up so a scholarship can be given in memory of someone. I made out one in honor of my sister Beatrice."*

Patton readily admits that he greatly misses the military life. *"If I were to say that I didn't miss the Army, I'd be lying. I didn't have any idea what it was that I would miss the most but it turns out to be the fellowship of the Army environment."* Patton muses, *"I remember that scene from the* Patton *movie when the German intelligence officer was burning the classified documents as they were about to surrender to the Allies. As he set fire to a photograph of my father he said, 'Peace will destroy you.' Well, he might have been right. It is somewhat true of me."*

Perhaps most of all, Patton is nostalgic for the command responsibilities. *"It's a privilege to be placed in command, but it is a sacred responsibility that you sense acutely twenty-four hours a day. I enjoyed being in uniform because I believe I made a difference. In every generation a certain group is selected to serve and I believe we are selected by some ethereal influence, the Almighty or whatever. There isn't much you can do about it when you're selected except to go and do the*

*best job you can. There's a sort of mystique about it.
I've often said war is an ugly thing and luckily, only a
few of us were chosen to engage in its practice."*

Having spent over three decades in uniform, Patton
looks back over a lifetime that witnessed a small boy
grow to manhood in the shadow of a famous father.
Patton once wrote that he had never known the problem of what the French call *"le fils de son père,"* meaning that the son of a famous father has a hard life,
although others including Ruth Ellen certainly felt so.
Yet they watched an outstanding officer emerge from
his father's footsteps to seize his own day, in his own
time and in his own way.

SELECTED BIBLIOGRAPHY

The following list contains selected books, magazine and newspaper articles, motion pictures, and other sources of information consulted in writing *The Fighting Pattons*. Additionally, I have listed numerous individuals who gave of their time to help tell the story of a father and son in war and peace.

BOOKS

Allen, Robert S. *Lucky Forward*. Vanguard Press, 1947.

Ayer, Frederick, Jr. *Before the Colors Fade*. Houghton-Mifflin, 1964.

Blumenson, Martin. *Patton: The Man behind the Legend*. Morrow, 1985.

Blumenson, Martin. *The Patton Papers, 1885–1940*. Houghton-Mifflin, 1972.

Blumenson, Martin. *The Patton Papers, 1940–1945*. Houghton-Mifflin, 1974.

Bradley, Omar, and Clay Blair. *A General's Life*. Simon and Schuster, 1983.

Codman, Charles R. *Drive*. Little, Brown & Co., 1957.

Crackel, Theodore J. *The Illustrated History of West*

Point. Harry N. Abrams, Inc. In association with the United States Military Academy Class of 1940.

Dunston, Simon. *Vietnam Choppers: Helicopters in Battle 1950–1975.* Osprey Publishing Ltd., 1988.

Dunston, Simon. *Vietnam Tracks: Armor in Battle 1945–1975.* Osprey Publishing Ltd., 1982.

Eisenhower, David. *Eisenhower at War 1943–1945.* Random House, 1986.

Eisenhower, Dwight D. *At Ease: Stories I Tell My Friends.* Doubleday & Company, 1967.

Eisenhower, Dwight D. *Crusade in Europe.* Doubleday & Company, 1948.

Eisenhower, John. *Strictly Personal.* Doubleday & Company, 1974.

Essame, H. *Patton: A Study in Command.* Charles Scribner's Sons, 1974.

*Farago, Ladislas. *Patton: Ordeal and Triumph.* Obolensky, 1964.

Farago, Ladislas. *The Last Days of Patton.* McGraw-Hill, 1981.

Forty, George. *Patton's Third Army at War.* Charles Scribner's Sons, 1978.

Hatch, Alden. *George Patton: General in Spurs.* Julian Messner, 1950.

Houston, Donald E. *Hell on Wheels: The 2nd Armored Division.* Presidio Press, 1977.

Irving, David. *The War between the Generals.* Congdon & Lattès, Inc., 1981.

Karnow, Stanley. *Vietnam.* Viking, 1983.

McWhorter, John C., Jr. *USMA: Class of 1946.* 1993.

Nye, Roger H. *The Patton Mind.* Avery Publishing Group, Inc., 1993.

Palmer, Bruce, Jr. *The 25-Year War: America's Military Role in Vietnam.* Touchstone, 1985.

* Although this book served as the basis for the Academy Award-winning movie starring George C. Scott, the family does not favor Farago's work as the most accurate. As for Scott's depiction of Patton, however, the family considers the performance an outstanding representation.

Patton, George S., Jr. *War As I knew It*. Houghton-Mifflin, 1947.

Patton, Robert H. *The Pattons*. Crown, 1994.

Province, Charles M. *The Unknown Patton*. Hippocrene Books, Inc. 1983.

Puryear, Edgar F. *Nineteen Stars*. Coiner Publications, 1971.

Semmes, Harry H. *Portrait of Patton*. Appleton-Century-Crofts, 1955.

Sorley, Lewis. *Thunderbolt*. Simon & Schuster, 1992.

Stanton, Shelby L. *Order of Battle WW II*. Presidio Press, 1984.

Stanton, Shelby L. *Vietnam Order of Battle*. U.S. News Books, 1981.

Starry, Donn A. *Armored Combat in Vietnam*. The Ayer Company, 1982.

Summers, Harry G., Jr. *On Strategy*. Presidio Press, 1982.

United States Military Academy. *Register of Graduates and Former Cadets*. Association of Graduates, West Point, New York, 1993.

Westmoreland, William C. *A Soldier Reports*. Doubleday & Company, 1976.

Williamson, Porter B. *Patton's Principles*. Management/Systems Consultants, 1979.

Yearbook of the Regular Course Students and Faculty of the Command and General Staff College. *The Bell*. United States Army at Fort Leavenworth, Kansas, 1958.

ARTICLES

Buckley, Kevin P. "General Abrams Deserves a Better War." *The New York Times Magazine* (October 5, 1969): 34, 36, 120, 122, 124–131.

DeMaret, Kent. "Fiery and Flamboyant, a Second George Patton Takes Command at Fort Hood." *People* (September 1975): 6–9.

Patton, George S. "Operation Crusader." *Armor* (May–June 1958): 6–19.

Patton, George S. "Pile On." *Armor* (January–February 1970; March–April 1970): 25–31, 26–31.

Patton, George S. "Some Thoughts on Cavalry." *Armor* (May–June 1979): 26–30.

Patton, George S. "Why They Fight." *Military Review* (December 1965): 16–23.

Patton, Joanne. "On Military Social Customs." *Armor* (July 1975): 33–34.

Patton, Joanne, and Mrs. Michael J. Fay. "Women's Liberation—Armor School Style!" *Armor* (May 1972): 30–34.

Sobel, Brian. "The Pattons of Hamilton." *Boston Herald Sunday Celebrity* (May 1983): 6.

Time. "The Growing U.S. Army" (October 13, 1961): 20–23.

PERIODICALS

Life. Patton Covers. January 7, 1945, and January 15, 1945.

Look. Various issues.

Newsweek. Various issues.

Saturday Evening Post. Various issues.

Time. Various issues.

NEWSPAPER LIST

Boston Globe. Clippings.

Los Angeles Times. Clippings.

New York Times. Clippings.

The Stars and Stripes. Clippings.

STUDY

Patton, George S. *Portrait of an Insurgent: A Study of the Motivation of the Main Force Vietnamese Communist Fighting Man.* U.S. Army War College, Carlisle Barracks, Pennsylvania, April 1965.

DOCUMENTS

Blackhorse Prayer. Bob Hawn, Chaplain, January 26, 1969.
Combat After Action Report—Operation Atlas Wedge, 11th Armored Cavalry Regiment. Period 17–24, March 1969.
Letter, George S. Patton to General Abrams, drafted but not sent, June 1956.
Letter, George S. Patton to General Davidson, re: Deployment of 11th ACR, January 1966.
Letter, George S. Patton to General Edward C. Meyer, August 1980.
Letter, George S. Patton to Secretary Callaway, re: Volunteer Army, December 1973.
Letter, George S. Patton, Jr., to George Patton, June 6, 1944.
Letter, Richard Nixon to Brian Sobel, January 1991.
Letter, Ruth Ellen Patton Totten to George Patton, January 21, 1969.
Patton, George S., Major General. Personnel (201) File. Federal Records Center, St. Louis, Missouri.
Patton, George S. Daily Diaries, various entries, 1947–1986.
Patton, George S. 2nd Armored Division—Commanding General's Notes. Various, 1975–1977.
Patton, George S. Speeches. Various, 1977–1983.
Patton, George S. Year End Report—Academic Year 1956–1957. To: Commandant of Midshipmen.
Patton Centennial Celebration. General Information and Contact List. November 1985.

Senior Officer Debriefing Report, 11th ACR, April 7, 1969.

MOTION PICTURES AND TELEVISION PRODUCTIONS

The Last Days of Patton. Chrysler Showcase Presentation, CBS, 1985.
Patton. Twentieth Century–Fox, Starring George C. Scott, 1970.

PRIMARY INTERVIEWS—SELECTED LIST

Doolittle, General James.
Dozier, Major General James L. (USA, Ret.).
Gay, Lieutenant General Hobart.
Kerwin, General Walter T. (USA, Ret.).
McEnery, Lieutenant General John W. (USA, Ret.).
Mims, John.
Nixon, Richard M.
O'Meara, Colonel Andrew P. (USA, Ret.).
Patton, Joanne.
Patton, Major General George S. (USA, Ret.).
Totten, Ruth Ellen Patton.
Westmoreland, General William C. (USA, Ret.).
Woodring, Horace L. "Woody."

INDEX

ABOUT THE AUTHOR

BRIAN M. SOBEL owns and operates a media consulting firm in Petaluma, California. He is the author of a previous book and is a frequent contributor to magazines and newspapers. A former news director for two California radio stations, Sobel held public office for nine years.